the
PIANO

the
PIAN

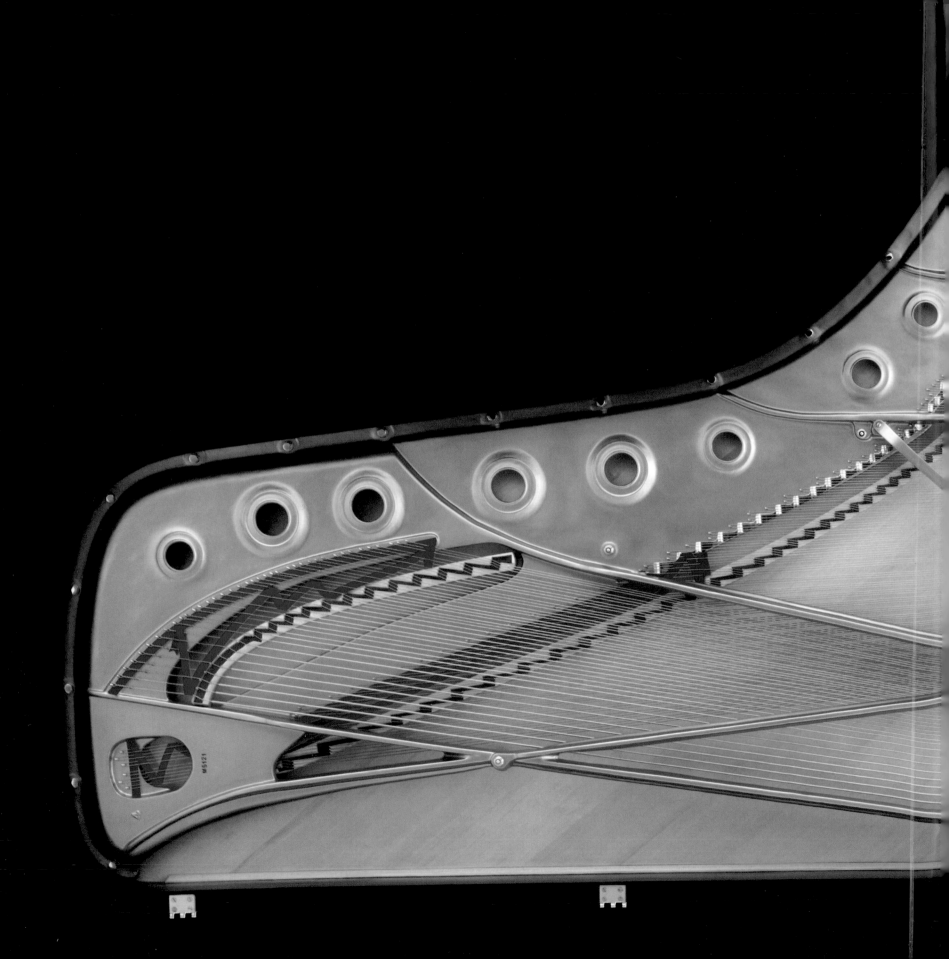

the
PIANO

john-paul williams

BILLBOARD BOOKS
An imprint of Watson-Guptill Publications
NEW YORK

First published in 2002 in the United States by
Billboard Books,
An imprint of Watson-Guptill Publications,
A division of VNU Business Media, Inc.
770 Broadway, New York, NY 10003

Library of Congress Cataloging-in-Publication Data for
this title can be obtained from the Library of Congress.

ISBN: 0-8230-8151-6

QUAR.PIAN

Conceived, designed, and produced by
Quarto Publishing plc
The Old Brewery
6 Blundell Street
London N7 9BH

Senior Project Editor   **Nicolette Linton**
Senior Art Editor   **Penny Cobb**
Designer   **Tanya Devonshire-Jones**
Photographer   **Paul Forrester**
Illustrator   **Kuo Kang Chen**
Picture Research   **Sandra Assersohn, Anna Carr,**
Image Select International
Text Editors   **Gillian Kemp, Pat Farrington**
Indexer   **Dorothy Frame**

Art Director   **Moira Clinch**
Publisher   **Piers Spence**

Manufactured by **Regent Publishing Services Ltd, Hong Kong**
Printed by **Star Standard Industries (Pte), Singapore**

First US printing 2002

1 2 3 4 5 6 7 8 9 / 10 09 08 07 06 05 04 03 02

AUTHOR'S ACKNOWLEDGMENTS
For the loving encouragement of my mother, father, brother,
and sister; the tremendous support of my friends, and colleagues
both at London Metropolitan University (formerly London
Guildhall University) and within all areas of the piano trade;
and a special thank you to Malcolm McKeand, whose expert
knowledge, tuition, and friendship inspired me to become
a piano technician.

contents

HISTORY and development

In this section we chart the historical development of the piano, from its remarkable conception by Cristofori in the 1690s, through the golden age of piano making, to the present day. We reveal the close relationships between the great composers and the early makers, and explore in detail the anatomy of the piano.

Introduction

Ancient Egyptian musicians.

HISTORY RELATES THAT NICOLAS FOUQUET, THE SPLENDID YET ILL-FATED TREASURY MINISTER OF KING LOUIS XIV OF FRANCE, ONCE EXCLAIMED TO A MUSICIAN OF THE COURT: "HOW NOW, MONSIEUR, YOU CARE NOT FOR MUSIC? YOU DO NOT PLAY THE CLAVECIN! I AM SORRY FOR YOU: YOU ARE INDEED CONDEMNING YOURSELF TO A DULL OLD AGE."

There was a time, not so long ago, when you could find a piano in almost every home. Many people's memories hold vivid pictures of an old piano standing in the corner of their parents' or grandparents' house. In its flexibility as a solo instrument or for accompaniment, leading an orchestra or as a tool in the hands of the composer, or simply as a nice piece of furniture, the piano was unrivaled, as too is the claim that everybody can play something on the piano, even if it is only "Chopsticks."

Millions around the world—young and old—still experience the joy of picking out their favorite tunes or accomplishing a well-loved masterpiece. To many, the piano in the home is a comforter and companion, always ready to give its best, unchanging, and patient.

No musical instrument is as easy to handle and so quick to produce a note for the beginner. None has attained such universal popularity. Given its special status, it is perhaps not surprising that every pianist should want to know not only how to choose and care for a piano, but also to understand its development, working, and individual maker's characteristics.

The piano's ancestors can be classified into two types of stringed instruments: those that are plucked and those that are struck. Most early civilizations used harps and lyres for musical

A Greek vase painting from around 490–480 B.C. Apollo (left, holding the lyre) and Artemis offer a sacrifice at the altar of Jupiter (Zeus). A lyre is a stringed instrument whose strings are attached to a yoke, which lies in the same plane as the sound table.

A double zither of the Salzburg shape made prior to 1800. The two sets of strings are stretched over a sound box; the melodic strings are run over a fretted fingerboard and the open strings are used for accompanying purposes.

timeline

The piano has developed over many centuries against a backdrop of war and change. The earliest record of anything resembling such an instrument is in 1426; by the early twenty-first century, many pianos incorporate digital technology.

1426
• exchange of musical instruments from Burgundy to the court of Niccolò d'Este in Ferrara containing an "instrumento pian e forte."

1440
• detailed manuscript written by Henricus Arnault describing stringed keyboard instruments and their mechanisms.

c.1490
• earliest extant example of a "clavicytherium."

accompaniment, and these simple plucked instruments were modified to include a soundboard positioned underneath the strings for greater resonance. Called the psaltery, this plucked instrument would be the inspiration for the harpsichord, while the struck version, the dulcimer, would later inspire some of the first piano experimenters.

Although keyboards had been used with organs since 221 A.D., and had been chromatic since 1361, it is not until 1425 that the first representations of stringed keyboard instruments are found. From this year survives a carving in the altarpiece of Minden Cathedral, Germany, depicting both a clavichord and a harpsichord. In 1440, a manuscript written by Henricus Arnault describes many stringed keyboard instruments, and gives comprehensive details of their mechanisms. The earliest extant example, however, is a German clavicytherium—an upright stringed keyboard instrument based on the psaltery whose strings were plucked by keyboard-operated jacks—made around 1490, now exhibited in the Donaldson Collection of the Royal College of Music, London.

By the mid-sixteenth century, stringed keyboard instruments were widely known throughout Europe, with the sensitive and

A small dulcimer with crook-shaped hammers made in Italy in the mid-eighteenth century. The dulcimer—often associated with country folk music—became fashionable in the royal courts of Europe during the early eighteenth century due to some remarkable performances on the instrument by Pantaleon Hebenstreit.

The fourteenth-century painting "Concert of Angels" by Paolo Veneziano depicts angels playing an assortment of instruments including the plucked psaltery (middle two angels in the bottom row). The psaltery was played by the ecclesiastical and aristocratic class, either held with one hand and played with the other, or rested on the lap leaving both hands free to play.

Lady playing a harp.

1521

• *earliest extant example of a harpsichord, made by Hieronymus Bononiensis, Italy.*

1523

• *earliest extant example of a spinet, made by Franciscus de Portalupis, Italy.*

Learning to play the harpsichord.

A spinet is a small keyboard instrument with a plucking mechanism. Spinetta was the original term for the rectangular virginal, derived from its inventor Giovanni Spinetti in 1503. This beautiful example was made in 1571 by Benedict Floriani.

A sixteenth-century harpsichord made by Domenico Pisaurensis in 1546 with contemporary Renaissance scores. The harpsichord, an ingenious interpretation of the plucked psaltery, employs plectrums (traditionally crow quills) attached to wooden jacks that sit on the back of each key. The jack is designed so that the quill only plucks the string as the key is depressed, and not when it returns. A small felt pad on top of the jack acts as a damper. The silvery sound is appreciably louder than that of the clavichord but the sonority of each individual string is not variable.

inexpensive clavichord predominantly used in churches and schools—particularly in Germany—and the harpsichord proving popular as a performance instrument within the royal courts. Contemporary with the harpsichord was a group of smaller plucked keyboard instruments: the spinets and the virginals that were reserved mainly for domestic use. But the harpsichord's inability to create dynamic variation and the clavichord's low volume were placing limits on their usefulness in the expressive vocal music that was developing at the time. During the eighteenth century, a proliferation of musical amateurs among the rising middle classes, frustrated at the shortcomings of the available keyboard instruments and the high maintenance they required, created a climate favorable to a new form of instrument. Enter Bartolomeo Cristofori, an Italian keyboard instrument maker, who had already anticipated the new sentiment. By 1700, Cristofori had designed and made his *gravicembalo col pian e forte*; this struck keyboard instrument would combine the expressive potential of the clavichord, but maintain the sonority and volume of the harpsichord. The age of the piano had arrived.

timeline

1700

• *the Medici court inventory includes an* arpicembalo che fa il piano e il forte *made by Bartolomeo Cristofori.*

1711

• *Scipione Maffei publishes an article describing Cristofori's invention; his visit took place in 1709.*
• *John Shore invents the tuning fork.*

It is hard to pinpoint exactly when the piano took on the mantle of popularity. Many makers carried on experimenting to improve the dynamic control of the harpsichord. Some even supplied gadgets, including strips of metal lowered onto the strings, in order to make the piano sound more like a harpsichord! Most workshops throughout the middle of the eighteenth century continued to produce all types of stringed keyboard instruments, and a number of combination harpsichords were made with two manuals, one employing a plucking mechanism and the other operating striking hammers.

In the 1770s much opposition still existed to the pianoforte. Voltaire in 1774 called it a "boiler maker's instrument in comparison to the harpsichord," and throughout the decade harpsichord production continued to increase, with the output and sales of makers such as Burkat Shudi and Jacob Kirkman unaffected by the emergence of the new instrument. At the same time, composers such as Clementi, Haydn, and J. C. Bach had started to produce music with both harpsichord and pianoforte mentioned on the title pages; and the piano's dynamic sensitivity

The seventeenth-century painting "Woman at a Virginal with a Man" by Jan Vermeer. The virginal is a small rectangular harpsichord with only one string per note that runs parallel to the keys. The name derives from the Latin virginalis *meaning "maiden" and contemporary paintings show virginals being played only by young women. The instrument lying on the floor is a viola da gamba.*

1716

• *Jean Marius produces four ideas for a harpsichord with hammers.*

1717

• *Christoph Gottlieb Schröter claims to have produced two models for a striking mechanism.*

1720

• *earliest extant example of a Cristofori pianoforte.*

1722

• *Cristofori develops "una-corda" mechanism.*

1725

• *Maffei's article is published in Germany.*

The top view of a clavichord by Johann Hass. The name "clavichord" was first used in 1404 in the rules for the Minnesingers, but the instrument existed in various forms throughout Western Europe as early as the fourteenth century. Of all the keyboard instruments, the clavichord is the simplest in construction and the most sensitive in its musical qualities. At the end of each key is a metal tangent that strikes two strings; acting as a bridge, the tangent sets the speaking length of the strings vibrating, producing a quiet, delicate sound that sings as long as the key remains depressed. Peculiarly touch-sensitive, the performer can vary the slight pressure on the key to produce a vibrato called Bebung.

as both an accompanying and a solo instrument was beginning to achieve widespread recognition.

By the end of the century the piano was credited as an instrument in its own right. Charles Burney, an English historian, exclaimed in 1803, that "the harsh scratching of the quills [of the spinet] could no longer be borne." Freed from comparisons with other wooden keyboard instruments, pushed by the expectations of the new composers, and aided by the advances of the industrial revolution, the pianoforte's development could proceed unhindered.

During the first half of the eighteenth century, while Cristofori's ideas were spreading across southern Europe, another instrument—inspired by one Pantaleon Hebenstreit, a traveling entertainer—was causing a sensation in Germany. Hebenstreit toured the royal courts of Europe playing a giant dulcimer that was over 9 feet (275cm) long and covered a compass of fifty-five notes.

During his virtuoso performances he would leap from one end of the instrument to the other, striking the 186 gut and metal strings with wooden and cloth-covered hammers to obtain a range of different tones. It was Louis XIV himself who, in 1704, suggested the novel instrument should be called the "Pantaleon," after its inventor. In Saxony Hebenstreit's talent impressed further, and the Dresden court appointed him—on a salary that matched that of the Kappelmeister—as Court "pantaleonist." The enormous job of maintaining the instrument fell to Gottfried Silbermann and he became the supplier of duplicate instruments until 1727 when, after a disagreement, Hebenstreit obtained a royal writ stopping Silbermann from making any further copies.

The tonal effects that Hebenstreit's instrument was capable of producing, together with the sheer difficulty of mastering it, inspired others to create a more manageable version. The pantalon built by many independent German makers throughout the eighteenth century was shaped like a harpsichord or clavicytherium, had no escapement or damping mechanism, and employed a keyboard to propel wooden faced hammers to the strings.

There are various claims to the title of "inventor" of the piano. Jean Marius, a lawyer and versatile inventor, showed four drawings of a "Clavecin à Maillets" (keyboard instrument with hammers) to the Académie Royale des Sciences in Paris, 1716. They were crude

timeline

1726
• *first hammer mechanisms made by Gottfried Silbermann, but unsuccessful.*

1732
• *first music published specifically for piano in Italy; Twelve Sonatas for loud and soft harpsichord by Ludovico Giustini.*

c.1736
• *Silbermann shows his pianos to J. S. Bach, whose criticism spurs on the maker to improve his instruments.*

1739
• *earliest extant example of upright piano, made by Domenico del Mela.*

1745
• *earliest extant example of a pyramid piano, made by Christian Ernst Friederici.*

designs, two of which had downstriking actions and no dampers or escapement, while another resembled the clavichord in which the hammers struck the strings directly. The instruments never went into production as Marius failed to win the protection of a royal privilege, but his ideas were groundbreaking at the time. In 1738 Christoph Gottlieb Schröter, organist, writer, and instrument maker, claimed to have produced two action models for use in a struck keyboard in 1717, and maintained until his death in 1782 that he was the inventor of the piano. By the time of his claim his models were lost, and so are only known through his own declaration.

It is, though, the pianoforte credited to Bartolomeo Cristofori that was steadily improved over 150 years of design modifications into what we now recognize as the modern piano. But there is no simple linear path of development from Cristofori to Steinway; many different styles, types, and designs of pianos were being made and used, all at the same time, throughout the whole of the period.

evolution of the keyboard compass

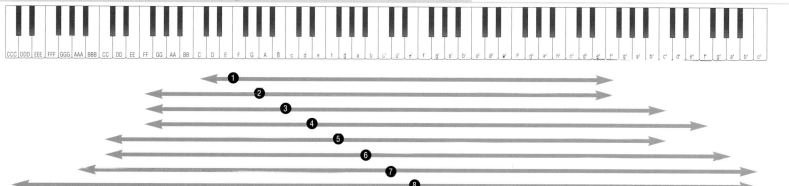

The piano keyboard's compass (range) has grown steadily since Cristofori's time, when pianos had a range of 4 ½ octaves (54 notes); today, the standard is 7 ¼ octaves (88 notes). Some manufacturers, most notably Bösendorfer and Stuart & Sons, continue to push the boundaries and employ an even greater span in an attempt to improve the sustain and tone of the regular end notes, AAA and c⁵.

1. the keyboard compass of a Cristofori gravicembalo col pian e forte, around 1700 (C to f³)
2. the keyboard compass of Silbermann, Stein, and the English piano (FF to f³) until the 1770s
3. a 5 ½-octave compass was first achieved by Broadwood around 1792 (FF to c⁴)
4. the 6-octave compass commonly found in Viennese pianos around 1805 (FF to f⁴)
5. the 6-octave compass commonly found in English pianos around 1805 (CC to c⁴)
6. the compass of a typical mid-eighteenth century piano
7. today's standard compass of 7¼ octaves (AAA to c⁵)
8. the 8-octave compass used in the Bösendorfer Imperial Concert Grand (CCC to c⁵)

concert pitch

Today, all musical instruments are tuned to the international standard pitch of a¹ = 440 Hz (A above middle C vibrating at 440 times per second), which was agreed upon at the International Tuning Pitch Conference in London in 1939. This is so that concert instruments, when played, will be in tune with each other. Until then, concert pitch had fluctuated according to the parameters in which musical instruments could be made, but also to popular taste.

a¹ = 392 Hz [modern G]: Baroque French pitch (late seventeenth century)
a¹ = 403 Hz: higher Baroque French pitch (early eighteenth century)
a¹ = 422 Hz: Baroque/Classical pitch (1740–1820)
a¹ = 452 Hz: former "sharp pitch" (mid-nineteenth century)
a¹ = 466 Hz [modern A#]: reached in some historical pitches
a¹ = 415 Hz [modern G#]: present usual historical Baroque pitch
a¹ = 440 Hz [modern A]: standard pitch (since 1939)

Development
of the piano

ALTHOUGH CRISTOFORI IS WIDELY ACCEPTED AS THE INVENTOR OF THE PRECURSOR TO TODAY'S PIANOFORTE, EVIDENCE SUGGESTS THAT STRINGED KEYBOARD INSTRUMENTS THAT WERE STRUCK EXISTED AS EARLY AS THE FIFTEENTH CENTURY.

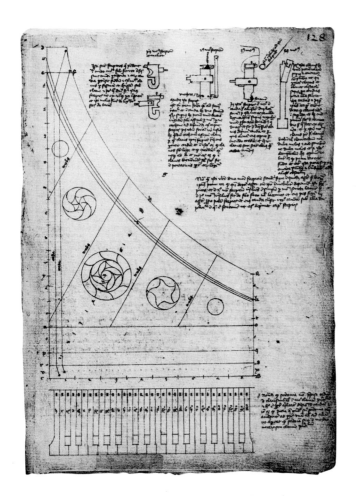

A detailed manuscript on instrument making written by Henricus Arnault, in Burgundy in 1440, includes a full-scale working drawing that depicts a rebounding striking mechanism to be fitted to a stringed keyboard instrument that should "make it sound like a hammered dulcimer." It is possible that an exchange of musical instruments as early as 1426, from Burgundy to the court of Niccolò d'Este in Ferrara, contained such an instrument. In 1598 a series of letters by the organist and instrument carer for the Italian court mentions an *instrumento pian e forte*, and from the brief description that exists of this instrument, it seems likely that it was a stringed keyboard instrument with a striking mechanism.

It was, however, Bartolomeo Cristofori's ingenuity in designing a working striking mechanism at the end of the seventeenth century that began a continuous process of development to the modern piano.

An anonymous portrait of Bartolomeo Cristofori holding a drawing of his hammer mechanism in 1726. The painting, formerly shown in the Staatliches Institut für Musikforschung in Berlin, was destroyed during the Second World War.

A page from the Henricus Arnault manuscript showing details of a clavisimbalum and four types of mechanism. The mechanism shown on the top-right hand side depicts a rebounding striking action.

timeline

1747
• *in the presence of Frederick the Great, J. S. Bach plays Silbermann's pianos and is, this time, impressed.*

1753
• *C. P. E. Bach publishes the first work to include a reference to piano technique, "An essay on the true art of playing keyboard instruments."*

1762
• *Johann Christoph Zumpe builds his first square piano in England.*

the wing-shaped piano

The first record of Bartolomeo Cristofori's "invention" is documented in *The Medici Inventory of Diverse Musical Instruments* of 1700 as an *arpicembalo che fa il piano e il forte* (a large keyboard instrument that produces loud and soft). It was an ingenious assembly of levers and hammers, set in a strengthened harpsichord case, that produced a sound capable of subtle nuances. Although it is not known precisely how many pianofortes Cristofori made in his lifetime, the total is thought to be in the region of twenty, of which three survive today.

Cristofori was born in Padua, Italy, in 1655. Little is known of his early years but it is thought that he began his working life as an instrument maker, specializing in fine harpsichords. In 1688, a growing reputation earned him employment as the keyboard instrument curator and maker to the court of Prince Ferdinando de Medici at Florence, where his duties were to include the repair, tuning, and safe transportation of the court's collection of thirty-five keyboard instruments. Bearing in mind the heavy use that these instruments would have received, it is staggering to think that he maintained them all while still finding the time to make new instruments.

Cristofori started out sharing a workshop with 100 other artisans, all engaged in various trades for the royal court, and in his first weeks complained bitterly of the noisy conditions he had to work in. Although the many different crafts practiced under the same roof must have influenced Cristofori's own projects, by 1690 he had transferred his tools and his workshop to his house.

It is thought to have been during this period that Cristofori began to experiment with new hammer mechanisms. Prince Ferdinando was himself a keen musician and had a deep interest in complex mechanical devices, so there is little doubt that he and Cristofori would have had conversations about the possibility of an improved stringed keyboard instrument. Although the concept of such an instrument is relatively straightforward, in practice it is highly complex. Cristofori began with the strung back, case design, and keyboard from an Italian harpsichord, all of which he could use with a few modifications. His notion of using hammers to strike the strings to create the desired tone might have been influenced by the dulcimer, or by reports of the instruments from Ferrara, although there is no hard evidence of either; in any case, the combining of these ideas into a working instrument was a stroke of genius. It soon became clear that a hammer mounted directly on the back of the key would travel and strike the string, but would then block the string and damp its vibration for as long as the key remained depressed. By 1700 Cristofori had overcome this problem by introducing an intermediate lever that could escape from underneath the hammer just before it struck the string, decoupling it from the pressed key and so letting the string vibrate freely.

First published in the Giornale de' Letterati d'Italia *in 1711, Maffei's enthusiastic article, together with a sketch and explanation of Cristofori's hammer mechanism, was translated into German by Johann Ulrich König and published in the* Critica musica *in 1725.*

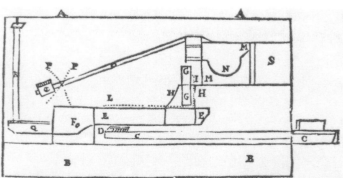

A. Die Saite.
B. Der Boden zu den Clavieren oder dem Anschlag.
C. Die Claviere, oder die ersten Heber, welche mit den Pflöckgen die andren in die Höhe treiben.
D. Das Pflöckgen, Zäpfen oder Holz-Schu an dem Anschlag.
E. Die zweyte Hebe, wo, auf jeder Seiten, eines von den Neben-Stützgen fest gemacht ist, die das Züngelgen halten.
F. Der Angel oder Stifft in der zweyten Hebe.
G. Das bewegliche Zünglein, welches, wann es mit der zweyten Hebe sich in die Höhe schiebt, auf das Hämmerchen anstößt.
H. Die Nebenstützgen auf beyden Seiten, worin das Züngelchen eingefaßt ist.
I. Ein fester Messing-Drat, oben an der Spitze breit geschlagen, der das Züngelchen fest hält.
L. Eine Feder von Messing-Drat, die unter dem Züngelchen liegt, und es gegen dem festen Drat angestoßen hält, den es hin'en hat.
U u 2

1767

• *piano first used as an accompanying instrument in Covent Garden Theatre, London.*

1768

• *Johann Christian Bach gives the first solo performance on a piano in London.*

This use of an intermediate lever also had the advantage of increasing the distance through which the hammer traveled for the same depth of key travel, giving a much increased impact velocity and so attaining a volume louder than that of the clavichord. Cristofori also found that using heavier gauge strings wound to a higher tension not only further augmented the volume but also increased the speed at which the hammers rebounded from the strings. This gave much faster repetition, and allowed an increase in the depth of key travel.

In 1711 Scipione Maffei, following a visit to the Medici workshop in 1709, published an article in the *Giornale de' Letterati d'Italia* describing Cristofori's invention. As well as including a detailed drawing and explanation of how the instrument worked, he was sufficiently impressed to exclaim: "So bold an invention has been no less happily conceived than executed in Florence, by Signor Bartolomeo Cristofali,* of Padua. The production of greater or less sound depends on the degree of power with which the player presses on the keys."

From the three instruments that survive today and the detailed drawing and explanation by Maffei it is clear that Cristofori constantly modified his invention, perfecting a design that by 1726 would already have many of the basic features of a grand piano.

However bold the invention, the instrument was not readily accepted in the country of its birth. Italian music was dominated by opera and the climate was not suited to home-centered activities, Cristofori's piano did cause much debate in its native land, where it was eventually considered to be at its best as an accompanying chamber instrument.

In 1732 the first piece specifically written for the piano was published in Florence, *Sonata da Cimbalo di pian e forte detto volgarmente di martelletti* by Ludovico Giustini. Bartolomeo Cristofori died in the same year, bitterly disappointed that his invention had not received the wide acclaim that he felt it deserved, and with him died any major Italian involvement in piano making until the late twentieth century.

In his will, Cristofori left his tools and supplies to the Del Mela family. Domenico del Mela is thought to have been one of Cristofori's two students, and the only known instrument bearing his name is an ingenious upright piano made in 1739. Cristofori's primary student was Giovanni Ferrini and it was he who continued work on his master's invention, producing several instruments retaining the same action and case structure, until three years before his own death in 1758.

Orthography was inconsistent in the late seventeenth century and Cristofori's name appears in various records as Cristofali and Cristofani.

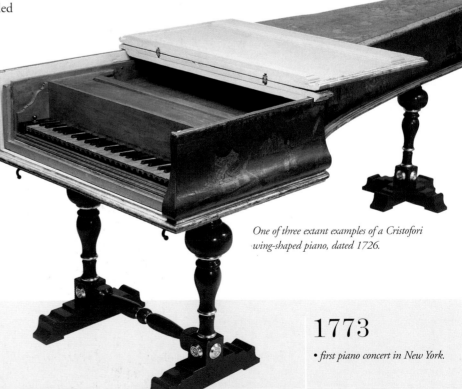

One of three extant examples of a Cristofori wing-shaped piano, dated 1726.

timeline

1770
• *Americus Backers builds a grand piano employing the English grand action.*

1771
• *square pianos are first made in Russia.*

1773
• *first piano concert in New York.*

the spread of an idea

Cristofori's instruments and ideas were dispersed around Europe, not only by Maffei's article but also by migrating Italian musicians and singers employed by the various royal courts. They found a particular welcome in Portugal, home to a vibrant musical society during the wealthy reign of King João V. The King, his coffers bursting with money raised from the reexport of goods from South America, such as tobacco and sugar, and the wealth of gold and diamonds mined in Brazil, went on a spending spree and undertook numerous extravagant projects. One of these was the building of an opera house, which attracted many Italian singers and musicians who brought with them stories and examples of Cristofori's fabled instrument. These were highly sought after and King João himself bought pianos directly from Cristofori for a staggering amount of money, perhaps five times as much as the cost of a good harpsichord. In the wake of the King's patronage Cristofori's instrument gained rapid popularity, particularly with singers such as the famous castrato Farinelli, and court records of the time suggest that piano making was widespread in Portugal and Spain. It is thought that many of the early Portuguese pianofortes were destroyed in an earthquake in 1755, and the dislike of music shown by King Carlos III of Spain between 1759 and 1788 may have led to more being destroyed, leaving few surviving examples.

The two oldest surviving Iberian pianos, both anonymous, are attributed to Francisco Perez Mirabel of Seville and date from around 1745. One is in the collection of Señor Bartolome March of Madrid; the other in the Museo Provincial de Bellas Artes in Seville. Both are meticulously well crafted and have actions that are very similar to Cristofori's. Of three surviving Portuguese pianofortes, two are by Henrique van Casteel, who made instruments in Lisbon between 1757 and 1767 before settling in Brussels. The other is inscribed in 1767 by Antunes, who in 1760 received a royal

The eighteenth-century music room of the Palacio da Ajuda in Lisbon, Portugal. Under the reign of King João V, Portugal became one of Europe's most vibrant musical centers. Possessing many keyboard instruments, including pianofortes by Cristofori, the royal court gave patronage to—among others—Domenico Scarlatti, today recognized as one of the great eighteenth-century keyboard composers.

1775
• *Johann Behrent of Philadelphia builds the first square piano in America.*
• *James Watt improves the steam engine.*

1776
• *American Declaration of Independence.*

1777
• *Robert Stodart is issued a patent for improvements to English grand action. This is the first use of the term "grand piano."*

• *from Augsburg, Mozart writes to his father praising the advancements of Johann Andreas Stein's pianos.*

1782
• *Montgolfier brothers construct a hot air balloon, and make the first ascent the following year.*

This 1746 grand piano by Gottfried Silbermann is one of fifteen that belonged to Frederick the Great. It is exhibited in the music room of the New Palace in Potsdam, Germany.

privilege that gave him sole authority to make pianofortes with his improved action for ten years.

Word of Cristofori's invention traveled not only west but also north. Maffei's article was published in German in 1725 and instrument makers in that country were aware of Cristofori's advances; it is curious, therefore, that no German instrument that follows his designs has survived. Yet piano making was adopted relatively quickly in Germany: Schröter alleged that by 1721 he knew of "more than twenty towns and villages in which the usual manufacture of harpsichords has been replaced by the manufacture of keyboard instruments equipped with hammers or striking tangents." The lasting names from this period are those of Gottfried

Silbermann, who worked in Freiburg and his student, Christian Friederici, in Gera. In Germany, Silbermann was regarded as the inventor of the piano: as late as 1806 a commentator wrote, "This admirable instrument—hurrah! Another invention of the Germans. Silbermann perceived the failing of the harpsichord which could not express color at all." Silbermann's earliest pianos were made during the 1730s and although the tone of these instruments was admired by J. S. Bach, the composer's criticisms of a heavy touch and weak treble spurred on the maker to improve his designs. By the 1740s, Silbermann's instruments had reached high office, and Frederick the Great had commissioned fifteen of them. The action of the two surviving instruments made by Silbermann in 1746 and 1749 is a replica of that on Cristofori's 1726 piano, and not the earlier design that Maffei documented. From this we can assume that prior to 1746 Silbermann had access to one of Cristofori's pianofortes.

Until the 1740s only one pianoforte existed in England, a copy of a Cristofori instrument made by an English monk, Father Wood, in Italy. The proud owner was Samuel Crisp, and it is recorded that, although the "tone was superior to that of the harpsichord, its touch was imperfect so that nothing fast could be played on it." In 1756 the Seven Years War started, leading to an exodus of piano builders from Saxony. Twelve good makers fled to safety in England, where they set to work making harpsichords. Of this group of makers—known as the Twelve Apostles—it was Johann Christoph Zumpe who started the great tradition of piano making in England.

Entertaining on the clavichord.

timeline

1783
• *John Broadwood makes significant improvements to the square piano's damping mechanism and includes a pedal to replace knee levers.*

1789
• *the French Revolution begins.*
• *Charles Albrecht opens a piano factory in Philadelphia.*

1790
• *John Broadwood builds a piano with a five-and-a-half octave compass.*

the square piano

Despite the limited success in Germany of Silbermann's wing-shaped pianofortes, German music revolved around the church and school, and not the royal courts as it did elsewhere in Europe. So it was the rectangular clavichord rather than the harpsichord that was the inspiration for Zumpe's "invention." Combining a strengthened rectangular cabinet with a novel bridge and string design to produce a sonorous tone, and including an action inspired directly by the hammered dulcimer rather than the mechanism of Cristofori, the entire design of Zumpe's square piano was unique.

The reputation of this instrument was greatly enhanced in 1768 when J. C. Bach played one in the first concert performance of a piano in England. As square pianos were much cheaper to produce than single manual harpsichords, and perfectly designed to match English taste in furniture, other English instrument makers soon began to turn these instruments out in quantites that could not be matched by makers of the more time-consuming wing-shaped piano. Zumpe's workshop became the first in England to produce solely pianos and he was the first maker to advertise his address on the instrument's name board, sensing that his piano's fine tone would bring buyers flocking to his door.

Zumpe's original design was improved in 1783 by John Broadwood,* a former apprentice and by now partner of the Swiss-born harpsichord maker Burkat Shudi, and in 1786 John Geib patented a more notable improvement, introducing a mechanism derived from Cristofori's later action that gave Geib's instrument a more expressive touch. Both of these modifications were adopted in all square pianos made until the 1860s.

By the turn of the nineteenth century the square piano had attained a phenomenal degree of popularity in England and France, with Broadwood at one point producing 1,300 square pianos in a year. But the demand for an enlarged compass and a fuller tone meant that a stronger supporting structure had to be devised. In 1820 the inventive William Southwell (who in 1784 used wires for the first time to support the damper heads) employed metal braces on the frame of the instrument. In 1825, Alpheus Babcock patented a full iron frame for the square piano, allowing it to take the strain imposed by the string tension of a seven-octave compass.

By the 1850s, in Europe at least, the square piano had all but been replaced by the next

John Broadwood improved the damper mechanism, placing the dampers below the strings, to which they were held firmly by a counterweight.

In this 1766 square piano by Zumpe, the natural keys are covered in ebony while the stained fruitwood accidentals are covered in ivory. This reversal of the keyboard coloring was quite common in the eighteenth century.

1792

• *Sebastien Erard flees the revolution in France and sets up a factory in London.*

1797

• The Pianoforte, *the first magazine devoted exclusively to the piano, is first published in London.*

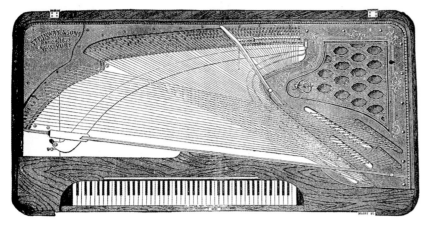

A square piano by Steinway & Sons won a gold medal at the Fair of the American Institute in New York. It employed a full iron frame and, for the first time, over-stringing.

square piano action

1 hammer head
2 hammer rail
3 leather hinge
4 metal guide pins

5 hammer shank
6 damper
7 hitch pin block

development of the instrument, the cottage upright. In America, meanwhile, its popularity had still not hit its peak. Steinway & Sons launched their business with a square piano in 1855, exhibiting one at the World Fair held at Crystal Palace in New York. The amazing tone emitting from this instrument did wonders for the popularity of the square piano in America, and this growing market fueled local piano makers to persevere with what they felt was a superior instrument compared to the upright. By the 1870s, however, the emergence of concert tours featuring grand pianos, together with further developments to the upright alternative, caused the fortunes of the square piano to wane. Its demise was signaled dramatically in 1903 when the Society of American Piano Manufacturers lit a 50 foot-high bonfire of square pianos to publicize the financial problems facing their industry.

The square piano action by Zumpe (1767–82)
A small leather hammer, attached to a rail by a thin leather hinge and guided by a metal pin, was pushed toward the string. The key reached the limit of its travel when the hammer was about a quarter of an inch (0.5cm) away from the string and the momentum of the hammer carried it the remaining distance. The vellum-hinged dampers were strengthened by small whalebone springs (not illustrated) that pushed them firmly onto the strings, while whalebone stickers that ran through the hitch pin block lifted them from the back of the key. Hand-operated stops were employed to lift the dampers off the strings either in the treble section or the bass, or both.

The square piano action by John Geib, 1786
With a design capable of attaining a more expressive touch, John Geib introduced an action in 1786 that would be the pattern on which all square pianos would be made until the 1860s. Employing an easily regulated hopper to push an intermediate lever that shared the same guide pin as the hammer, the accuracy and consistency of the action's performance was greatly improved. All parts, including the heavier hammers, pivoted on vellum hinges. Turning a brass eyelet screw regulated the hopper's leather-button rest.

english square piano action

1 hopper
2 leather button
3 screw threaded wire
4 vellum hinge
5 brass eyelet screw
6 guide pin
7 hammer head

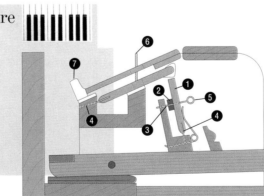

timeline

1798
• the first Giraffe upright is built in Vienna.

1800
• *John Isaac Hawkins of Philadelphia and Mattias Müller in Vienna independently produce two upright pianos in which the strings extend down to the floor.*

1804
• *compass extended to six-and-a-half octaves.*
• *Napoleon Bonaparte declares himself emperor of the new French Republic.*

1807
• *William Southwell introduces the cabinet piano.*

1808
• *Sebastien Erard patents the agraffe.*

piano making
in england and vienna

By 1780 two clearly defined types of wing-shaped piano had emerged and, although both featured hammer mechanisms, their differences signify two distinct lines of development germinating from separate inspirations.

In London, in 1770, Americus Backers, another exile thought to be from Holland, designed a Cristofori-derived wing-shaped pianoforte constructed in the fashion of an English harpsichord. The instrument had a distinctive hammer mechanism that was to prove significant in the development of the wing-shaped pianoforte in Europe, and make it a creditable alternative to Zumpe's popular square pianos. In a previously untried publicity stunt, Backers introduced his instrument to the London public by way of an exhibition lasting three weeks, in which a professional musician played his pianoforte on Monday, Tuesday, Friday, and Saturday mornings at an advertised address.

Backers' piano was notable in many ways. Employing an arched soundboard, it used heavier-gauged trichord strings, and the narrow, firm hammer heads struck the treble strings very close to their ends—innovations pivotal in creating a fuller tone. It also employed pedals rather than knee levers for the sustain and una-corda effects. The action, known as the English grand action, was criticized for having a heavy touch and a slow repetition, although the design did allow for easy regulation in situ. Key travel was, in fact, longer than in previous designs and the key had to return fully before the note could be repeated. Backers made twenty-one pianos before he died in 1778, but his action design, further improved by Robert Stodart, was used by Broadwood and Sons in their pianos until the 1880s.

In Germany meanwhile, Johann Andreas Stein was producing pianofortes during the 1770s in Augsburg that were very different from the legacy of Cristofori, and which would become known, somewhat oddly, as the Viennese piano. The instruments were lightly built (about a tenth of the weight of a modern concert grand) and were bichord strung throughout. They had a thin flat soundboard and leather-covered hammers, producing a beautiful, even, thin tone, efficiently stopped by wedge-shaped dampers. With a touch only half the depth of a modern grand piano, the action (initially called the German action, before being known as the Viennese action and termed, in the twentieth century, Prellmechanik), simply had a hammer mounted in a pivot at the back of the key, with no intermediate levers or repetition aids. It was capable of being accurately regulated and had no need for any lost

The oldest surviving English grand piano, dated 1772, this Americus Backers fortepiano was probably the first to employ foot pedals. It is exhibited in the Russell Collection of Early Keyboard Instruments, University of Edinburgh, Scotland.

1810
• *Sebastien Erard designs what would become the modern pedal mechanism.*

1811
• *Robert Wornum develops a small upright "cottage" piano.*

1815
• *Battle of Waterloo.*

1820
• *Allen and Thom in London patent a grand piano including a compensating iron frame.*

1821
• *Sebastien Erard patents a repetition grand action.*

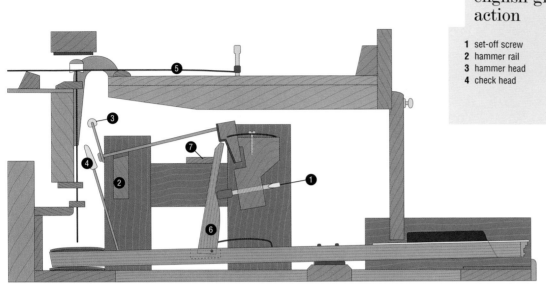

english grand action

1 set-off screw
2 hammer rail
3 hammer head
4 check head
5 string
6 escapement hopper
7 comb register

The English grand action by Americus Backers, around 1772
A simple action with no intermediate lever, the hammer was supported on the rest rail and the hopper guided in a comb register sat fractionally below the hammer butt. This left a small amount of lost motion in the action. The action's regulation was easy: by using a tuning hammer to turn the set-off screw, the escapement of the hopper from the hammer butt could be accurately adjusted with the action remaining inside the piano. Employing a check head to catch the returning hammer both aided repetition and allowed the more consistent return of the hopper beneath the hammer butt. Each hammer sat on its own axle and the resistance on this pivot could be adjusted by tightening the brass cover-plate to increase the pressure on the cloth bushing.

German action by Johann Andreas Stein, around 1785
With no intermediate lever or repetition aids, the hammer was simply mounted in a pivot on the back of the key and could be regulated to rise to within 0.04 inch (1mm) from the string without the fear of blocking or double striking. Requiring no lost motion, the action's performance was famously touch-sensitive and very light, attributes recognized by many of the greatest composers of the time. The action and keyboard were a complete unit that could easily be slid out of the front of the piano, requiring no tools, and the dampers could also be lifted out individually.

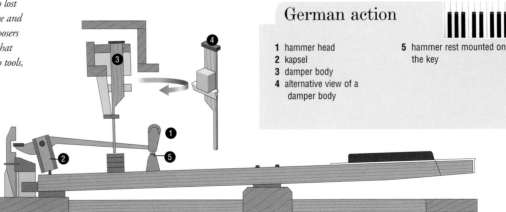

German action

1 hammer head
2 kapsel
3 damper body
4 alternative view of a damper body
5 hammer rest mounted on the key

timeline

1825
• Alpheus Babcock patents a one-piece cast iron frame for a square piano.

1826
• Robert Wornum patents the tape-check action for upright piano.
• Jean-Henri Pape patents designs for graduated felt covered hammers and uses tempered steel piano strings.

1827
• *invention of photography by Joseph Niepce.*
• *James Stewart, partner of Chickering, develops a method of using one length of wire as two strings.*

1831
• *Michael Faraday makes important discoveries about electricity and magnetism.*

1835
• *introduction of an automated hammer covering machine in Germany.*

During the 1790s Anton Walter, in Vienna, significantly improved Stein's construction designs, primarily by increasing the strength of the instrument's wrest plank and supporting structure. His use of heavier hammers and small improvements to the repetition of the action meant that, by 1800, the only makers in Vienna not following Walter's lead were Stein's son, Matthäus, and more notably his married daughter, Nanette Streicher. The Prellmechanik action was commonly made by independent Austrian firms into the 1920s but with the continued use of the double escapement action by all other makers, the action eventually became obsolete.

A pianoforte by Johann Andreas Stein, dated 1782. One of the most inventive and renowned instrument makers of the eighteenth century, Stein's pianos were presented to the royal courts of Paris and Vienna, and were Mozart's preferred make. The piano employs a knee lever to simultaneously lift the trebles, and is treble-strung in the top treble. It also includes the South German action that is attributed to Stein.

motion between the key and the hammer, and thus allowed a more direct way of playing. Although it required a different technique to master its percussive touch, Stein's piano had a greatly extended dynamic range and it was admired by many of the great composers. How Stein came upon his idea is unclear, as he was a contemporary of both Zumpe and Silbermann, but at the end of the eighteenth century independent makers in southern Germany were producing many forms of hammered instrument inspired by the hammered dulcimer of Pantaleon Hebenstreit, and this may be an explanation.

comparison of english and viennese grand pianos

• *CASE: Although similarly wing-shaped, the case of the English instrument was made to take the strain of the strings (like the harpsichord), while in the Viennese piano the case was merely decorative, the string tension being taken by a separate system of braces on a solid base.*

• *STRINGS: The English makers preferred to use three strings per note, whereas the Viennese makers employed just two. Some Viennese makers employed three strings per note in the top treble. The wire used by the English makers was typically fifty percent larger in diameter.*

• *SOUNDBOARD: English pianos employed a slight crown, while the Viennese makers used a flat soundboard.*

• *HAMMERS: English pianos employed much heavier hammers; the Viennese touch weight was only about 1 ounce (28 grams).*

• *DAMPERS: English dampers rested lightly on the strings; Viennese dampers, using wedge-shaped felt and weighted bodies, worked much more efficiently.*

1836

• *Serialization of Charles Dickens'* Pickwick Papers *begins.*

1838

• *Pierre Erard patents the pressure bar.*

1842

• *J. C. L. Ishermann, in Hamburg, becomes the first specialized action-making firm.*

the grand piano

It is thought that the term "grand pianoforte" was coined by Robert Stodart in 1777. His improvements to the English grand action, together with John Broadwood's tonal improvements during the 1890s, meant that the power and depth of tone created by English pianos in 1800 was like nothing heard before. Broadwood's main contribution to the development of the grand piano was a succession of methodical improvements to the bridge. He made it square in cross section, with a flat top, carved so that all three strings of a trichord could have the same speaking length, a technique (still used today) that improved the piano's tuning and tone. To increase the resonance of the bass register, Broadwood employed a separate bass bridge that would eventually allow the idea of cross-stringing to be realized. But it was Sebastien Erard, in France, with his ingenious inventions, who elevated the piano to a plane where it became the favored instrument of the nineteenth-century composers for the expression of tone poems.

In 1808 Erard patented the agraffe, a brass stud that accurately determined the strings' speaking length while preventing them from being driven upward by the blows of the hammers; this improved tuning stability. In 1822 the firm patented its double escapement action, a development of a mechanism it had first patented in 1808. The origins of this lay in Cristofori's action, but the hammer on return from the string was not only caught close to the string by a check head, but also landed on an oblique sprung lever that would throw the hammer in the air once the key was released to aid the speed of repetition. When compared with the English grand action, Erard's design was not only acclaimed for its faster repetition but also for its lightness and reliability, and it became the basis of the grand piano action still used today. Erard not only developed the hammer mechanism but also, less successfully, experimented with the damper mechanism. In an attempt to create the popular

A grand piano by Robert Stodart built in 1784. The oak case is veneered in mahogany, satinwood, and other exotic timbers. The piano originally had two pedals suspended between its front legs.

By 1820, when this piano was produced, Broadwood and Sons were making grand pianos that were able to withstand a fifty percent increase in string tension than those made in 1800, thus creating a fuller and brighter tone.

timeline

1843
• Jonas Chickering produces first grand piano to employ a one-piece iron frame.

1844
• Jonas Chickering exports the first pianos from America, to India.

1855
• Steinway & Sons exhibit a square piano with full iron frame and overstringing.

double escapement action

1 hammer head
2 intermediate lever
3 jack
4 key
5 check head
6 damper head
7 repetition spring

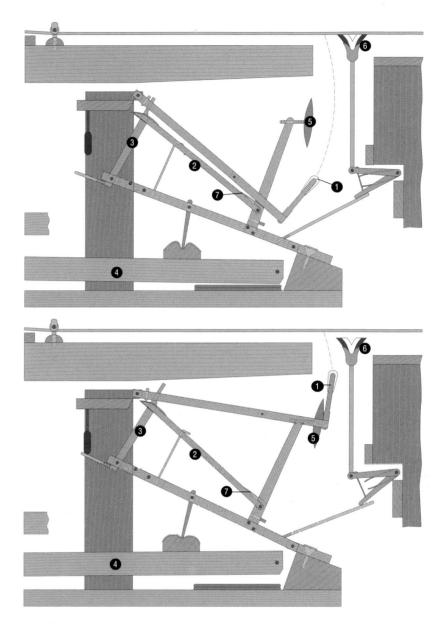

resonant sound of early English pianos, they employed dampers that operated below the strings. This radical approach obtained from the instrument a very different tone, quickly eliminating the fundamental frequencies of a note while leaving the higher harmonics to sound slightly longer, creating a harmonic shimmer.

With a reliable action, a fuller sound was required to accommodate changing musical tastes and give the piano more power. Antoine Bord patented the capo d'astro bar in 1840 and Jean-Henri Pape, working for Pleyel, developed a dense felt hammer covering using rabbit hair and lamb's wool as a replacement for doeskin. But with heavier hammers, stronger strings, and a greater compass, the supporting structure of the grand piano had to be improved. In the eighteenth century, wing-shaped pianos had been made almost entirely out of wood, with metal bracings employed only between the wrest plank and the rest of the frame. In 1800 John Isaac Hawkins, an engineer, was first to introduce a full iron frame into a cabinet piano. To many musicians and piano makers, steeped in the tradition of working in wood, the idea of using so much metal in a musical instrument was anathema. Throughout the 1820s a stream of patents were taken out on designs employing iron braces bolted to metal hitch plates; these were known as composite frames. Although continuous cast-iron frames were used in square

The double escapement action by Erard, 1822
Aware of the need for an improved grand piano action that did not block or double strike, Sebastien Erard patented his first escapement action in 1808. By 1822 he had developed the "double escapement" action that would become the basis for the modern grand piano action. The design included a spring, adjustable in strength, that could support the weight of the hammer after it had struck the string, so permitting the repeated sounding of the note without the key necessarily returning to rest. The top figure shows the key at rest, while the bottom figure shows the action when the key has been played. Note that the action is fixed (tied) to the top of the key and that the damper acts beneath the string.

1859
• *Steinway & Sons receive a patent for overstringing in grand pianos.*
• ***Charles Darwin publishes his*** Origin of Species, *putting forward a revolutionary theory of evolution.*

1860
• *Ernest Kaps in Germany builds the first 5-foot (152cm) grand piano.*

1861
• ***the start of the American Civil War.***

1863
• *Fourneaux develops the pianista, the first pneumatic piano player mechanism.*

1868
• *Steinway & Sons receive a patent for a tubular iron frame.*

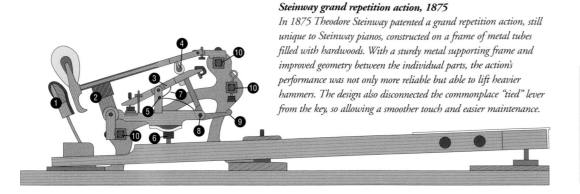

Steinway grand repetition action, 1875

In 1875 Theodore Steinway patented a grand repetition action, still unique to Steinway pianos, constructed on a frame of metal tubes filled with hardwoods. With a sturdy metal supporting frame and improved geometry between the individual parts, the action's performance was not only more reliable but able to lift heavier hammers. The design also disconnected the commonplace "tied" lever from the key, so allowing a smoother touch and easier maintenance.

steinway grand repetition action

1 back check
2 hammer
3 repetition lever
4 roller
5 repetition spring center
6 capstan
7 repetition V string
8 jack center pin
9 jack
10 tubular metal action rails

pianos as early as 1825 they were not used in grand pianos until 1843, when Boston-based piano maker Jonas Chickering fitted one. It comes as no surprise to learn that working for Chickering at that time was one Alpheus Babcock, the first maker to use a full iron frame in a square piano in 1825.

Theodore Steinway realized the modern grand piano in 1876 with the launch of Steinway's Centennial concert grand. This outstanding instrument was the culmination of intensive development work and employed many patented design improvements, including a developed repetition action capable of lifting heavier hammers, a duplex scale, and an improved "cupola" iron frame and bent-rim case that superseded the ground-breaking cross-strung and full iron frame grand piano that the company exhibited at the Paris Exhibition of 1867. A tide of change was running throughout Europe and America that saw almost universal adoption of the grand piano with overstringing and full iron frame by the end of the

nineteenth century. Some European makers, such as Blüthner, Broadwood, and Bösendorfer carried on making actions to their own designs, but the emergence of specialized action manufacturers such as T. & H. Brooks in London and Herrburger Schwander in Paris meant that eventually action design too became standardized across the majority of makes.

The top view of a Steinway & Sons Centennial concert grand, 1876, showing the patent duplex scaling, cross-stringing, and double cupola metal frame.

steinway concert grand, 1876

1 duplex bridges
2 double cupola metal frame
3 continuous soundboard bridge

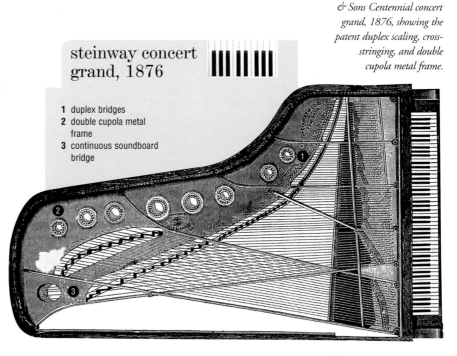

To improve the grand piano structurally and sonically, Steinway patented improvements to the piano rim and supporting braces. Instead of using several jointed short lengths, the rim was made using a series of layers of continuous lengths. The rim was formed around the piano belly using powerful metal presses.

timeline

1872
• *Theodore Steinway patents the duplex scale.*

1874
• *Steinway & Sons perfect the sostenuto pedal.*

1887
• *Yamaha produce their first pianos.*

1890
• *Seven-and-a-quarter octave keyboards become standardized.*

1903
• *the Society of American Piano Manufacturers burn a bonfire of square pianos at Atlantic City Convention.*

piano frames through history

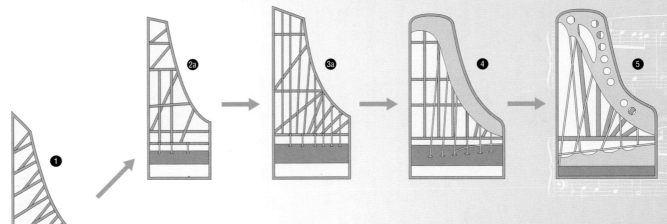

For many years it was against piano makers' principles to use metal in their frames, as it was thought to be detrimental to the tone. However, with the increase in the pitch of other instruments, the introduction of metal supports in the traditional wooden structure of the piano not only allowed the strings to be tuned to a higher tension and withstand the onslaught of heavier hammers, but it also made it possible to increase the instrument's compass.

1. Early eighteenth-century frame built from wood (Cristofori and Silbermann).

2a. Iron bars are positioned across the gap between the piano belly and the wrest plank, for many years the Achilles heel of the wing-shaped piano (England, around 1880).

2b. A single iron bar is positioned between the piano's belly and the wrest plank, (South Germany and Austria, around 1890).

3a. Due to the increased compass, additional support is given to the treble section (England and France, around 1820).

3b. A stronger wooden structure limits the use of metal to the minimum of one iron bar (Vienna, around 1820).

4. With an increased compass, heavier gauge strings tuned at higher tensions, and larger hammers, pianos soon require the extra support of a metal hitch plate and longer stress bars (around 1850).

5. The full iron frame introduced in America in 1843 is used today, bolted to a much simpler wooden supporting structure.

bridge positions through history

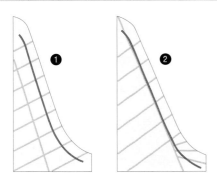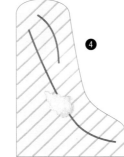

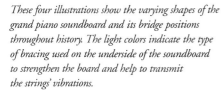

These four illustrations show the varying shapes of the grand piano soundboard and its bridge positions throughout history. The light colors indicate the type of bracing used on the underside of the soundboard to strengthen the board and help to transmit the strings' vibrations.

1. Cristofori, 1720
2. South German, around 1780
3. English, around 1790
4. 1880 to the present day

1910

• *a Broadwood player piano accompanies Captain Scott on his Antarctic Expedition where it is played on the ice at the first base camp.*

1912

• *Aeolian Duo-Art reproducing system introduced.*

the upright piano

With the sonorous wing-shaped pianoforte taking shape and the economic and space-saving square piano proving immensely popular throughout Europe, demand for an upright alternative was slow. The upright form did have certain structural advantages: its soundboard faced the pianist rather than the ceiling, and it could be built without the weakening gap between the wrest plank and the soundboard, the Achilles heel of the horizontal piano. Better still, a vertical piano could be made with a symmetrical case, an aesthetically desirable characteristic in the eighteenth century.

The earliest upright piano still in existence was made in 1739 by the Florentine maker Domenico del Mela. Based on the clavicytherium, it resembles a grand piano

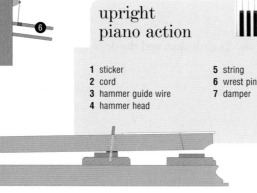

upright piano action

1 sticker
2 cord
3 hammer guide wire
4 hammer head
5 string
6 wrest pin
7 damper

Domenico del Mela, 1739 *In the earliest extant example of an upright piano's action, the vertical sticker lying on the rear of the key is connected to an intermediate lever that shares a pivot with the hammer. The hammer is made of two long sections joined at right angles and resting on a woven pad set on the intermediate lever. The hammers are thrown toward the string through a comb of arced brass guiding rods and, after striking the strings through momentum alone, they return with the aid of gravity to rest on the intermediate lever. The damper is hooked to the intermediate lever and is lifted from the string when the key is depressed.*

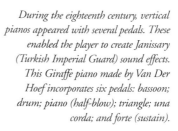

During the eighteenth century, vertical pianos appeared with several pedals. These enabled the player to create Janissary (Turkish Imperial Guard) sound effects. This Giraffe piano made by Van Der Hoef incorporates six pedals: bassoon; drum; piano (half-blow); triangle; una corda; and forte (sustain).

tipped up onto its keyboard and mounted on a stand. To create a symmetrical form, the strung back was modified into a triangular case that gave rise to the name "pyramid piano." Christian Ernst Friederici, in Germany, also made pyramid pianos and their ornate case designs were soon adapted to different shapes such as the lyraflügel, so named because its upper case resembled a large lyre.

The end of the eighteenth century brought new styles of vertical piano, such as the Giraffe. Styled in Vienna, the highly decorated case followed the grand piano's shape with a long, gentle curve leading to a scroll at the top of the instrument. Giraffe pianos typically incorporated between four and seven pedals to make an amazing range of sounds, including Turkish Janissary effects.

In England, various initiatives were taken to develop an upright piano. In 1795, William Stodart introduced his "upright-grand" to the English market and in 1798 William Southwell sold, in his London shop, a square piano tipped onto its side. Although these

The semi-elliptical shape of a demi-lune piano meant that, with the lid shut, the piano became a side table. Southwell's 1785 version is veneered in mahogany, satinwood, and amboyna.

timeline

1923

• *Reproducing mechanisms incorporated into ten percent of total piano sales.*

1925

• *A-440 established as concert pitch in the United States.*
• *137,000 conventional pianos and 169,000 player pianos are produced in the United States.*

tape check action

1 intermediate lever
2 escapement regulating screw
3 tape
4 damper

5 damper wire
6 string
7 check head
8 jack return spring

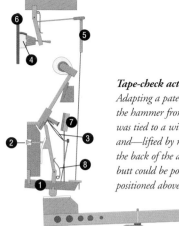

Tape-check action, Robert Wornum, 1842
Adapting a patent of Hermann Lichtenthal's, Wornum employed a tape to prevent the hammer from bouncing back on the string after it had initially struck. The tape was tied to a wire set into a rocking lever, which also housed the jack, check head, and—lifted by means of a long wire—the damper. A set-off screw, regulated from the back of the action, controlled the jack's escapement, and—so that the hammer butt could be positioned as close to the string as possible—the dampers were positioned above the hammers, resulting in the term over-damper action.

ideas generated some degree of interest, the great height of many of these instruments (some were over 8 feet, or 2.5 meters, tall) fatally hindered their future prospects.

The evolution of the modern upright piano began—simultaneously in Vienna and Philadelphia—in the year 1800. Matthias Müller and John Isaac Hawkins both produced vertical standing pianos in which, for the first time, the strings were extended behind the keyboard to the floor. Although Hawkins's 4½-foot (137-cm)-high piano was not rated highly for its sound, it was still an ingenious engineering feat that included an iron frame, and a check action mounted in front of the vertical strings.

In 1811, Robert Wornum patented a reduced height "cottage" piano, which he started manufacturing with much success in London in 1814. Like Hawkins's piano, it had a sticker action, and Wornum improved this in 1826; by 1842, Wornum's tape-check action had become the basis of the present upright piano action. The popularity of the cottage piano was almost immediate and other makers, including Broadwood and Clementi, were quick to see the possibilities. But it was in France that the instrument met with widest approval. Since the turn of the century architects in Paris had been

building small apartment houses, and the lack of space in these to accommodate a grand or a square piano encouraged French makers to produce this new type of piano. Pleyel were the market leaders, manufacturing "pianinos" based on the cottage pianos of Robert Wornum and the 1828 patents of Jean-Henri Pape; these patents described a 40-inch (102-cm) console piano that, for the first time, included cross-stringing to increase the string length and so improve the piano's tone. The architectural fashions of Paris soon spread through German and English cities and the desire grew for space-saving instruments. By the 1830s the domestic European market for pianos had shifted radically from the square piano to the upright.

By 1860, a few American makers had begun to pay attention to the perfected vertical system, which at its best employed overstringing and a full iron frame. But it took another decade before the trend caught on and it was Steinway & Sons who capitalized on it. An increase in city living encouraged makers such as Baldwin, Kimball, and Decker Brothers to produce vertical pianos out of necessity rather than visual wonderment, and the instruments' lower production cost ensured that, by the dawn of the twentieth century, the upright piano had become the only alternative to the grand.

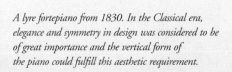

A lyre fortepiano from 1830. In the Classical era, elegance and symmetry in design was considered to be of great importance and the vertical form of the piano could fulfill this aesthetic requirement.

1931

• *Neo-Bechstein piano produced.*

1934

• *Brasted brothers introduce the Swedish designed "minipiano."*

piano making
in the twentieth century

By the turn of the twentieth century, the design of the piano as a musical instrument was essentially complete. The actions of the grand and upright piano could scarcely be improved and the use of the iron frame was already universal, as too was cross-stringing. The small piano workshops had grown into a massive industry, with many manufacturers owning more than one factory and employing mass-production techniques. In 1911, America boasted 301 piano manufacturers producing approximately 370,000 instruments, more pianos than in Germany (334 makers), England (136 makers), Austria (79), and France (37) put together; only 19 builders were known in Italy.

For the companies that survived the disruptions of the First World War (during which many helped with national war efforts making, among other things, aircraft parts), the peak years of piano building occurred in the 1920s, with a worldwide output of 600,000 pianos in 1920 alone. But the Great Depression of the 1930s, combined with the advent of radio and the gramophone, radically changed the piano industry's market and many of the firms that were not closed were forced into larger conglomerates. By 1935 the worldwide output of pianos was only about 144,000. If the effects of the Second World War were easier on the industry than the First, it was only because there were fewer makers to be affected. The subsequent reinvestment, particularly in Japan and Korea,

helped open new markets for the piano and today the largest producers of pianos are in the Far East.

With ever greater demands placed on the piano, twentieth-century makers have had to concentrate on improving the robustness of the instrument. Many of the core materials used in pianomaking remain unchanged but, with the export of pianos to climates very different from where the instrument was designed and made, tougher glues, finishes, and laminate woods have had to be developed and employed to cope with extreme levels of humidity and punishing long-distance freight. Some traditional materials are now so scarce that alternatives have had to be found, with plastic making a reasonable substitute for ivory and ebony key coverings, and composite boards often replacing solid wood cases.

To accommodate popular taste and smaller living quarters, makers have had to adjust the strung back so that pianos can be made in a myriad of sizes. The 4-foot (122-cm) "baby" grand was created by Albert Webery at the beginning of last century, but the most dramatic decrease in size affected the upright piano. In 1934, an English piano maker called Brasted discovered in Sweden a miniature piano made by Messrs. Lundholm of Stockholm. Brasted bought the rights to the design and began to manufacture it in England under the "Minipiano" name; the popularity of this instrument led to his being praised in the *Piano Trades Magazine*

The mechanism of a German player piano from the 1920s. Player pianos used paper rolls pierced with holes that corresponded to the pitch and duration of notes; this allowed pressurized air to pass through and mechanically play the piano's action.

timeline

1935

• largest ever grand piano made by Challen for the Silver Jubilee of King George V: 11 ft 8 in (355cm) long and weighing 1.25 tons.

• worldwide output of pianos falls to just 144,000.

Many piano companies employ leading architects and designers to create exciting and visually stimulating case designs. The case of this Sauter piano was designed by Peter Maly.

of America as having "revolutionized and saved the piano trade." The piano was so low that its action had to be dropped below the keyboard, from where its hammers were lifted to the strings rather than pushed. The advantages of its small size combined with Brasted's fashionable case designs soon led to other companies, such as Eavestaff, Kemble, and Barratt and Robinson, joining the trend.

The most significant piano innovation of the twentieth century was the player piano. Their pneumatic mechanisms, operated either by pedals or pumped air, read punched-paper rolls to perform pieces of music. By the 1920s, the dramatic rise in their popularity meant that almost half the pianos produced were player pianos. The gramophone, the radio, and the Great Depression of the 1930s led to their demise until the 1980s, when a pedigree returned to combat the threat of electric keyboards, this time driven by electric switches.

To meet worldwide demand, the piano industry has become highly automated, and production levels have increased gradually throughout the past century. Today, some companies produce a staggering 200,000 pianos a year. Increasing automation has not only led to a dramatic rise in output but it has also standardized further the design of the instrument. Many manufacturers, though, still pride themselves on producing instruments that create their own tone color through the use of various scale designs, and the tradition of art cases has continued, with many companies producing runs of commemorative instruments designed by modern architects and artists. The intrument's future appears to be in safe hands.

Bösendorfer's Chrysler piano was created as a tribute to the famous New York Art Deco skyscraper. The legs are shaped after the building itself, and the lyre and prop are inspired by the lobby vases. The decoration on the inside of the piano's top is a copy of the design on the elevator doors.

1956
• *Young Chang is the first piano manufacturer in Korea.*

1960
• *Yamaha produce 2,200 pianos a month.*

1986
• *Yamaha introduces the Disclavier.*

Pianos of the great composers

ENTIRE LIBRARIES OF MUSIC HAVE BEEN WRITTEN FOR THE PIANO BY THE FINEST COMPOSERS. WHILE THESE COMPOSITIONS WERE UNDOUBTEDLY INFLUENCED BY THE INSTRUMENTS AT THEIR DISPOSAL, THE DESIRE TO EXPLORE THE LIMITS OF MUSICAL EXPRESSION IN TURN DEMANDED FURTHER TECHNICAL DEVELOPMENTS IN PIANO BUILDING. ONE OR TWO COMPOSERS WERE THEMSELVES PIANO BUILDERS (MUZIO CLEMENTI AND IGNAZ PLEYEL ACHIEVED WIDESPREAD RECOGNITION IN BOTH SPHERES), AND MANY MAKERS THROUGHOUT HISTORY HAVE BEEN ADVANCED PIANISTS, USING THEIR MASTERY OF TECHNIQUE AS AN INSPIRATION FOR THEIR DESIGNS.

Franz Schubert was satisfied with the pianos made in Vienna, for their light touch and clear tone gave him the sense of intimacy he longed for. He wrote to his parents in 1825: "I performed my variations not unsuccessfully, since several people assured me that my fingers had transformed the keys into singing voices. If this is actually true, then I am highly delighted, since I cannot bear to listen to the damnable thumping which is peculiar to even the most distinguished pianists and which pleases neither the ear nor mind."

When Charles Burney declared that "the harsh scratching of the quills could no longer be borne" he may or may not have known that he was calling time on the age of the harpsichord and ushering in the age of the piano. The revised and strengthened piano with its extended compass was rapidly exploited by the compositions and performances of Chopin, Schumann, and Liszt. Its repertoire was sizable and growing all the time, and by the turn of the twentieth century the piano was poised to become the most commonly used musical instrument in both Europe and America. Further demanding and inspirational compositions from the likes of Ravel and Debussy in Europe, and Scott Joplin in America, together with the development of jazz, pushed the piano onto center stage. Demand grew exponentially, and manufacturers were forced to adopt mass-production techniques that were to standardize the instrument in the form in which we know it today.

In this chapter we are less concerned with the great manufacturers of the late nineteenth and the twentieth century than we are with the ones involved in the historical development of the piano. Before notions of power and evenness throughout the piano's entire range took hold, individual makers were valued for the particular character of their instruments, which quite intentionally displayed wide variations in touch preferences and tone color. It is a compliment to the piano makers of Vienna that many of Europe's musicians and composers preferred the light touch and clear tones of these instruments to the English and French styles of piano that would eventually be adapted to suit the large concert hall performances of later times. Even so, to hear Debussy's *Estampes* of 1903 played on a Blüthner grand of about the same age is to experience a richness and warmth that is absent when the same piece is played on a brighter modern piano. With successive eras donating various pitches and tuning temperaments, and a wealth of different actions and tone colors, it is interesting to see the wide selection of instruments that these musicians chose both for musical inspiration and character.

Schubert's living room in Wipplingerstrasse, Vienna, in 1821.

johann sebastian bach 1685–1750

*Johann
Sebastian Bach*

J. S. Bach spent his later years as a great enthusiast for the new form of keyboard instrument that had emerged during his own lifetime; he was acting as an intermediary in the sales of Gottfried Silbermann's pianofortes as late in his life as 1749. His initial introduction to the German maker's instrument was to prove pivotal in Silbermann's progress.

Silbermann had been making pianofortes since the early 1730s, and he first persuaded Bach to play one of his instruments around 1736. When asked for his reactions to the piano, Bach was said to have admired the tone of the new instrument, but heavily criticized the weak nature of the top treble and claimed the action was too difficult to play. A bitterly disappointed Silbermann, sensing the truth of the criticisms, set about remedying the problems. Using Cristofori's 1726 piano as a model he went back to the drawing board, and by the end of the decade was producing instruments that met with widespread approval. Much esteemed by Frederick the Great, king of Prussia, Silbermann's piano replicated Cristofori's inverted wrest plank and action, but used a soundboard of thin spruce instead of cedar, and included a decorative rose. The structure was still that of a heavily built harpsichord and, using local oak and walnut for the case and a heavier bridge, the instruments were aesthetically more Germanic than Italian. The hammer heads, like Cristofori's, were hollow rolls faced with a soft leather covering, and the compass of the keyboard was just fifty-six notes, FF–d3 (F9–D66). Tuned using a well-tempered scale, the instruments' pitch might possibly have been as low as A415 Hz (in 1770, Silbermann built the organ in the Roman Catholic church in Dresden, which had a pitch of A415 Hz), although in England at this time Handel's tuning fork was made at A422.5 Hz.

In 1747 "the Old Bach," as he was now being called, was invited by Frederick the Great to perform on all fifteen of his court's pianos. Bach responded, and on the final instrument famously improvised a six-part fugue. Bach's ability to entertain the Royal Court playing an instrument radically different in touch to the organ, clavichord, or harpsichord leads us to believe that he was, by then, used to playing the improved Silbermann action. Johann Friedrich Agricola, Bach's pupil between 1738 and 1741, claimed that Bach had at his disposal a Silbermann piano that satisfied him; this may very well be the "clavecin" that was mentioned in Bach's last will.

Bach's youngest son, Johann Christian, helped the progress to popularity of the early pianoforte, becoming among the first to exploit the instrument in performance and composition to its full potential. In 1768 he performed the first piano solo in England and the title pages of his two sets of Sonatas state they are "for the Harpsichord or Piano-forte."

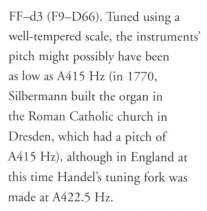

Bach plays in front of Frederick the Great in the music room at Sanssouci Castle.

on record

The "on record" box that appears with each composer highlights a recommended recording of their work.

Piano played: the 1726 Cristofori wing-shaped piano.

• Historische Tasteninstrumente aus dem Musikinstrumenten Museum der Universität Leipzig, *played by Walter Heinz Bernstein, and Christine Schornsheim. Label: Verlag K.-J. Kamprad.*

joseph haydn 1732–1809

Early forms of struck keyboard instruments existed in Vienna as far back as 1725, and Joseph Haydn would have been aware of the emerging pianoforte during his studies in the city in the 1750s. In 1773, while he was the Kapellmeister to Prince Esterhazy, a concert was performed featuring a pianoforte, and it is possible that Haydn played the instrument himself. In a letter to his publisher in 1788, he wrote: "In order to compose your three pianoforte Sonatas particularly well I had to buy a new pianoforte." Debate centers on whether this was a replacement for an existing piano or for the five-octave Viennese harpsichord he owned. His letters mention that the piano bought was by a Viennese maker, Wenzel Schantz, but it is not known whether this was a square or wing-shaped piano. A square piano by younger brother Johann Schantz is exhibited in the Kunsthistorisches Museum in Vienna, and it is claimed that this is the piano owned by Haydn during his time in Vienna. Although the square piano is not dated, its style suggests that it was made some time between 1785 and 1795, and it could be similar in construction to that made by the elder Schantz brother. It has a five-octave compass, FF–f3 (F9–F69), and employs a damper lift and moderator stop; but the most important design characteristic is within its action and keyboard. The action design is different from the Prellmechanik actions or the English style typically found in square pianos at this time: the keys are returned to their rest position by small brass springs fixed to the balance rail and connected to the underside of the keys through loops.

Haydn is known to have preferred a light touch—in a letter to Frau von Genzinger, for whom he wrote the Sonata Hob. XVI: 49, he wrote: "It's only a pity that your Grace does not own a Schantz fortepiano, on which everything is better

expressed—his pianofortes are particularly light in touch and the mechanism very agreeable." On his first visit to England in 1791, he lodged in Great Pulteney Street opposite the Broadwood workshop and salerooms, and composed in a private room of the Broadwood house. This, and the loan of a Broadwood grand for performances, accustomed Haydn to the English style of grand piano. From 1800, Broadwood's tuning fork was pitched at C505.7 Hz, about half a semitone lower than today's pitch, and the firm regularly tuned in Meantone temperament until 1846. The action would have required a much heavier touch, and the damping on English instruments was not crisp, giving the instrument a lingering, sustained tone. The bass register, although lush, was buzzy by modern standards, and the dry middle register allowed the elaborate ornaments to sing clearly. These differences, together with an enlarged five-and-a-half octave keyboard, may have provided Haydn with inspiration, as his later pieces feature thick chords and harmonized treble lines.

On his return to Vienna in 1795, Haydn bought a five-and-a-half octave Longman & Broderip grand, equipped with a compass FF–c4 (F9–C76) and an English grand action. Haydn played this until his final years, when it is said that he had to switch to the clavichord, as the fortepiano "proved too strenuous for his nerves."

A portrait of Joseph Haydn sitting at his piano, deep in thought.

on record

Richard Burnett's musical tour, *Richard Burnett. Label: Amon-Ra*

• Haydn Sonata in D *played on a Broadwood grand made in 1801.*

• Haydn Sonata in A *played on a Walter traveling square made in 1805.*

• Haydn: Variations in F minor, Three Sonatas, *Joanna Leach. Label: Athene.*

• Sonata in C *played on a Broadwood square of 1789.*

• Sonata in C minor *played on a Longman and Broderip square of 1787.*

wolfgang amadeus mozart 1756–1791

Recent evidence suggests that as early as the 1760s Leopold Mozart, father of Wolfgang Amadeus, owned a two-manual combination harpsichord made by Christian Ernst Friederici of Gera, as well as three clavichords. The smallest of these is certain to have been made by Stein, and another was acquired from Fishietti and Rust. The latter instrument Mozart favored throughout his life, and on it he composed and tested many of his works.

It is not until 1775 that the earliest account appears of Mozart playing a pianoforte in public. The *Deutsche Chronik* reports that an evening concert took place at the house of Herr Albert:

"I heard these two giants in contest on the clavier. Mozart's playing had great weight, and he read at sight everything that was put before him." The article says nothing of the piano or its make.

From Augsburg in 1777, Mozart wrote to his father praising Johann Andreas Stein's instrument: "Before I had seen any of his make, Spath's claviers had always been my favorites. But now I much prefer Stein's, for they damp ever so much better…whatever way I touch the keys, the tone is always even." The letter gives details of Stein's soundboard-making technique, and illustrates how frustrating and clumsy other pianofortes must have been at the time. A tuning fork belonging to Stein in 1780 was tuned to A422.6 Hz, and his instruments would have been tuned to a well-tempered scale.

Despite his continued association with Stein (he gave his daughter Nanette piano lessons), Mozart acquired a fortepiano made by Anton Walter some time between 1782 and 1785. Surprisingly, the instrument was not reserved for use in Mozart's house; a letter written by Leopold to his daughter Maria Anna in 1785 states: "Since my arrival, your brother's fortepiano has been taken at least a dozen times to the theater or to some other house." Walter's instrument extends five octaves and employs two knee levers, one on the left to raise the dampers simultaneously, and another on the right side that raises just the treble dampers. A moderator stop is placed centrally above the keyboard to create a softer sound. Despite the knee levers, Leopold goes on to say in his letter that his son "had a large pianoforte pedal made, which stands under the instrument and is about two feet longer and extremely heavy;" unfortunately this no longer exists. The Walter pianos of this time were known to have a bell-like tone, with a strong resonant bass and a precise response, ideal for fast runs and flourishes. The percussive type action accentuated dynamics and accents, and the tone remained clear even with prolonged use of the pedal.

This was the only pianoforte that Mozart ever owned, and in the inventory taken on Mozart's death in 1791 it is listed along with its pedal. Somewhat surprisingly his clavichord—of which his widow, Constanze, later wrote, "My dear clavier: upon which Mozart had played so often and had composed *Die Zauberflöte*, *La Clemenza di Tito*, the *Requiem* and *Eine Kleine Freimaurer Kantate*"—was not. Although four years later a notice was posted saying, "A large fortepiano and a clavichord of the late Mozart's are for sale each day," Constanze in fact gave them to her sons.

on record

Piano played: Paul McNulty after Johann Andreas Stein.

• Mozart: Six Violin Sonatas K.301-6, *Rumiko Harada*. Label: Globe.

Mozart's piano, made by Anton Walter of Vienna, now sits in the Mozart Museum in Salzburg, Austria, bequeathed by Mozart's sons.

Mozart's clavichord and an unfinished portrait of Mozart by his brother-in-law Josef Lange.

ludwig van beethoven 1770–1827

Beethoven is often considered the pianist and composer who was most influential in pushing forward the development of the piano. He wanted it to sound like an orchestra but his expectations were not always met, despite the efforts of Europe's finest makers. As a professor at the Paris Conservatoire recounted of a concert between 1803 and 1808: "One evening when Beethoven was playing a Mozart piano concerto he asked me to turn the pages for him. But I was mostly occupied in wrenching out the strings of the piano that had snapped, while the hammers struck among the broken strings. Beethoven insisted upon finishing the concerto, so back and forth I leaped, jerking out a string here, disentangling a hammer there, turning a page, and I worked harder than Beethoven."

Until 1800 Beethoven owned a pianoforte made by Anton Walter. Thought to be among the finest instruments, these pianos were characterized by Johann Ferdinand von Schönfeld in 1796 as having "A full, bell-like tone, a clear response, and a strong full bass. The tone is a bit dull at first, but later, after one has played the instrument for a certain time, the treble especially becomes very clear. After too much playing…the tone will be sharp and metallic, which can be remedied through the releathering of the hammers." The pianos by Walter were known to have had, for their time, a powerful bass, and the percussive attack of the Prellmechanik action gave accents and fortissimo markings a sudden boost, an effect well used by Beethoven.

"Beethoven in the morning grey in the study," a print from 1899 by Rudolf Eichstædt.

Beethoven was reportedly unimpressed by Haydn's English-style piano, but he craved an una-corda pedal and, Walter being reluctant to build an instrument with one, Beethoven took as a donation from Erard in 1803 the most advanced French grand piano of the time. It was triple strung with four iron arches across the gap between the wrest plank and the soundboard. It had a five-and-a-half octave range and four pedals, including an una-corda, as well as a damper lift, a lute stop, and a moderator for softening the tone. Beethoven disliked the heavy and deep touch and asked Stein's daughter Nanette and her husband, Johann Streicher, to modify the touch. Even after several attempts the modifications did not have the required effect, and although Beethoven continued to use the French instrument his affections remained with the type of pianofortes made in Vienna.

Although Beethoven never owned a Streicher pianoforte, he borrowed one whenever he could for his performances. In 1796 he wrote to the couple regarding a concert performed on one of their instruments: "I assure you in all sincerity that this was the first time it gave me pleasure to hear my trio performed; and truly this experience will make me decide to compose more for the pianoforte." Beethoven's continued friendship with the Streichers reveals his demands for a sturdier piano. In 1810, frustrated in his

Beethoven's Broadwood piano is made of Spanish mahogany, inlaid with marquetry and ormolu, and the laurel wreathed handles are made of brass. The six-octave compass was used by Beethoven to its limit, so too the pedals; the left operating an una-corda effect and the right interestingly being split, so that the right half raises the treble dampers and the left half raises solely the bass.

attempt to acquire the instrument he longed for, he wrote to Streicher: "You promised to let me have a piano by the end of October; and now we are already halfway through November and as yet I haven't received one—my motto is either to play on a good instrument or not at all. As for my French piano, which is certainly quite useless now, I still have misgivings about selling it, for it is really a souvenir such as no one here has so far honored me with." The Streicher instrument never materialized and the Erard piano was later given by Beethoven to his brother.

The English grand piano presented to Beethoven in 1818 by Thomas Broadwood was triple strung throughout, employed a full six octaves CC–c4 (C4–C76), and had a wood frame. The square-section bridge was carved to improve the accuracy of the strings' speaking lengths and the mechanism employed the English grand action. The piano's mellow and singing tone was suited to heavy chords rather than quick runs and the ineffective damping of the English system created more resonance. The tone of the instrument must have been difficult for Beethoven to judge, as by now he was increasingly deaf, but he responded to the gift, writing to the firm: "I shall look on this as an altar on which I shall place the most beautiful offerings of my spirit to the divine Apollo." The piano's journey from London took it by sea to Trieste and then overland by cart to Vienna. Broadwood's firm was by now expert in piano moving: the piano was packed in soft leather covers and contained in a zinc-lined crate. Specially knitted "socks" protected its legs.

Despite Haydn's having owned an English grand in Vienna by 1800, it appears that even at this late stage they were still regarded as an oddity in this city. Ignaz Moscheles held a demonstration concert in 1823, using a Viennese-made piano by Conrad Graf and the Broadwood piano owned by Beethoven. In his report he wrote: "I tried in my *Fantasia* to show the values of the broad, full, although somewhat muffled tone of the Broadwood piano; but in vain. My Viennese public remained loyal to their countryman—the clear, ringing tones of the Graf were more pleasing to their ears." The comparison of pianos may be harsh, as by this stage Beethoven's piano was almost certainly damaged through years of abuse and heavy playing; it proved no more resistant than any other piano

to Beethoven's heavy demands. In 1824 it was inspected by a noted instrument maker, Johann Andreas Stumpff, who reported: "Quite a sight confronted me: the upper registers are quite mute and the broken strings in a tangle, like a thorn bush whipped up by a storm."

To assuage Beethoven's by now almost complete deafness, Conrad Graf loaned him in 1825 a specially made piano that the composer used for the last years of his life. Eight feet (244cm) long with an extended six-and-a-half octave range CC–f4 (C4–F81), the piano employed quadruple stringing to produce a greater sonority (the bottom thirteen notes were triple strung). Fitted with a Prellmechanik action, the dampers were extended to the top string. It also employed three pedals: an una-corda, a moderator, and a damper lift. A year before his death Beethoven's frustration was evident as he expressed his view that the piano "is and remains an inadequate instrument."

on record

Piano played: Streicher, 1800.

• Historische Tasteninstrumente aus dem Musikinstrumenten Museum der Universität Leipzig; *includes Beethoven Sonata Opus 10 No. 1. Walter Heinz Bernstein and Christine Schornsheim. Label: Verlag K.-J. Kamprad.*

Piano played: Broadwood and Sons, 1817.

• The Beethoven Broadwood Fortepiano, *Melvyn Tan. Label: EMI Classics.*

Piano played: Conrad Graf, c.1830.

• Beethoven; Opus 109, 110, 111, *Paul Komen. Label: Globe.*

Beethoven's Amati violin rests on top of his piano, made by Conrad Graf, in the Beethovenhaus in Bonn.

frederic françois chopin 1810–1849

As one who continually explored the subtlety of the piano and its delicate effects, Chopin would exclaim to his students, "You must sing with your fingers!" Spending most of his adult life as a resident in Paris, Chopin owned two pianos, one by Pleyel and another by Erard. The instrument by Pleyel was by far his favorite, as it fulfilled his wish that any imperfection in a pianist's performance should be heard. Liszt felt that "Chopin was fond of Pleyel pianos because of their silvery and somewhat veiled sonority and their easy touch"; the silvery sound may be accounted for by Pleyel's employing a pitch of A446 for their pianos. The compass of Chopin's piano was CC–g4 (C4–G83); the single escapement action was based on the English grand action but was fitted with very light hammers that were shaped to a point rather than a curve. The effect was to offer a touch weight similar to that of a piano from Vienna and Chopin's regulation preference of a shallow after-touch led his technician to comment that the piano achieved "a facility and evenness and rapidity of repeated notes previously thought unobtainable."

Chopin had an ambiguous and often frustrating relationship with the instrument he called his "perfidious traitor" but he also

The Broadwood piano that Chopin played in 1848.

said, "When I feel in good form and strong enough to find my own individual sound, then I need a Pleyel piano."

The Erard piano he owned was reserved for off days. His student Emilie Gretsch quoted him as saying, "You can thump it and bash it, it makes no difference: the sound is always beautiful and the ear doesn't ask for anything more since it hears a full, resonant tone."

In France, Chopin was quickly adopted by Pleyel; the company donated a piano to him on his arrival in the French capital. His first public performance was at Pleyel Hall, on the same bill as the famous six-piano concert; but away from Paris he was courted by other piano makers. In a letter from London in 1848 he wrote, "I have at last managed to get a foothold in this abyss called London. I have only just begun to breathe more freely these last few days, now that the sun has begun to shine. Erard hastened to offer his services and he has placed one of his pianos at my disposal. I have a Broadwood and a Pleyel—three pianos in all, but what's the use of them since I have no time to play."

At his last performances in England in 1848 he played a Broadwood grand. Still made with a traditional English grand action and predominantly wood-framed, this piano was fitted with five iron bars, and tuned to a pitch of A436 using equal temperament, as had been all Broadwood instruments since 1846.

This Pleyel upright piano was sent to Chopin during his stay at the Abbey of Valdemosa, Mallorca, in 1838.

on record

Piano played: Chopin's Broadwood grand of 1848.

• Chopin, Piano Concerto No.1, *Weber.*
Label: Nimbus.

franz liszt 1811–1886

The nineteenth century saw the appearance of the piano virtuosos, and for the makers, although often they were not able to match the demands of the new style of performance, it became essential to have their instruments demonstrated on the concert platforms of Europe. In 1824, at the same time as Pleyel adopted Chopin, the piano house of Erard had the good fortune and vision to adopt under contract a young Hungarian piano prodigy whose name was Franz Liszt. The young Liszt was donated Erard's new patent grand piano that featured the double repetition action and a full seven-octave compass, and his first engagement was a tour of England. In the following years, aided by their responsive instruments and by Liszt's growing popularity, Erard would take from Broadwood the title of Europe's most sought-after concert piano.

Franz Liszt, though, did not confine himself to one make of piano for long, and wherever he could, he used a piano built by a local maker for his concerts. In a letter addressed to Erard in 1850 he wrote that it was his duty "not to hinder the soaring of local and national industries." In Vienna he was known to have used pianos made by Graf and Streicher; in England by Broadwood; and in the South of France, Spain, and Portugal by Boisselot.

Liszt's ability to play on any make or type of piano was aided by a practice regime on a heavy keyboard, and the power with which he attacked the keyboard—together with his extravagant and flamboyant style—left many of his chosen concert instruments with broken strings, keys, and action parts. The suffering pianos would require retuning at intervals throughout the performance and on some occasions it is known that spare pianos stood at the side of the stage, ready to take over if the performance instrument was too badly broken to continue. Liszt's reputation grew to the extent that the audience felt let down if a piano survived the evening intact.

Although not a piano technician, Liszt was interested in technological innovations. Once admitting that "without the pedal the piano is only a dulcimer," he employed dummy keyboards to practice on during long voyages, experimented with bass pedals, and owned a combination piano-harmonium.

By 1841, Liszt was considered the Paganini of the keyboard: the increased compass of the piano to seven octaves showed his dexterity and musicality, while the stronger framing of the instruments was more able to withstand the weight of his shoulders, arms, and wrists. By now he was an admirer of the lingering tone of Bösendorfer pianos, and a visitor to his home in 1850 reported that he owned one of that make, together with a Bechstein, a Boisselot, and a Streicher, in addition to Beethoven's Broadwood.

Toward the end of his life Liszt was less eager to provide testimonials for piano companies but, always in touch with developments, in 1884 he praised the American firm of Chickering. Such was the company's enthusiasm for his endorsement that they transported their piano from America through Europe and across the Alps to set it up in Liszt's Rome apartment. But the effect of the complimentary remarks was lost when Liszt went on to say, "When Mr. Steinway gets here I shall have a piano shop talk with him, about the construction of his grands." In his apartment in Rome he had a Steinway piano.

on record

Piano played: Erard concert grand of 1889.

• Liszt: Sonata in B minor, Prelude and Fugue, Csárdás Macabre, Norma Fantasy, *Alexei Orlowetsky.* Label: *Globe.*

In a rare performance later in life, Franz Liszt plays a Bösendorfer grand piano before the Imperial family in Budapest in 1872.

robert and clara schumann 1810–1856 & 1819–1896

Robert and Clara Schumann

Clara's father, Friedrich Wieck (1785–1873), an enlightened piano tutor and instrument retailer who also sold practice contraptions such as leaded gloves, finger stretchers, and practice keyboards, bought his eight-year-old daughter a piano made by Stein. It is said that he preferred the English style of piano, yet sensing that the keys were too heavy for such a young girl's practice he concluded that a Viennese-made piano was better suited. The acquired piano, upon which Robert Schumann was taught, had a Prellmechanik action, a six-octave range, and three pedals—two types of soft effect and the common sustaining pedal. In 1839, while studying in Paris, Clara wrote to Robert complaining of the heaviness of the Erard piano she had to play; she further commented that the Pleyel pianos that she had come across were a touch lighter. However, she acquired a six-and-a-half octave piano CC–g4 (C4–G83) made by Conrad Graf, with leather-covered hammers, and an action weight closer to that on which she had first learned. She kept this instrument throughout her marriage, even though Robert gave her a Hartel grand piano as a wedding present.

During the 1840s, despite Clara's misgivings, Robert was an advocate of the emerging upright piano. In 1845 he acquired a pedal piano by Louis Schone, for organ practice as well as composition, with a twenty-nine note pedal board. Schuman wrote many pieces for the pedal piano, most notably *Six Studies Op. 56, Four Sketches Op. 58,* and *Six Fugues on Bach Op. 60.*

After Robert's death in 1856 Clara gave her cherished Graf piano to her friend Johannes Brahms. Clara now preferred the pianos made by Grotrian-Steinweg, who were producing instruments with a deep bass and a bright singing treble, but her preferred domestic sound took getting used to on the concert platform. In reviews of her later concerts, she was heavily criticized for playing too fast. The thicker tone of the developed piano not only helped her approach a fresher perception of composers' ideas, but also muddled the sound, compelling many of her husband's pieces to be played at a slower tempo than on a clear-toned piano. It was widely thought at the time that maybe Robert Schumann's metronome was faulty, and so affected the tempo markings he chose.

At the age of seventy-seven, Clara's passion for the instrument still seemed defiant: while purchasing a cover for her daughter's piano she unexpectedly found a new Grotrian-Steinweg grand that so enchanted her that she bought it on the spot.

A pedal piano dating from 1800. Initially intended for organ practice, pianos, harpsichords and clavichords were occasionally equipped with pedal boards. These were connected with an action placed at the back of the piano, where a special soundboard, covered with 29 strings, was built into the case.

on record

Piano played: Graf grand, 1826.

• Richard Burnett's musical tour *includes Schumann,* Piano Quintet in E flat major, Opus 44. *Richard Burnett. Label: Amon-Ra.*

Piano played: Broadwood cabinet piano, 1850.

• Seven Broadwoods: The evolution of the English piano, *includes Schumann, from* Kinderszenen Opus 15. *Richard Burnett. Label: Sonic Culture Design.*

johannes brahms 1833–1897

Throughout his life Johannes Brahms played publicly on a multitude of different pianos. He is known to have played the American instruments of Steinway and Knabe, and those of the old and new makers of Europe, including Broadwood, Bechstein, Blüthner, Ibach, and Erard; but his preference for Viennese-made pianos lasted until his death. An amazing loyalty to Streicher culminated in the loan of a piano in 1864, about which Brahms wrote to Clara Schumann: "I have a beautiful grand from Streicher on which to practice. He wanted to share his achievements with me." In the 1880s, due to their emerging control of piano making in Vienna, Brahms regularly chose a Bösendorfer grand for his performances. The company were still making pianos with the Prellmechanik action but their inherent tone was far more smoky and lingering than a present-day Bösendorfer.

Johannes Brahms owned just two pianos in his lifetime. The first was the piano by Graf owned by Clara and Robert Schumann, and given to Brahms by Clara in 1856. Although this piano was much loved by Brahms, its six-and-a-half octave compass was limiting his compositions; but its sentimental value led it to be exhibited by Brahms at the Vienna Exposition of 1873, after which it was donated to the Gesellschaft der Musikfreunde in Vienna.

In the same year, Brahms received as a gift from the Streicher firm a grand piano they had made in 1868, and he kept this piano in his study until his death in 1897. The seven-octave piano, AAA–a4 (A1–A85), was conservative in design, employing a partial metal frame and using tensioning bars bolted to the hitch plate to hold the tension of the straight-strung strings. The action was a single escapement Prellmechanik design with leather-covered hammers. The sound of this piano was unique to the Viennese maker, producing a clear, sweet tone. The softer sound was created by a very quick decay rate after a forceful attack, particularly in the bass strings. The piano's compass had three distinct sounds, with the full middle register easily dominating, but its clarity of pitch meant that melody lines played in the tenor and bass were outstanding. The action's lighter and shallower touch allowed a small amount of pressure to produce vast dynamic response. Unfortunately the piano was destroyed in a bombing raid during the Second World War.

on record

Piano played: Streicher grand of 1839.

• Mendelssohn: Works for Cello and Piano, *Melvyn Tan. Label: RCA Victor Red Seal.*

The Graf piano that Clara Schumann gave to her dear friend Brahms in 1856. Despite a brief experiment with quadruple stringing in the treble end of his pianos, the design of Conrad Graf's instruments remained relatively unchanged throughout his life. As late as 1839, Graf refused to employ any metal in the structure of his pianos, feeling that it would have a harmful effect on the instruments' tone.

Anatomy
of the piano

EVERY PART OF THE PIANO HAS A SPECIFIC NAME RECOGNIZED BY TECHNICIANS AND
DEALERS THE WORLD OVER. A KNOWLEDGE OF THESE TERMS WILL HELP
READERS GET THE MOST FROM THE CHAPTERS THAT FOLLOW, AND
WILL ENABLE THEM TO DESCRIBE ACCURATELY ANY
PROBLEMS ARISING WITH THEIR INSTRUMENT.

As the piano developed, the materials used for its parts were
carefully chosen to fulfill specific tasks. The essential woods,
metals, and felts have now become standard in piano
making and, despite the obvious difference in their
vertical and horizontal forms, the upright and
grand pianos can each be divided into three
main component systems: the casework,
the strung back, and the
playing mechanism.

*An exploded view of a grand piano
showing the action and keyboard,
soundboard, iron frame, and case
with supporting braces.*

anatomy of the grand piano

1 action
2 keyboard
3 piano case
4 wrest plank
5 wooden braces
6 soundboard
7 long bridge
8 iron frame

the piano case

The piano's shapes and parts are governed by the instrument's musical function, but—as it is both a musical instrument and a piece of furniture—it is in the piano case that one finds a marriage of acoustics, aesthetics, and engineering.

cabinet finishes

Casework finishes are required to be especially attractive to the eye. The case may be covered in exotic wood veneers or finished in almost any flat color, and the choice is staggering.

Most piano cases are put through an elaborate finishing process, often consisting of over twenty stages, from sanding through staining to applying and polishing the final finish coats. Traditional finishes, such as French polish, are today used only in restoration workshops; in the factory, they have largely been replaced by sprayed-on finishes, such as lacquer or polyester. These can be produced with a satin or gloss effect and tinted with various colors. A black piano is often described as having an ebonized finish.

the case finish

To arrive at a flawless finish, the casework parts go through a multi-stage finishing process.

1. The case is veneered on both sides.
2. If necessary, it is stained or grain-filled.
3. The parts are coated with several layers of clear or tinted polyester or lacquer.
4. The surface of the final coat is sanded with ever-finer-grit abrasive paper and then burnished using a high-speed buffing mop to a mirror-like sheen.

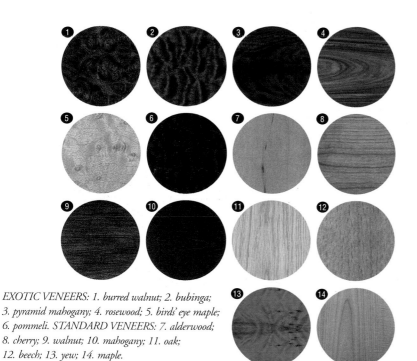

EXOTIC VENEERS: *1. burred walnut; 2. bubinga; 3. pyramid mahogany; 4. rosewood; 5. birds' eye maple; 6. pommeli. STANDARD VENEERS: 7. alderwood; 8. cherry; 9. walnut; 10. mahogany; 11. oak; 12. beech; 13. yew; 14. maple.*

the properties of wood

The species and cut of wood employed in any part of piano making must fulfill numerous criteria, of sound, strength, stability, and longevity. Every piece of wood has its own distinct characteristics and properties, and the true piano craftsman can select these to suit a particular requirement. Many years are required to season this increasingly rare material to a stable condition before it can be used in musical instrument making, and piano manufacturers have to hold huge stocks of various timbers. The *Timber Trade Times* reported, with amazement, on John Broadwood's timber yard at the end of the nineteenth century, "This Thames wharf offers therefore an unique object-lesson in dendrology. Inside, we were brought face to face with fallen giants from the tropical jungle, from the silent Australian bush, from the dense back-woods of the wild west, from the stately and historic wealds of England."

wood for the case

The upright piano's case, although primarily decorative, does have to support and protect the keyboard and action. In the grand piano, the case is an essential part of the instrument's resonant body, with a continuous rim running around the strung back and a top that deflects the sound toward the listener.

The maker must give as much consideration to how the piano's case will stand the test of time as he does to the instrument's mechanics. Solid wood has wonderful acoustic properties, but it is also a hygroscopic material—it shrinks and expands across its grain as humidity levels around it change—and it is therefore inimical to the stability required in a piano case. Wood is, however, much less likely to shrink and warp if it is laminated, that is, made up of layers whose grain alternates in direction. That is why, since the piano's earliest beginnings, its makers have favored for the casework the use of a solid wood core covered on both sides with veneer, for the optimum combination of stability and tonality. Today plywood or particleboard is more commonly used as the core material and it is this that is veneered. Solid wood is still used for some casework parts, such as grand legs and moldings.

the upright's pedals

- *Upright piano pedals are mounted on the bottom board of the piano, and are connected to the action by means of various levers and dowels called the trapwork.*

- *The pedal on the left is called the half-blow pedal. When depressed it pushes the hammers closer to the strings, thus reducing the power with which they can hit the strings. The disadvantage of this pedal is that, by moving the hammers closer to the strings, it creates lost motion between the jack and the hammer butt, leaving an uncomfortable and less controlable touch for the pianist.*

- *The sustaining pedal is always on the right, and when depressed, it simultaneously lifts all the dampers off their strings, thus leaving the strings to vibrate until the pedal is released.*

- *More often than not, the middle pedal is a celeste pedal. When depressed, it locks down and lowers a thin strip of felt between the hammers and the strings, muffling the piano's tone. Although good for note-bashing practice at a quieter volume, it is not possible to use it for practicing the subtle nuances of tone that make music played on a piano so beautiful.*

- *On more expensive upright pianos, the middle pedal controls a sostenuto mechanism, an effect of selective damping similar to that found on many grand pianos.*

Truss leg

upright piano casework names

1 top	**10** castor
2 top door	**11** plinth
3 treble end	**12** lock rail
4 fall	**13** nameboard rail
5 cheek	**14** music desk
6 bottom door	**15** bass end
7 column (or if connected to case sides, trusses)	**16** keyblock
8 toe	
9 pedal feet	

grand piano casework names

1 rim	**9** leg (bass, point, and treble)	**17** keyblock
2 spine (or long side)	**10** ferrule	**18** cheek
3 tail (or point)	**11** castor	**19** music shelf
4 bent side	**12** lyre	**20** music desk
5 treble end	**13** pedal feet	
6 top	**14** backstays	
7 front half	**15** fall	
8 prop and half-prop	**16** keyslip	

the grand's pedals

• *The grand piano's pedals are suspended from the underside of the key bottom and are housed in the pedal lyre. The lyre is either bolted to the underside of the key bottom or attached using cleats and wedged into place; either way it is important for the lyre to be fitted with backstays, which withstand the enormous pressure exerted on the lyre by the pianist's foot. Although the lyre is heavily built, it can easily be broken by continued use with poorly fitted backstays or if it is allowed to bear the weight of the piano when it is moved. It is therefore essential that it is removed prior to any moving of the piano and refitted with its backstays once the piano has been relocated.*

• *The left pedal on the grand piano is called the una-corda pedal. Its function is to shift the entire keyboard to the right, forcing the hammers in the treble section to miss one of the three strings and in the bass to strike a fresh area of the hammer nose, which is toned differently. The effect of this is to create a different tone, one that may be perceived as being quieter. Once the pedal is released, a spring on the inside of the treble cheek returns the action and keyboard to the normal position.*

• *The pedal on the right side is called the sustain pedal; it lifts all the dampers off their strings simultaneously, allowing the strings to vibrate even if the key is released. The middle pedal normally operates the sostenuto mechanism. If the pedal is activated while a key is depressed, the sostenuto rod engages with a lip on the damper body, preventing it from falling when the key is released. Any keys depressed after the sostenuto pedal has been depressed function normally, allowing for selective damping.*

• *In some grand pianos the middle pedal operates a bass sustain effect.*

• *Some companies have started to introduce a fourth pedal, which operates a half-blow mechanism. Commonly found in the upright piano, this is sometimes referred to as the real soft pedal.*

Lyre

the strung back

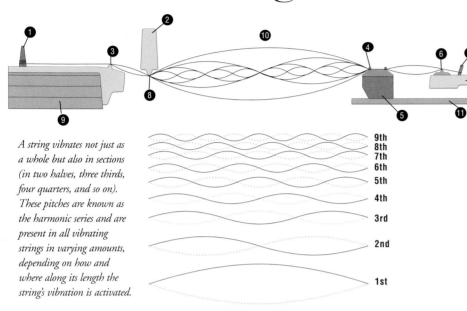

A string vibrates not just as a whole but also in sections (in two halves, three thirds, four quarters, and so on). These pitches are known as the harmonic series and are present in all vibrating strings in varying amounts, depending on how and where along its length the string's vibration is activated.

9th
8th
7th
6th
5th
4th
3rd
2nd
1st

string vibrations (below left)

1	tuning pin	6	rear duplex bridge
2	capo d'astro bar	7	hitch pin
3	front duplex bridge	8	front aliquot
4	rear aliquot	9	pin block (wrest plank)
5	bridge	10	string vibrating pattern
11	soundboard		
12	hitch pin plate (frame)		

As a sonorous musical instrument the piano is a set of strings, held at a massive tension by a supporting structure, which when struck produces a sound recognizable the world over. The brain recognizes sound through the oscillatory motion of excited air particles via the ear; the greater the air particle displacement, the louder the sound. A narrow string is only capable of moving a small amount of air, so if one is set to vibrate without amplification, its sound would be almost inaudible. By laying the strings across a soundboard, their vibration is coupled to a greater amount of surrounding air, thus making it louder.

the vibrating strings

Early piano strings were made of either brass or iron wire, but with the development of high-tensile steel in the 1820s, piano builders were given a much stronger material with which to work. This strength could withstand the impact of larger hammers and be tuned to a higher tension, so starting a process of improvements to produce a louder sound. Today the piano's treble strings are still made from high-tensile steel and the wire diameter is called a gauge. In order to encompass the

range of frequencies required in a piano, however, strings of different gauges must be used. The physics of sound dictates that if the length of a string is doubled and its diameter and tension are constant, it will vibrate at the frequency of a note one octave below. Thus if the same gauge wire were to be used for the entire seven and a quarter octaves of the piano, the bass strings would need to be almost 30 feet (9m) long! A string's vibration is slowed down by adding mass, so to keep the strings to a managable length the thickness of the wire gradually increases from treble to bass. The piano's strings are made from over twenty gauges of wire, from a diameter of 0.7mm in the top treble to 1.6mm in the region below middle C. At this stage physics intervenes once again: above a certain thickness, the string becomes stiff and unresponsive, which means that the piano's strings cannot simply go on increasing in diameter indefinitely. To get around this problem, the tenor and bass strings are covered with a copper winding that increases the strings' mass per unit length

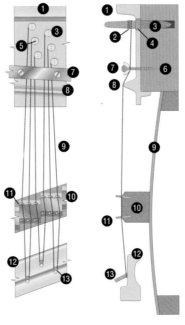

pressure bar—return stringing system

1	header bar	8	top (or iron) bridge
2	coils	9	soundboard
3	wrest pin	10	soundboard bridge
4	plate bushing	11	bridge pins or sidegraft pins
5	beckett or tag	12	hitch plate
6	pin block (wrest plank)	13	hitch pin
7	pressure bar		

without perceptibly increasing its stiffness. In the extreme bass the strings often have a double winding of copper.

At the correct pitch, the string that sounds as C88 vibrates at 4138.44 Hz and A1 at just 27.18 Hz. The vibrating portion of the string, called the "speaking length," is determined by the distance apart of the two bridges. The relationship between a string's tension, speaking length, and diameter is all part of the piano's "scale design" and this is critical to the instrument's inherent tone and sustain.

The compass of a modern piano is either eighty-five or eighty-eight notes, with at least one string per note (usually three strings per note in the treble, two in the tenor, and one in the bass), which means that there are a total of approximately 220 strings. With a tension on each string of about 160–200 pounds (about 75–100kg), the total pulling stress over the entire compass is about 35,000 pounds (16,000 kg). A cast-iron frame and a strong braced back are required to take this massive strain.

the supporting structure

The iron frame is designed to hold the tension of the strings while masking as little of the soundboard as possible. It is cast in sand to eliminate the possibility of its "whistling" (vibrating at certain frequencies) and then sprayed gold or bronze. Cast iron can withstand a great deal of compression but it is brittle and cracks relatively easily if twisted or dropped. The frame is bolted to the back structure, both around its edge and by central rose bolts fitted through a hole in the soundboard, thus allowing the belly to vibrate.

The back structure consists of large wooden posts that help the iron frame take the strain of the strings by preventing it from twisting. Spruce is the wood most often used for backposts, as it has a high strength-to-weight ratio and resists splitting or cracking after it is seasoned.

The strings are stretched between the hitch pins, which provide a firm anchorage for the strings, and the wrest pins (or tuning pins), which permit the strings to be tuned by altering their tension. The hitch pins are fitted into the iron frame and the wrest pins are driven into a block made of quarter-sawn beech, called the pin block or wrest plank, which is firmly secured to the frame to ensure

iron frame anatomy

1	space for pin block or wrest plank web	8	hitch pins
2	front flange	9	flange
3	capo d'astro bar	10	lag screw hole
4	agraffes	11	nose bolt hole
5	treble end bar	12	bass registry hole
6	stress bars		
7	web		

tuning stability. The wrest pins must be a snug fit in the pin block to prevent them unwinding—they have a fine thread to aid extraction. The block itself, drilled with up to 240 holes, is laminated to prevent it from splitting. The number of laminations does not necessarily determine the strength of the pin block; some manufacturers use as few as three layers, others as many as forty, but five or seven laminations is considered the optimum.

the piano's belly

The strings pass over two bridges that define their speaking length. The top bridge, nearest the tuning pins, is either cast into the iron frame or mounted onto the frame within brass agraffes, and the strings are deflected either up or downward to ensure adequate bearing. The bridges attached to the soundboard are made of hardwood, most commonly beech, and the strings are deflected sideways as well as downward to ensure adequate coupling.

For their sound to be audible the strings have to be coupled to a resonant board capable of vibrating freely; this is called the soundboard. Made of spruce, the board is crowned, or domed slightly, to resist the down-bearing force of the strings through the bridge, and additional support is given by carved spruce braces, or belly bars, glued to the underside of the soundboard at 90 degrees to its grain direction. The bars are spaced about 4 inches (10cm) apart and are scalloped at their ends so that the soundboard is not too rigid around its edge.

soundboard material

When spruce is quarter-sawn it offers a high strength-to-weight ratio, is stable after seasoning, and, due to its light weight, responds quickly and evenly over its entire surface to vibrations. Only top-grade selected wood is used for piano soundboards: any resin ducts would inhibit the transmission of vibrations across the board and the evenness of the wood's grain is critical. As no two trees are alike, each soundboard will have its own characteristic tonal qualities. Sitka spruce is the largest of the spruce family and it is the most commonly used, as it offers long lengths of fault-free wood.

bridge material

Piano bridges were traditionally made of solid quarter-sawn beech or maple—hard, strong woods that resist the strings' cutting action and give support to the many pins inserted into the bridge. Today most bridges are made using a vertically laminated beech base, with a solid quarter-sawn beech or maple cap. Stronger and easier to produce than a solid bridge, the laminated format allows little of the strings' vibrational energy to be lost traveling through layers of glue. The solid cap still offers resistance to cuts made by the strings and can be suitably carved and pinned. The bridges are notched on both sides to provide a precise termination point for the string's speaking length and to reduce the mass of the bridge, allowing it greater freedom to vibrate.

down-bearing and bridge pitch

The vibrations of the strings pass through the bridges before being dispersed over the soundboard, so it is essential that there is a good connection. The bridges should be higher than the path of the string by about $\frac{1}{16}$ inch (2mm) or, more accurately, so that the string is displaced by 1.5 degrees. If the down-bearing pressure of the strings is too great then it will clamp the soundboard, making it difficult for it to vibrate. The balance of the strings' down-bearing pressure on the bridge is a critical aspect in piano making and rebuilding. The front edge of the wooden bridges should be slightly higher than the back edge, ensuring that the speaking length of the string is accurately terminated. This slight angle on the top surface of the bridge is known as its "pitch."

Made of top-grade spruce, the piano's soundboard is responsible for the amplification of the strings. The two bridges are glued on the topside (far left) and the belly bars on the underside (left), at right angles to the soundboard's grain.

the playing mechanism

We have seen how the strung back—the set of vibrating strings that are the heart of the piano, the iron frame that supports their tremendous tension, and the soundboard that amplifies the string's minute vibrations—is capable of generating the wide range of tones that are the hallmark of the instrument. But to sound at all, the strings must first be struck, and the complicated mechanism that achieves this is called the action. As the action is the principal interface between player and instrument, it follows that its quality is responsible not only for elements of the sound but also for much of the "feel" of the piano to the musician, and is therefore a critical part of the set-up. The piano action has seen an enormous amount of technical development over the years. Although the basic layout has changed little since the mid-nineteenth century, there have been countless minute improvements in design, construction, and materials, with the result that today's piano actions are precision instruments in their own right. This is such a complicated part of piano making that many manufacturers employ specialist firms to make their actions.

the hammer head

The hammer head, so critical to the tone and volume of a piano, is made up of a wooden molding covered in dense, hard felt. The size of the hammer set gradually increases from the bass hammer to the treble hammer, and its shape also changes from being more rounded in the bass to being more pointed in the treble. The quality of the felt is important; it has to be very dense to prevent the strings from cutting into it but not so hard that it produces a metallic sound, and it is considered to have a superior tone quality if it is made of long wool fibers.

Upright piano hammer heads taken from three different sections of the piano; they graduate in size and shape from the bass to the treble end. The overall length of the bass hammer head is shorter than the two treble hammer heads due to the raised positioning of the bass strings in a cross-strung piano.

Grand piano hammer heads —the arc shaped on the end of the molding allows the hammer head to be securely caught by the back check.

The hammers are made from one length of felt that is thicker down the middle and tapered toward its sides, and this is glued to the molding, creating a tension running around the outside of the hammer and compression through the middle. To create enough clamping pressure a hydraulic press has to be used. After the glue has dried the tapered strip is cut into individual hammers and the felt is stapled to give further strength and prevent the felt from unwrapping. Some hammer manufacturers include colored underfelt on their hammers; this has no bearing on the resulting tone that the set offers.

The point where the hammer contacts the string is called the hammer nose and its striking position along the length of the string is critical to the volume and quality of tone produced. It is agreed that the best strike position is at a point between one-seventh and one-ninth of the way along the speaking length. A string struck here will produce a fuller tone, enriched with desirable harmonics.

flanges

Most of a piano action's moving parts are mounted on little hinges called flanges. The flange and moving part are pinned together using center pins, which fit tightly in the wood of the moving part and rotate in a cloth-lined hole, called a bushing. To allow the part to move freely in the direction of travel but with no sideward play means that the manufacturing tolerances between the pin and bushing are critical.

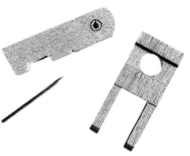

The piano action's moving parts pivot on a center pin that rotates in a cloth-lined hole in a flange.

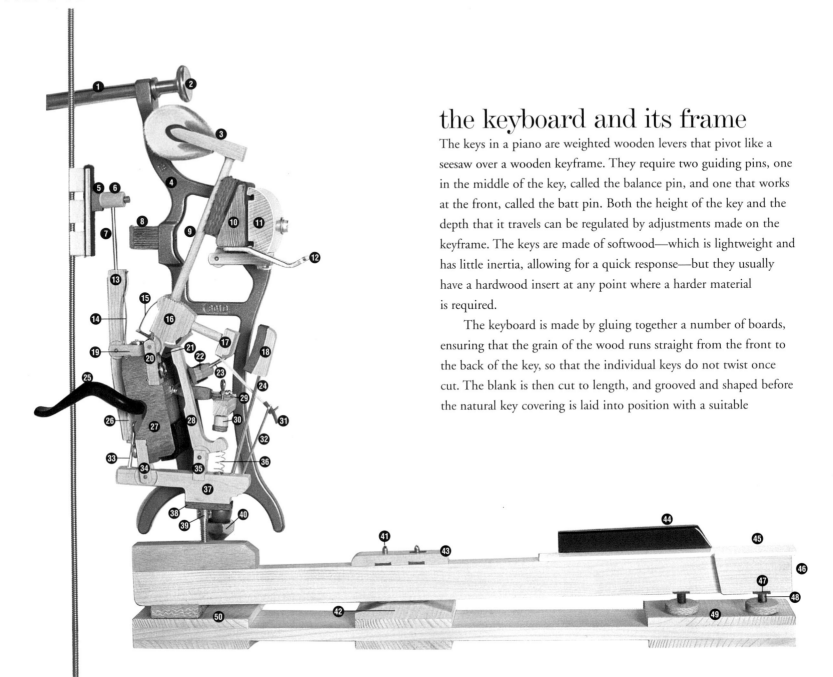

the keyboard and its frame

The keys in a piano are weighted wooden levers that pivot like a seesaw over a wooden keyframe. They require two guiding pins, one in the middle of the key, called the balance pin, and one that works at the front, called the batt pin. Both the height of the key and the depth that it travels can be regulated by adjustments made on the keyframe. The keys are made of softwood—which is lightweight and has little inertia, allowing for a quick response—but they usually have a hardwood insert at any point where a harder material is required.

The keyboard is made by gluing together a number of boards, ensuring that the grain of the wood runs straight from the front to the back of the key, so that the individual keys do not twist once cut. The blank is then cut to length, and grooved and shaped before the natural key covering is laid into position with a suitable

cross section of the upright piano playing mechanism

1 action standard bolt	**10** half blow rail	**19** damper flange	**27** beam rail, main action rail	**36** spiral (jack) spring	**45** key top
2 action standard nut	**11** hammer rest rail	**20** hammer flange	**28** jack	**37** lever body, wippen	**46** key front
3 hammer head	**12** half blow arm	**21** cushion pad	**29** set-off rail	**38** heel of action	**47** front mortise
4 action standard	**13** damper body	**22** jack skip rail	**30** set-off button	**39** capstan, pilot or dolly	**48** bat pin
5 damper head	**14** damper spring	**23** jack slap rail screw or left	**31** tape (bridle strap)	**40** action standard cup	**49** front-touch rail
6 damper drum	**15** butt spring	and right screw	**32** tie wire (bridle wire)	**41** balance pin	**50** back-touch rail
7 damper wire	**16** hammer butt	**24** check wire	**33** spoon	**42** balance rail	
8 damper slap rail	**17** balance hammer	**25** simultaneous lift rod	**34** lever flange	**43** chasing	
9 hammer shank	**18** check head	**26** damper tail	**35** jack flange	**44** sharp	

cross section of the grand piano playing mechanism

1 key front	**19** repetition lever adjusting screw	**37** spoon
2 key top	**20** repetition spring	**38** damper lever body
3 front mortise	**21** bottom lever (wippen)	**39** damper slap rail
4 bat pin	**22** lever block or heel	**40** lead weight
5 chasing	**23** heel of action	**41** lift rail lever
6 balance pin	**24** capstan	**42** damper lift rail
7 balance rail	**25** hammer shank	**43** damper flange
8 hammer flange	**26** repetition lever	**44** damper lever rail
9 hammer rail	**27** lever rail	**45** sostenuto rod
10 set-off rail	**28** hammer rest rail	**46** sostenuto tab
11 set-off dolly	**29** lever flange	
12 jack	**30** hammer head	
13 action standard, bracket	**31** back check	
14 drop screw	**32** back check wire	
15 roller, knuckle	**33** damper head	
16 jack regulation screw	**34** damper guide rail, socket rail	
17 jack regulation button	**35** damper wire	
18 spoon	**36** damper wire block or knuckle	

adhesive. The exact position of each note is marked on this key blank and numbered before the board is cut into individual keys. After the individual keys have been spaced on a keyframe the sharps are fitted.

The traditional materials for covering piano keys were ebony and ivory, chosen not only for aesthetic reasons but also for their natural properties. Both materials are warm to the touch, and have a natural absorbency, which is essential for reducing sweat on a key top. During the 1980s, essential laws were enacted to protect the world's elephants and, because ivory can no longer be imported, piano manufacturers have researched many different plastic alternatives that offer the same qualities that ivory possesses. Strict controls in many countries even forbid the import of existing ivory keyboards that might be hundreds of years old, making the moving of older pianos with ivory keyboards from country to country all but impossible. Because of its scarcity and escalating cost, ebony wood is now reserved for use on top-range instruments; all other pianos are fitted with plastic or stained hardwood sharps.

Fitted to the rear of the key is a capstan, a dome-topped screw that can be regulated in height so that the back of the key meets the heel of the action. The keys are plugged with lead to reduce the action weight that the fingers have to press. Since the bass hammers are larger than the treble hammers, the bass keys require more lead weights to match the resistance in the treble. Even so, a typical touch weight will graduate from 1.7 ounces (48g) in the top treble to 1.8 ounces (52g) in the extreme bass.

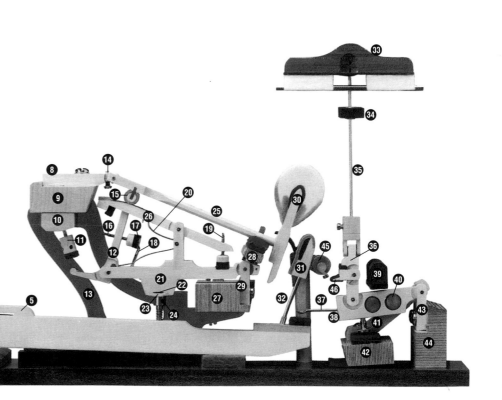

the upright piano action

The action parts are screwed onto a beech or maple rail secured to the piano's strung back by two, three, or four die-cast metal action standards. The bottom of each standard locates into a metal cup, which is screwed into the keybed, while the top is slipped over an action standard bolt and is secured by a knurled nut. The action can be removed quickly and easily in one piece by undoing these nuts, whereupon it is lifted out, leaving the keys behind. In some cases it may be necessary to disconnect the trapwork dowels before removing the action.

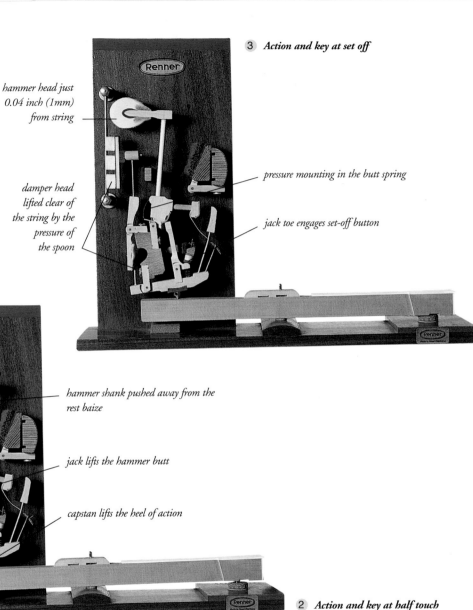

3 *Action and key at set off*

hammer head just 0.04 inch (1mm) from string

pressure mounting in the butt spring

damper head lifted clear of the string by the pressure of the spoon

jack toe engages set-off button

hammer shank pushed away from the rest baize

spoon engages the damper trail

jack lifts the hammer butt

capstan lifts the heel of action

2 *Action and key at half touch*

damper head firmly pushed onto the string by its spring

hammer shank lies on its rest baize

whippen supported by the capstan mounted in the back of the key

back of the key lies on the back-touch baize

1 *Action and key at rest*

4 *Action and key at full touch*

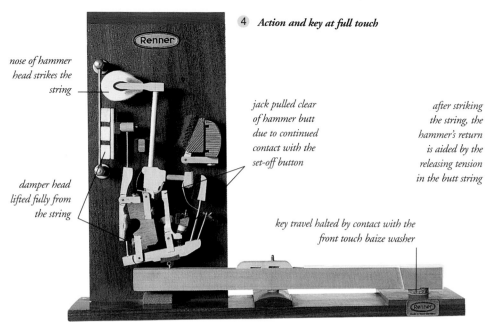

nose of hammer head strikes the string

damper head lifted fully from the string

jack pulled clear of hammer butt due to continued contact with the set-off button

key travel halted by contact with the front touch baize washer

5 *Action and key in check*

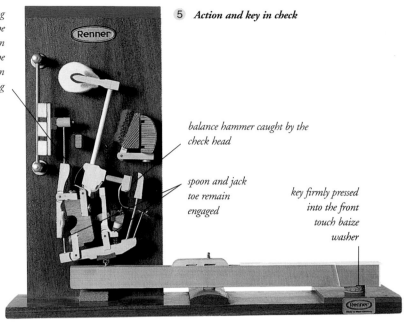

after striking the string, the hammer's return is aided by the releasing tension in the butt string

balance hammer caught by the check head

spoon and jack toe remain engaged

key firmly pressed into the front touch baize washer

how the upright piano action works

So that the weight of the action does not prove too much for the pianist's fingers, its various connections and tasks are distributed throughout the key's travel.

1. Action parts at rest.

2. When the key is depressed, it rocks on the balance rail and rises at the back. The back of the key pushes up the whippen on which is pivoted the jack. This pushes on the hammer butt and the hammer is pushed toward the string. When the key is halfway down, the spoon—situated at the rear of the lever—connects with the damper tail, lifting the damper clear of the string.

3. When the hammer is almost in contact with the string, the jack toe contacts the set-off button.

4. The jack is pushed from underneath the hammer butt, leaving the hammer's momentum to carry it the short remaining distance to the string.

5. On striking the string, the hammer rebounds and is caught by the check head, stopping it from bouncing back onto the string. As long as the key is held down, the hammer will stay in check and the damper will be kept fully released from the string, allowing the string to sustain its vibration.

6. When the key is released, the whippen drops and the jack spring resets the jack ready for a next blow. The balance hammer is released from the check head and the butt spring aids the hammer back to its rest rail. The damper spring returns the damper back onto the string, applying a pressure to stop it from vibrating.

7. The weight of the action parts returns the key to its rest position.

6 *Action and key returning to rest*

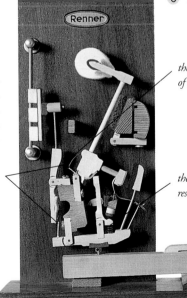

the releasing pressure of the spoon allows the damper spring to return the damper head to the string

the butt spring aids the return of the hammer

the spiral spring returns the jack to its resting position

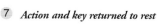

7 *Action and key returned to rest*

the grand piano action

The action parts in a grand piano are also screwed onto beech or maple rails supported by three, four, or five metal action standards. Two screws hold each standard to the floating key frame, so that the action, keys, and key frame can be removed via the front of the piano as one piece, leaving the damper mechanism behind.

Many of the action parts share the same name as those used in the upright piano action but note the inclusion of the repetition lever, which enables the grand piano action to produce a much faster repetition than an upright.

damper lifted clear from the string

hammer strikes the string

drop screw remains fully engaged

jack fully escaped from beneath the roller

key travel halted by front touch baize washer

hammer head is still 0.04 inch (1mm) from the string

4 *Action and key at full touch*

damper head lifted clear of the string by the back of the key

repetition lever contacts the drop screw so it cannot rise any further

jack toe contacts the set-off dolly

3 *Action and key at set-off*

repetition lever and jack push the hammer to the string

capstan lifts the heel of action

back of the key engages the spoon

2 *Action and key at half touch*

damper head sits on the string

hammer roller rests on the jack and the repetition lever

damper lever is supported by the damper wire

whippen supported by the capstan mounted in the back of the key

back of the key lies on the back-touch baize

1 *Action and key at rest*

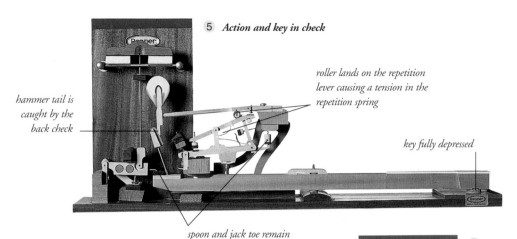

5 *Action and key in check*

hammer tail is caught by the back check

roller lands on the repetition lever causing a tension in the repetition spring

key fully depressed

spoon and jack toe remain fully engaged

how the grand piano action works

1. Action parts at rest.

2. When the key is depressed, the capstan on the end of the key pushes up on the whippen. Pivoted on the whippen are the jack and a repetition lever, that connect with the roller and push the hammer towards the string. When the key is halfway down, it picks up the damper body, lifting the damper clear of the string.

3. When the hammer is almost in contact with the string, the drop screw halts the rise of the repetition lever momentarily before the jack toe contacts the set-off dolly.

4. The jack is pushed from underneath the roller, leaving the hammer's momentum to carry it the short remaining distance to the string.

5. On striking the string, the hammer rebounds, lands on the repetition lever, and is caught by the check head, stopping it from bouncing back onto the string. The force of the hammer landing on the repetition lever pushes it down, installing a tension in the repetition spring.

6. As the key is released, the check head releases the hammer. The spring, relieved of its tension, throws the hammer into the air, allowing the jack, with the aid of a spring, to return underneath the roller.

7. As the key returns to its rest position the parts fall to rest, including the damper, which falls back onto the string, thus stopping its vibration. The hammer and jack are in position for a repeated note when the key has only returned halfway, allowing a grand action to be repeated at half touch.

8. The weight of the action parts returns the key to its rest position.

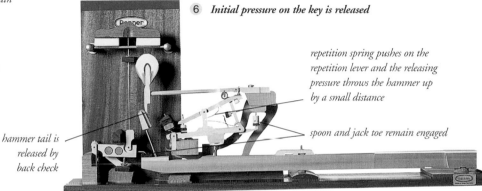

6 *Initial pressure on the key is released*

repetition spring pushes on the repetition lever and the releasing pressure throws the hammer up by a small distance

hammer tail is released by back check

spoon and jack toe remain engaged

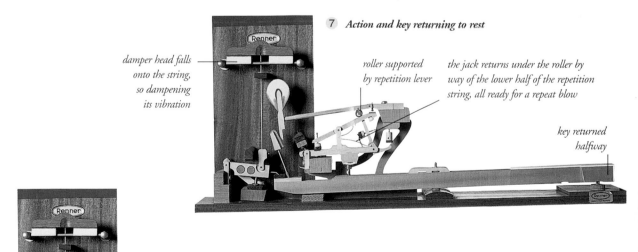

7 *Action and key returning to rest*

damper head falls onto the string, so dampening its vibration

roller supported by repetition lever

the jack returns under the roller by way of the lower half of the repetition string, all ready for a repeat blow

key returned halfway

8 *Action and key returned to rest*

piano makers

This section draws together comprehensive portraits of over 40 major piano manufacturers from around the world, giving an overview of the history of each company. The directory includes lists, charts, tables, and specifications to help identify and date your piano.

directory of Piano makers

IN 1900 THE WORLD'S TALLY OF PIANO MANUFACTURERS EXCEEDED 1,000, BUT HUGE SOCIAL AND ECONOMIC UPHEAVAL DURING THE TWENTIETH CENTURY HAS CAUSED THAT NUMBER TO DECLINE DRAMATICALLY. THE DIRECTORY FOCUSES ON FORTY OF THE BEST-LOVED MAKERS OF THE LAST CENTURY, MOST OF WHOM—DESPITE TWO WORLD WARS AND CRIPPLING ECONOMIC DEPRESSION—ARE STILL PRODUCING TOP-QUALITY INSTRUMENTS TODAY.

From the beginning of the twentieth century, when the development of the piano was pretty much complete, many of these makers concentrated on engineering a trademark tone. In the 1920s, Blüthner pianos were as renowned for their warmth as Steinways were for their power. Today—with new pretenders to the piano-making throne such as Fazioli and Stuart & Sons making stunning debuts—the drive to innovate continues. Add in Far Eastern manufacturers such as Yamaha, Samick, and Young Chang, all of whom have made the piano more accessible through mass-production techniques and the introduction of digital technology, and the industry, far from appearing in decline, seems to live and breathe with a new vigor.

how to use the directory

Each entry gives the following information:

1. A brief history of the founder and the company.

2. The company address.

3. A portrait of the founder of the company.

4. An additional anecdote about the founder or the company.

5. A map showing the location, historic or present, of the company.

6. A chart showing the production history of the company over the years.

7. The serial numbers of the pianos. Every instrument leaving the factory is issued with a number that is stamped on the piano's frame or strung back. This number can be used to date the instrument.

8. The company logo.

9. The specifications of a selection of pianos made by the company, including the model name; the type of casework;

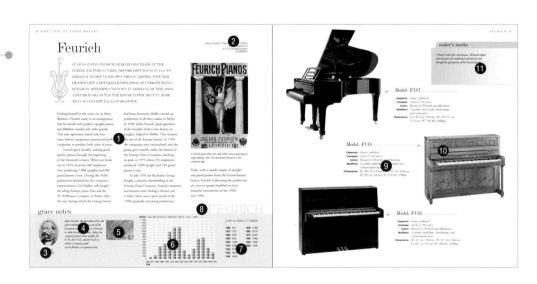

the compass; the type of action; the modifiers; and the piano's dimensions.

10. A photograph of the piano described.

11. The "Maker's Marks"—all pianos are expected to produce a familiar sound and required to fulfill the

function of a musical instrument, and are therefore essentially the same. However, each and every maker has his own ideas on design and manufacture, and this column notes the special characteristics of the company's pianos.

Astin-Weight

Astin-Weight
120 West 3300 South
Salt Lake City, Utah 84115
UNITED STATES

IN AN AGE WHERE PIANO MANUFACTURERS UTILIZE SIMILAR DESIGNS IN AN ATTEMPT TO CREATE A PERFECT STANDARIZED PIANO, ASTIN-WEIGHT OFFER A UNIQUE APPROACH. THE RESULT IS A TONE CHARACTER, CASE DESIGN, AND FINISH THAT IS TOTALLY UNLIKE ANY OTHER INSTRUMENT.

maker's marks

• *The novel strung back design creates an unusual tone character that is made up of many overtones. This can confuse or add an extra vitality to the sound of these pianos.*

• *The use of a soft-sheen oil finish gives this piano a look very different from the typical high-gloss polyester or lacquer shine most commonly associated with the piano.*

Edwin Astin and Don Weight formed Astin-Weight in Salt Lake City in 1959, and in 1978 Ray Astin took up the reins. The firm produces a limited number of well-made grand and upright pianos, but it is the design of the strung back that makes their pianos unique.

To increase the volume and the fullness of tone they designed an upright piano in which the soundboard could be extended to fill the entire case, rather than just to the height of the pin block, as is the case in other pianos. This, in effect, means that a piano can be 10 inches (25cm) shorter in height and still have the sounding area of a taller piano. This novel approach does indeed sound different, although some critics suggest that the increased height of the bridges to facilitate the design absorbs much of the strings' energy and distorts the tone. It is

widely agreed that the strings' speaking length, rather than the size of the soundboard, has the greater bearing on the quality of a piano's tone.

In order to maintain a suitable depth, the back posts have been dispensed with. Instead, the piano incorporates a full-perimeter iron frame to withstand the strings' tension. Although this type of construction has been used in Europe for over fifty years, some technicians believe that the omission of back posts has a detrimental effect on tuning stability.

Astin-Weight also produce a limited number of 5-foot 9-inch (176cm) grand pianos that are even more radical than their uprights. The piano has no long side and is almost symmetrical in shape. This allows the bass bridge to be positioned further down the soundboard, creating a much longer string length, closer to that

found on a 7-foot 6-inch (230cm) piano, and a larger soundboard area. It is a strange-looking instrument: the lid is hinged on the treble side of the piano rather than the bass side.

Model: X Professional U-500

Casework:	hand-rubbed oiled oak
Compass:	AAA–c5, 88 notes
Action:	Pratt Read and U10 to Astin-Weight specifications
Modifiers:	3 pedals: half-blow, sustaining, and bass sustain
Dimensions:	H: 50 in (127cm); W: 60½ in (145cm); D: 24½ in (62cm); W: 640lb (290kg)

grace notes

Astin-Weight's small output of high-quality, hand-crafted pianos have found their own niche in a market dominated by mass production. It is perhaps even more notable that the names inscribed on the wall still work in the factory making instruments.

Salt Lake City

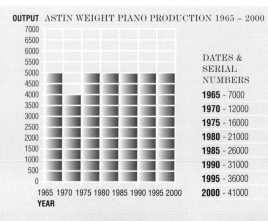

OUTPUT ASTIN WEIGHT PIANO PRODUCTION 1965 – 2000

DATES & SERIAL NUMBERS	
1965	7000
1970	12000
1975	16000
1980	21000
1985	26000
1990	31000
1995	36000
2000	41000

Baldwin Piano and Organ Company
4680 Parkway Drive
Mason, Ohio 45040
UNITED STATES

**Owned by: Gibson Guitar Corporation
Incorporating: Chickering and Wurlitzer**

Baldwin

BALDWIN MANUFACTURES PERHAPS THE MOST DIVERSE RANGE OF PIANOS AVAILABLE TODAY. THEY PRODUCE GRAND AND UPRIGHT PIANOS FOR CONCERTS, DECORATED DOMESTIC INSTRUMENTS, AND STUDIO UPRIGHTS FOR SCHOOLS, AS WELL AS PLAYER PIANOS AND ELECTRIC KEYBOARDS FOR STUDIO AND TEACHING SYSTEMS.

In 1873, prominent Midwest music teacher Dwight Hamilton Baldwin founded the Baldwin Piano Company, a retail store selling pianos and organs. Toward the end of the century, as the business grew, he contracted the Ohio Valley Piano Company to produce upright and square pianos "built exclusively for D. H. Baldwin & Co." By 1891, the Baldwin Piano Company had started to make low-priced upright pianos and two years later were producing moderately priced uprights under the Ellington Piano Company name. By the end of the century, they had designed and produced a high-quality instrument called the Baldwin, which won the Grand Prix at the Paris Exposition of 1900.

D. H. Baldwin died in 1899, leaving the company to the Presbyterian Church.

The former office clerks, Lucien Wulsin and George Armstrong, bought control of the company in 1903. Lucien Wulsin, Jr., became chief executive officer in 1926, staying with the company until his death in 1964.

During the 1920s, Baldwin became well known as a builder of automated pianos using the Manualo player mechanism, and they experimented with electronics aided by the physics department of the University of Cincinnati. It was not until 1936 that the company found financial stability by producing small upright pianos, such as the 36-inch (90cm) Acrosonic spinet and the 40-inch (100cm) Acrosonic console. These led to the design and production, from 1938, of the popular 44-inch (112cm) Hamilton studio upright, one of the most popular upright pianos

As well as Baldwin pianos, the firm also produces pianos under the illustrious names of Chickering and Wurlitzer.

ever sold. After the Second World War, during which time the company helped with the war effort by making wooden aircraft pieces, the company mushroomed with the production of the successful Baldwin electric organ.

Throughout the 1960s and 1970s, the Baldwin Piano Company acquired 42 companies, including those involved

grace notes

*Dwight Hamilton
Baldwin*

Acclaimed in 1900 for making the first American piano to earn the coveted Grand Prix at the Paris Exposition, Baldwin's 9-ft (274-cm) concert grand was designed by John Warren Macy, whose challenge—set by D. H. Baldwin—was to "build the best piano possible and worry about the cost later."

Mason •

OUTPUT BALDWIN PIANO PRODUCTION 1890 – 2000

substantial growth from 1995

(chart y-axis values: 160000, 150000, 140000, 130000, 120000, 110000, 100000, 60000, 50000, 40000, 30000, 20000, 10000, 0)

(chart x-axis) 1890 1900 1910 1920 1930 1940 1950 1960 1970 1980 1990 1995 2000
YEAR

DATES & SERIAL NUMBERS

1890 - 3890	**1960** - 145002
1900 - 10400	**1970** - 190028
1910 - 16400	**1980** - 236654
1920 - 35800	**1990** - 290656
1930 - 63000	**1995** - 328780
1940 - 88700	**2000** - 480000
1950 - 110243	

Baldwin

Model: Baldwin Artist Series L1

Casework: traditional ebony
Compass: AAA-c5, 88 notes
Action: Baldwin
Modifiers: 3 pedals: una-corda, sustaining, and sostenuto
Dimensions: L: 6 ft 3 in (190.5cm); W: 4 ft 10⅞ in (149cm); W: 688 lbs (312kg)

maker's marks

• A patented "Acu-Just" hitch pin arrangement is fitted to Baldwin grand pianos. This enables the adjustment of the downbearing of each individual string.

• Baldwin have patented a treble termination piece for use on their concert grand series to provide extra clarity, power, and duration to the piano's treble section.

in finance and electronics, becoming Baldwin United. In 1963, they acquired Bechstein, the well-loved German firm; this association, which was to last until 1987, gave them an international piano service for concert artists. In 1965 they produced their first concert grand, the SD-10. Their rise continued until 1983 when, due to rising interest rates, Baldwin United filed for bankruptcy. The profitable piano division was bought by its executive staff and in 1984 the Baldwin Piano and Organ Company once again became privately owned.

Between the 1980s and early 1990s, Baldwin, in association with Samick, formed the Korean American Music Company and between them they produced the Howard grand piano. During the late 1980s Baldwin enlarged again, buying piano-related firms such as Wurlitzer, the American piano and organ firm. On November 1, 2001, nearly a month after filing for bankruptcy, the Baldwin Piano and Organ Company was acquired by the Gibson Guitar Corporation, starting a new and exciting chapter in the history of the two firms.

Model: Baldwin 248

Casework: American walnut
Compass: AAA-c5, 88 notes
Action: Baldwin full blow action
Modifiers: 3 pedals: half-blow, sustaining, and celeste/moderator
Dimensions: H: 48 in (122cm); W: 59¾ in (152cm), D: 26 in (66cm); W: 528 lbs (240kg)

Model: Wurlitzer 1175

Casework: American country regal oak
Compass: AAA-c5, 88 notes
Action: Wurlitzer
Modifiers: 3 pedals:, half-blow, sustaining, and celeste/moderator
Dimensions: H: 37 in (94cm); W: 57 in (145cm); D: 24 in (61cm); W: 337 lbs (153kg)

WURLITZER

C. Bechstein

C. Bechstein Pianofortefabrik GmbH
Reichenberger Strasse 124
1000 Berlin 36
GERMANY

Incorporating: Hoffmann and Zimmermann

THE NAME OF BECHSTEIN HAS FOR GENERATIONS BEEN SYNONYMOUS WITH EXCELLENCE IN PIANO BUILDING. COMPOSERS SUCH AS LISZT, WAGNER, AND BRAHMS ALL EXPRESSED THEIR DELIGHT IN THESE GERMAN-MADE INSTRUMENTS.

Carl Bechstein was born in 1826 in Gotha, Germany, and until the age of twenty-seven he traveled widely to serve a complete apprenticeship in piano building, working at the famous nineteenth-century firms of Pleyel, Perau, and Pape and Kriegelstein, in Paris and Germany. After thoroughly learning all aspects of the trade, he settled in Berlin to establish his own piano factory, where he was to revolutionize the way the piano was made.

Bechstein produced his first upright pianos in 1853, but on learning that Liszt frequently broke pianos during his concerts, he set out to design and build a grand piano strong enough to withstand the abuse imposed by the modern way of playing, yet which sounded as sweet as the French pianos that he had been instrumental in making. Employing the cross stringing system used in America, the powerful tone of the English pianos, and the fast repetition of the French makes, he succeeded in building an instrument that won silver and gold awards in London and Paris exhibitions, and by 1867 his pianos were considered to be among the very best.

By the time the company was handed down to Carl's three sons, Edwin, Carl, and Johann, Bechstein was known throughout the world as a master maker, and this reputation lasted through the beginning of the twentieth century with the opening of branches in London, Paris, St. Petersburg, and Moscow. The company also established Bechstein concert halls, such as the one in Wigmore Street, London, now called the Wigmore Hall.

Factory output also reached new heights: in its first seven years Bechstein made just 176 instruments, but by the 1920s up to 5,000 pianos a year were being produced, including player pianos, double manual pianos, and a short grand called the Lilliput.

Like all piano makers, Bechstein was affected by the Great Depression of the 1930s. In addition to this, the introduction in 1933 of the unpopular "neo-Bechstein" grand piano—in which fewer strings were used per note, strung over an amplified soundboard—had an adverse effect on the company and in that year Bechstein only produced 600 pianos. The brothers had died, leaving control to Helene Bechstein, whose association with German political figures brought further pressures. The factory was almost completely destroyed during the Second World War, along with its materials and

C.BECHSTEIN

grace notes

Carl Bechstein

Bechstein has a long tradition of supporting piano culture, especially by assisting young pianists. The Bechstein Haus in Berlin houses a recital hall that has been described as the center of Berlin's music scene.

• Berlin

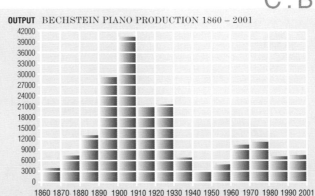

OUTPUT BECHSTEIN PIANO PRODUCTION 1860 – 2001

YEAR

DATES & SERIAL NUMBERS

1860 - 300	**1950** - 147000
1870 - 4196	**1960** - 151950
1880 - 11676	**1970** - 162300
1890 - 24958	**1980** - 173785
1900 - 54181	**1990** - 180312
1910 - 94753	**2001** - 187538
1920 - 115783	
1930 - 137446	
1940 - 143890	

Model: Bechstein M180

Casework: mahogany with inlaid panels
Compass: AAA-c5, 88 notes
Action: Renner to Bechstein specifications.
Modifiers: 3 pedals: una-corda, sustaining, and sostenuto
Dimensions: L: 5 ft 9 in (180cm); W: 59 in (150cm)

production machinery, and it was not until 1951 that Bechstein was again making grand pianos. However, needing an urgent injection of capital, it was sold in 1963 to Baldwin, under whose control it was able to operate autonomously.

In 1987, Bechstein was sold to a well-known German piano master craftsman, Karl Schulze. The original Bechstein scale designs and techniques were reintroduced and, combined with modern factory methods, pianos were again produced to a very high quality and sounding in the Bechstein tradition. In the early 1990s, after the acquisition of Hoffmann and Zimmermann, the name changed to the Bechstein Gruppe, and Bechstein's image as one of the best piano makers was restored.

Model: Bechstein Arts Noveaux

Casework: semi-oval shaped cabinet, sides black, high gloss
Compass: AAA-c5, 88 notes
Action: Renner to Bechstein specifications
Modifiers: 3 pedals: half-blow, sustaining, and celeste/moderator
Dimensions: H: 49 in (124cm); W: 60 in (152.5cm); D: 25¼ in (64cm)

maker's marks

• The tonal characteristics of a Bechstein piano can be described as clean and thin in the treble with the bass offering a strong fundamental frequency rather than harmonics.

• All new Bechstein pianos have Renner actions, solid Bavarian spruce soundboards, and Delignit pin blocks, and are strung using agraffes throughout.

• A Bechstein concert grand is single strung throughout, which improves tuning stability and is of advantage in the event of a broken string.

• Upright pianos built around the turn of the twentieth century included an extra spring fixed on the jack and connected to the hammer butt to allow faster repetition.

Model: W. Hoffmann Trend 120

Casework: cherry
Compass: AAA-c5, 88 notes
Action: Renner to Bechstein specifications
Modifiers: 3 pedals: half-blow, sustaining, and celeste/moderator
Dimensions: H: 47 in (120cm); W: 59 in (150cm); D: 23.7 in (60cm)

Blüthner

Julius Blüthner Pianofortefabrik GmbH
Franz-Flemming-Strasse 39
04179 Leipzig
GERMANY

IN A TIME WHEN MOST MANUFACTURERS ARE COMPETING TO PRODUCE THE MOST POWERFUL PIANO, BLÜTHNER ARE COMMITTED TO PRODUCING A LESS DOMINATING AND MORE ROUNDED SOUND, ABLE TO BLEND EASILY WITH THE HUMAN VOICE AND OTHER INSTRUMENTS. BLÜTHNER'S ROUND AND WARM TONES ARE PARTICULARLY SUITED TO CHAMBER MUSIC AND ACCOMPANIMENT ROLES.

Julius Blüthner, a cabinetmaker from Falkenheim, Germany, founded his own business in 1853 making pianos. Although he started with limited funds, his pianos were well received at the Industrial Exhibition of 1854 in Munich, and this led to a commission from the practice rooms of the Leipzig Conservatory of Music. Within a short time Blüthner pianos were known throughout the world as quality instruments. The production of upright pianos began in 1864 and the firm, with its 137 employees, moved into a larger factory on the outskirts of Leipzig.

By the end of the nineteenth century, Blüthner had become the second largest European piano producer and had made some 50,000 instruments, all of which, it is said, were personally checked by Julius before leaving the factory. After the death

of Julius Blüthner in 1910, the company was taken over by his sons, Max, Robert, and Bruno, and it expanded steadily until the Second World War, when the factory was destroyed in an air raid.

The company was reconstructed after the war by Rudolph Blüthner-Hæssler, but this took many years, and for a short time Blüthner shared Bechstein's facilities under GDR government control. This created organizational problems, but the pianos were still handcrafted and lost none of the quality for which they were admired. Blüthner was reprivatized in 1989, and its pianos, cherished by music lovers everywhere, are still manufactured in Leipzig under the directorship of Julius Blüthner's great-great-grandson Ingbert, and his sons Christian and Knut.

In 1935, the German Admiralty asked Blüthner to make a lightweight grand piano to be played on the Hindenburg airship. The concert susequently performed on the airship was broadcast on radio and created enormous interest in Blüthner pianos.

Blüthner

grace notes

Julius Blüthner

Julius Blüthner found Leipzig an ideal city to establish his business. In those days, it was a cultural center equal to Paris, London, and Vienna. It was also a well-developed trade center, and its prosperous inhabitants showed the same cultural aspirations as the country's nobility. Blüthner's business blossomed as a result.

OUTPUT BLÜTHNER PIANO PRODUCTION 1853 – 2000

(bar chart, y-axis OUTPUT from 0 to 28000 in increments of 2000; x-axis YEAR: 1853 1860 1870 1880 1890 1900 1910 1920 1930 1940 1950 1960 1970 1980 1990 2000)

DATES & SERIAL NUMBERS

1853 - 700	**1940** - 125500
1860 - 2500	**1950** - 128800
1870 - 9200	**1960** - 133006
1880 - 18500	**1970** - 140000
1890 - 31000	**1980** - 145000
1900 - 55000	**1990** - 148300
1910 - 81000	**2000** - 150100
1920 - 100000	
1930 - 115000	

Model: 4 SPS

Casework: ebony, polished
Compass: AAA–c5, 88 notes
Action: Renner to Blüthner specifications
Modifiers: 3 pedals: una-corda, sustaining, and sostenuto
Dimensions: L: 6 ft 10 in (210cm); W: 5 ft 1 in (156cm)

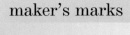

maker's marks

• *Good-quality handcrafted pianos with a warm and well-balanced sound. Much extra work is done to ensure an even tone, such as the balancing of the pitch of the hammer shanks before they are fitted.*

• *Wood is carefully selected: pine from Mecklenburg, beech from the Low German mountain ranges, and spruce, maple, and alder from the eastern Alps.*

• *Single stringing is used throughout, which improves tuning stability and is of advantage in the event of a broken string.*

• *The aliquot scaling system uses a fourth string located above the treble strings, which is not struck by the hammer but free to vibrate in sympathy. The extra strings are tuned an octave higher than the actual note and offer enriched overtones and harmonics to the piano's upper register.*

• *Blüthner patent action was used in grand pianos until the 1920s.*

Model: M6 PALI-1

Casework: jacaranda fitted with leather
Compass: AAA–c5, 88 notes
Action: Renner to Blüthner specifications
Modifiers: 3 pedals: una-corda, sustaining, and sostenuto
Dimensions: L: 6 ft 3 in (191cm); W: 4 ft 9 in (149cm)

Model: Model A

Casework: cherry, polished
Compass: AAA–c5, 88 notes
Action: Renner to Blüthner specifications
Modifiers: 3 pedals: half-blow, sustaining, and celeste/moderator
Dimensions: H: 49 in (124.5cm); W: 59.4 in (151cm); D: 24.6 in (62.5cm)

Bösendorfer

L. Bösendorfer Klavierfabrik AG
Bösendorferstrasse 12
A–1010 Vienna
AUSTRIA

SINCE 1827, BÖSENDORFER PIANOS HAVE BEEN USED AND ADMIRED BY MANY OF THE WORLD'S GREATEST COMPOSERS AND MUSICIANS. CLAIMING THE UNUSUAL DISTINCTION AS THE WORLD'S SLOWEST PIANO MAKER, BÖSENDORFER TAKE MORE THAN FOUR YEARS TO BUILD THEIR GRAND PIANOS, HALF OF WHICH IS SPENT WAITING FOR THE WOOD TO SEASON.

Ignaz Bösendorfer was born in 1794 in Vienna, then one of the great cultural centers of Europe and home to many musicians and composers. After serving an apprenticeship with the respected piano and organ manufacturer Joseph Brodmann, Bösendorfer founded his own company in 1827. The instruments he built were of high quality and robust construction, and his reputation was hugely enhanced when Franz Liszt, then only seventeen, endorsed his concert grand. Not only was Liszt an enthusiast for the instrument's tone; more to the point, it was strong enough to survive his forceful style of playing. Almost overnight the name Bösendorfer was elevated to the first rank of the world's piano manufacturers.

On the death of Ignaz Bösendorfer in 1859, the business was taken over by his son, Ludwig. He moved it to a larger factory, where the firm prospered to the extent that in 1870 it was forced to move again to larger premises, this time to its present site in Vienna's Fourth District. Ludwig had no direct descendants and upon his retirement in 1909 he sold the business to his friend Carl Hutterstrasser, whose sons Wolfgang and Alexander became partners in 1931.

Until the mid-1920s, Bösendorfer made only a few hundred pianos a year; this production fell rapidly during the Great Depression and ceased altogether in the final years of the Second World War, when the company's offices were destroyed by heavy fighting, and its wood reserves and pianos used for firewood.

Revival in the postwar period was slow and painful, with production not exceeding 100 pianos a year until 1950. Then in 1966 Arnold H. Habig, president of Kimball International Inc., bought the company with the aim of using Bösendorfer's expertise to revitalize the Kimball range of pianos. The acquisition, unlike many similar buyouts, turned out to be an extremely successful one for both companies until January 2002, when Bösendorfer broke ties with the Kimball organization. Today, backed by the Austrian banking group BAWAG-P. S. K., Bösendorfer have fully regained their position among the world's greatest makers of fine pianos.

grace notes

Bösendorfer

Ignaz Bösendorfer

In July 1828, Ignaz Bösendorfer was granted a decree for "manufacturing of pianos by trade and the right of citizen and master," ensuring that the name of Bösendorfer would always be associated with Vienna, the cultural heart of nineteenth-century Europe.

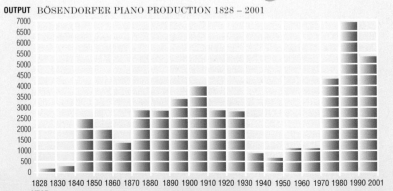

OUTPUT BÖSENDORFER PIANO PRODUCTION 1828 – 2001

7000 6500 6000 5500 5000 4500 4000 3500 3000 2500 2000 1500 1000 500 0

1828 1830 1840 1850 1860 1870 1880 1890 1900 1910 1920 1930 1940 1950 1960 1970 1980 1990 2001
YEAR

DATES & SERIAL NUMBERS

1828 - 4	**1920** - 22530
1830 - 200	**1930** - 25350
1840 - 490	**1940** - 26290
1850 - 3000	**1950** - 26960
1860 - 5000	**1960** - 28017
1870 - 6400	**1970** - 29109
1880 - 9300	**1980** - 33444
1890 - 12200	**1990** - 40384
1900 - 15640	**2001** - 45695
1910 - 19250	

Model: Johann Strauss

Casework: polished ebony
Compass: AAA-c5, 88 notes
Action: Renner to Bösendorfer specifications.
Modifiers: 3 pedals: una-corda, sustaining, and sostenuto
Dimensions: L: 6 ft 7 in (200cm); W: 4 ft 9 in (146cm); W: 754 lbs (342kg)

Model: Hollein

Casework: black and red lacquer; cover inlaid with gold
Compass: AAA-c5, 88 notes
Action: Renner to Bösendorfer specifications.
Modifiers: 3 pedals: una-corda, sustaining, and sostenuto
Dimensions: L: 6 ft 7 in (200cm); W: 4 ft 9 in (146cm); W: 754 lbs (342kg)

Model: 130 CL

Casework: black, polished
Compass: AAA-c5, 88 notes
Action: Renner to Bösendorfer specifications
Modifiers: 3 pedals: half-blow, sustaining, and celeste/moderator
Dimensions: H: 40½ in (132cm); W: 60 in (152.5cm); D: 25¼ in (64cm); W: 656 lbs (298kg)

maker's marks

• Bösendorfer pianos have a powerful, singing tone.

• The 7-foot (212cm), 7-foot 4-inch (225cm), and 9-foot (275cm) grands all have an extra four notes in the bass, while the 9-foot 6-inch (290cm) "Imperial" concert grand has nine extra bass notes extending down to CCC. Although these notes are rarely played, the presence of a longer soundboard and longer bridge adds to the power and sonority of the regular bass notes. The extra keys are normally covered to avoid confusing the pianist while playing.

• The rim of the grand is made of solid spruce sections so that the case becomes an extension of the soundboard. This, combined with the scale, is responsible for a sweeter, less powerful treble sound and a strong fundamental tone from the bass strings.

• A removable capo d'astro in the treble facilitates rebuilding and results in less sound absorption by the frame.

• Single stringing throughout improves tuning stability and presents a distinct advantage in the case of a broken string.

Broadwood & Sons

The British Piano Manufacturing Company Ltd
Woodchester Mills, Woodchester
Stroud, Glos. GL5 5NW
UNITED KINGDOM

JOHN BROADWOOD HAD A HUGE IMPACT ON THE TONE, APPEARANCE, AND PLAYING ACTION OF THE MODERN PIANO. SURROUNDING HIMSELF WITH LEADING MUSICIANS AND MASTERS IN HIS TRADE, HE WAS PERFECTLY POSITIONED TO COME UP WITH INNOVATIONS THAT WOULD PROVE TO BE OF PERMANENT VALUE.

Born in Scotland in 1732 and trained as a cabinetmaker, John Broadwood moved to London in 1761, where he began working for the illustrious harpsichord maker Burkat Shudi. He married Shudi's daughter in 1770 and a year later was entrusted his father-in-law's workshop at 33 Great Pulteney Street, London. Mozart had played in this workshop, and it was here that Handel, a good friend of Shudi, had written most of his compositions.

Throughout the 1760s, the newly introduced pianoforte was causing a stir in London, and it was this instrument that more and more intrigued John Broadwood. In 1773, the year of Shudi's death, "Johannes Broadwood" sold his first square piano; eight years later he would sell his first grand. Concentrating on this new market, Broadwood made his last harpsichord in 1793; and in 1807, with

the introduction of his sons James and Thomas to the business, the firm was renamed John Broadwood and Sons.

The output of pianos from the Broadwood factory was prodigious: between 1780 and 1867 they produced 135,344, of which 30,481 were grands. Broadwood were responsible for major improvements to all types of pianos: they patented designs for actions and the strung back; they were among the first to introduce steel bars and metal hitch plates to the traditionally all-wood piano; they were responsible for dividing the single bridge, thereby providing the bass section with its own separate bridge; and they replaced the awkward knee levers with patented "piano and forte pedals." Also, Broadwood improved the English grand action, which for the first time allowed rapid repetition without the hammers

blocking, a mechanism that the firm would use until the late nineteenth century.

The promising Broadwood domination never quite materialized, however, and in the nineteenth century the firm suffered two major blows to its public image as the world's greatest piano maker. The first was Erard's patent for a grand piano repetition action in 1821, and the subsequent order of an Erard instrument by King George IV, which Broadwood perceived as a threat to the coveted Royal Warrant that they had held since the reign of King George II. And in 1851 it was again Erard who embarrassed them, this time by winning the gold medal at the Great Exhibition of London.

Although the firm recovered from this humiliation by winning gold medals at other exhibitions in following years and supplying pianos to all the subsequent

grace notes

John Broadwood

During the nineteenth century, John Broadwood & Sons was the twelfth largest employer in London. Broadwood pianos were played by many of the great composers and crowned heads of Europe, and they have the distinction of being the oldest holder of a Royal Warrant.

• Stroud

BROADWOOD

OUTPUT BROADWOOD PIANO PRODUCTION 1932 – 2000

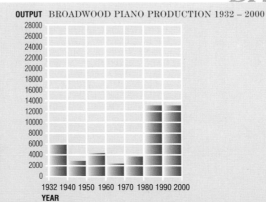

YEAR

DATES & SERIAL NUMBERS

1932 - 250000	**1980** - 269180
1940 - 256000	**1990** - 282500
1950 - 258832	**2000** - 283700
1960 - 263001	
1970 - 265336	

Serial numbers pre-1932 are not continuous and distinguish between upright, square, and grand pianos.

Model: Barless upright piano

Casework:	black polyester with rosewood veneered panels
Compass:	AAA-c5, 88 notes
Action:	Langer to Broadwood specifications
Modifiers:	3 pedals: half-blow, sustaining, and celeste/moderator
Dimensions:	H: 52 in (132cm); W: 60 in (152cm); D: 25½ in (64cm)

kings and queens of England, its fortunes had begun to wane. Production of a popular small upright piano in the 1860s helped improve the situation and a radical piano frame design, one made of rolled steel and requiring no stress bars, was introduced toward the end of the century.

In 1903 the historic buildings in Great Pulteney Street were demolished and the company moved to new premises in Hackney, East London, still under the ownership of the sixth Shudi-Broadwood generation. Production began of a player piano that was built entirely in-house, but even this offered no relief to the financial problems that beset the firm.

Ironically it was the outbreak of war in 1914, the ruin of so many piano manufacturers in Europe, that was to save Broadwood from financial disaster. The factory was cleared for aircraft production and, at £125 per plane, the company earned enough by the end of the war to be at last financially solvent. When the lucrative wartime work ceased,

piano production resumed. In 1939, the outbreak of war once again led to a government regulation that forced the amalgamation of piano manufacturers. Production of Broadwood pianos moved to the Whelpdale, Maxwell & Codd factory in Clapham, South London, where they were made under license until the end of the century.

With extensive restructuring, and changing production between grand, upright, and player pianos to suit the changing times, Broadwood and Sons has survived, marking an incredible 260-year history. Today Broadwood pianos are made by the British Piano Manufacturing Company, founded in 2000 in Stroud, who also make pianos to the specifications of other English firms such as Bentley, Knight, Welmar, and Woodchester. The Broadwood barless upright is made under license for John Broadwood & Sons by Ladbroke Pianos, founded some fifty years ago in Birmingham.

maker's marks

• In 1783 Broadwood started to make pianos that had two pedals, one for lifting the dampers clear of the strings and another for pressing a soft pad on the strings to soften them. The pedals replaced the awkward knee levers.

• In 1817 Thomas Broadwood visited Beethoven in Vienna and in 1818 presented him with a grand piano as a gift. The piano had an extended six-octave keyboard and was triple strung. It was later owned by Liszt, and is now in the National Museum of Hungary.

• In 1888 Broadwood patented a new design of frame called the "barless." Made of rolled boiler steel, it was strong enough to resist the strings' tension around its outer edge, and did not require the stress bars that compromise the mass of the bridges and thus weaken the tone of selected notes. Both grand and upright pianos were made.

• Chopin and Liszt both played their last concerts in England on Broadwood grand pianos. Liszt was encouraged to write that "no pianofortes last so well as those of Broadwood."

• In 1875, Captain Nares on the British Polar Expedition to the Arctic took a small Broadwood upright piano aboard the HMS Discovery. In 1910 a Broadwood player piano was taken on Captain Scott's Antarctic expedition, where it was played on the ice at the first base camp.

Vienna Music Sdn. Bhd.
45–47 Jalan SS 15/5A
47500 Subang Yaya
Selangor
MALAYSIA

Challen

**Other names used: Barratt & Robinson;
Witton & Witton; Brasted.**

THE ENGLISH PIANO MAKER CHALLEN AND SONS WAS FOUNDED IN 1830, ALTHOUGH IT IS BELIEVED THAT CHARLES H. CHALLEN BUILT HIS FIRST PIANO AS EARLY AS 1804.

For the last quarter of the nineteenth century through the first quarter of the next century, Challen produced around 500 instruments a year of above-average quality. The firm's fortunes changed in 1926, with the arrival of a new managing director, William Evans, formerly from Chappell, who redeveloped a 5-foot (152cm) "baby" grand piano, that Challen had produced earlier in the century. By employing large-scale production techniques, Challen was able to reduce the price of this instrument from £125 to £65 (US$175 to US$90) and it subsequently became so popular that it almost displaced the upright piano from English homes. The Great Depression that hit most piano manufacturers in the 1930s did not seem to affect Challen: production rose from 500 pianos in 1925 to 2,500

in 1935. The company took over the manufacturing of Broadwood pianos in 1932, and in 1936, along with Steinway and Bösendorfer, signed a contract with the BBC to supply pianos, a move that guaranteed the sound of their instruments in every home across the country. Upon William Evans's retirement in 1959, the Challen name was sold to the Brasted Brothers and upon their demise in 1970, went to Barratt and Robinson.

Since 1986, Challen pianos have been assembled in western Malaysia by Musical Products Sdn. Bhd., the factory division of Vienna Music Sdn. Bhd.

Model: 140

Casework:	polished ebony
Compass:	AAA-c5, 88 notes
Action:	Renner to Challen specifications
Modifiers:	3 pedals: una-corda, sustaining, and sostenuto
Dimensions:	L: 4 ft 11 in (150cm); W: 4 ft 10½ in (149cm); W: 772 lbs (350kg)

Challen

grace notes

Challen was best known for its small grand pianos, but it also made the world's largest grand piano in 1935 for the silver jubilee of King George V. Although the whereabouts of this instrument is not known today, it measured a remarkable 11 feet 8 inches (355cm) in length, with a 9-foot, 11-inch-long (302cm) bass string, and weighed 1¼ tons. The tensile stress of this piano was estimated at 30 tons.

Selangor

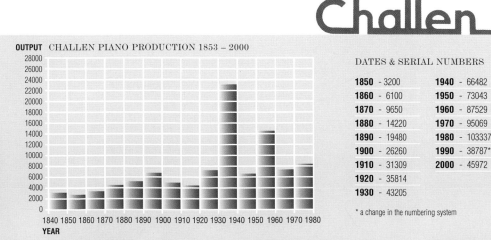

OUTPUT CHALLEN PIANO PRODUCTION 1853 – 2000

YEAR (1840 1850 1860 1870 1880 1890 1900 1910 1920 1930 1940 1950 1960 1970 1980)

DATES & SERIAL NUMBERS

1850	- 3200	**1940**	- 66482
1860	- 6100	**1950**	- 73043
1870	- 9650	**1960**	- 87529
1880	- 14220	**1970**	- 95069
1890	- 19480	**1980**	- 103337
1900	- 26260	**1990**	- 38787*
1910	- 31309	**2000**	- 45972
1920	- 35814		
1930	- 43205		

* a change in the numbering system

Chappell & Company

Chappell of Bond Street
50 New Bond Street
London W1Y 9HA
ENGLAND

Owned by: Warner Brothers

RICHARD STRAUSS WROTE OF A CHAPPELL PIANO: "I CONSIDER THE TONE OF A REMARKABLE SWEET AND SYMPATHETIC QUALITY... THE TOUCH VERY RESPONSIVE AND LIGHT... IT WAS A GREAT AND AGREEABLE SURPRISE TO ME TO FIND SUCH A PERFECT INSTRUMENT OF ENGLISH MANUFACTURE."

maker's marks

- *The name is famous for a rather peculiar square glass piano now housed in the collection of the Victoria & Albert Museum, London. The instrument has glass rods fitted instead of strings and these are struck by down-striking hammers.*

- *Chappell's concert grand was particularly unusual, since the notes in the top treble were made up of four strings, not three.*

Samuel Chappell, Johann Cramer, and Francis Latour, already a firm of music publishers, founded Chappell & Company in London in 1811. They did not start producing pianos until the 1840s, but began selling pianos in a special showroom called the Ware Room.

Cramer was a fashionable London composer and teacher, and the company used this as an advantage over rival firms by advertising that he personally selected every instrument in their shop. As well as publishing music and selling pianos, the firm produced concerts within London and became closely linked with the Philomonic Society. In 1840 Chappell began making pianos in a factory in Soho, London, and as production grew, they moved to a factory in Chalk Farm.

In 1901 the Chappell Piano Company

Model: Empire

Casework:	dark mahogany polyester
Compass:	AAA-c5, 88 notes
Action:	Yamaha
Modifiers:	3 pedals: half-blow, sustaining, and celeste/moderator
Dimensions:	H: 45½ in (116cm); W: 59½ in (151cm); D: 22 in (56cm)

and the Publishing Company separated and piano production increased to 1,000 pianos a year during the 1920s and 1930s. In 1929 they expanded, buying Allison Pianos and Collard and Collard, and in 1938 acquired John Strohmenger & Sons.

The Phillips Record Company

bought the Chappell Company in 1968 for £17.5 million (US$25.5). Owned by Warner Chappell, Kemble produced the Chappell pianos under license until 2000 (Warner continue to hold sole rights). Chappell of Bond Street still exists as a music and instrument retailer.

grace notes

• London

When Chappell & Company was founded in January 1811, the Morning Chronicle *contained this advertisement:*

Chappell & Co. beg to acquaint the nobility and gentry that they have taken the extensive premises lately occupied by Moulding and Co., 124 New Bond Street, and have laid in a complete assortment of music of the best authors, ancient and modern, as well as a variety of instruments, consisting of Grands and squires Piano-fortes, harps for sale or hire."

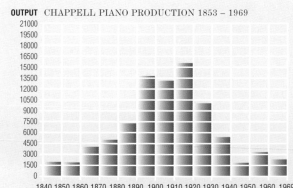

OUTPUT CHAPPELL PIANO PRODUCTION 1853 – 1969

YEAR: 1840 1850 1860 1870 1880 1890 1900 1910 1920 1930 1940 1950 1960 1969

DATES & SERIAL NUMBERS

Date	Serial	Date	Serial
1840	2000	**1920**	65000
1850	4000	**1930**	75250
1860	6000	**1940**	80870
1870	10000	**1950**	82500
1880	15000	**1960**	85832
1890	22376	**1969**	88200
1900	36100		
1910	49440		

Chappell pianos are not currently in production.

Fazioli

Fazioli Pianoforti S.R.L.
Via Ronche 47
33077 Sacile (Pordenone)
ITALY

AT THE FRANKFURT MUSIC FAIR IN 1981, FOUR NEWLY DESIGNED PIANOS WERE UNVEILED BY A PREVIOUSLY UNKNOWN ITALIAN MAKER. JUST TWENTY YEARS LATER, FAZIOLI PIANOS ARE NOT ONLY ACCEPTED IN WHAT IS STILL A VERY TRADITIONAL TRADE; THEY HAVE ESTABLISHED THEMSELVES AS SERIOUS CHALLENGERS FOR THE TITLE OF THE WORLD'S FINEST PIANOS.

Combining his knowledge of mechanical engineering with his piano-playing skills, in which he had a diploma from the Conservatory in Pesaro, Paolo Fazioli was in a unique position to know what he should expect from a piano. Never satisfied with the pianos he had previously tried, he decided at the age of 35 to abandon a promising career with the family's large furniture business and try his luck at designing and building a totally new piano.

Setting up shop in the corner of his family's factory, Paolo set about studying every existing make of piano. He assembled a team of experts from diverse fields ranging from wood seasoning to acoustics and, after much research and experimentation, he came up with four prototypes, all grand pianos measuring in length 5 feet (156cm); 6 feet (183cm); 7 feet, 6 inches (228cm);

and 9 feet (278cm). Paolo's biggest risk lay in using an Italian name, as the country's piano industry had been all but dormant since Cristofori's initial experiments. But he persevered, hoping that if the piano was good enough, it would find its place in the market. Few doubt that his enterprise was anything but a triumph. All four prototypes were sold after the fair in 1981, and in the first year of production, six further pianos were made. In 1986 production of two more models started, the 7-foot 6-inch (228cm), and the enormous 10-foot 3-inch (308cm) grand.

Fazioli pianos are still handmade and a successful move to a purpose-built factory in the summer of 2001 saw production increase from 80 to 120 instruments a year. The new site also includes a test and research area, and a concert hall.

maker's marks

- *Fazioli pianos have a rich tone, an evenness of sound and touch, and a resonance that can cut through a full orchestra without becoming harsh.*

- *Only grand pianos are made, all by hand and each individually checked by Paolo Fazioli as it leaves the factory.*

- *The 10-foot, 3-inch (308cm) grand is the largest concert piano available today. It includes a fourth pedal, which moves the hammers closer to the strings, thus offering a softer sound without altering the tonal characteristic as the una-corda pedal does.*

- *Fazioli pianos have a choice of two actions and two lyres to allow a performer more voicing options.*

grace notes

Paolo Fazioli

Paolo Fazioli makes his pianos in Sacile, about 40 miles (60km) north of Venice. It is an area close to the Val di Fiemme, a rich forest of slow-growing spruce where Stradivarius and other violin-makers sourced their wood. The wood's tight and dense annual rings make it perfect for piano soundboards, the heart and soul of the instrument.

• Pordenone

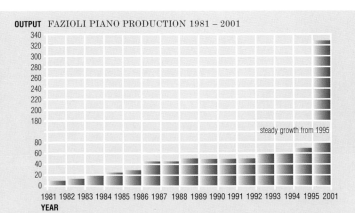

OUTPUT FAZIOLI PIANO PRODUCTION 1981 – 2001

steady growth from 1995

YEAR

DATES & SERIAL NUMBERS

1981 - 1		**1990** - 290
1982 - 10		**1991** - 340
1983 - 25		**1992** - 390
1984 - 45		**1993** - 450
1985 - 70		**1994** - 510
1986 - 100		**1995** - 580
1987 - 145		**2001** - 910
1988 - 190		
1989 - 240		

Model: F308

Casework:	black, high gloss polyester
Compass:	AAA-c5, 88 notes
Action:	Renner to Fazioli specifications.
Modifiers:	4 pedals: una-corda, half-blow, sustaining, and sostenuto
Dimensions:	L: 10 ft 3 in (308cm); W: 5 ft 1½ in (156cm); W: 1,520 lbs (690kg)

Model: F212

Casework:	black, high gloss polyester
Compass:	AAA-c5, 88 notes
Action:	Renner to Fazioli specifications
Modifiers:	3 pedals: una-corda, sustaining, and sostenuto
Dimensions:	L: 7 ft (212cm); W: 5 ft (153cm); W: 640 lbs (290kg)

Model: F156

Casework:	black, high gloss polyester
Compass:	AAA-c5, 88 notes
Action:	Renner to Fazioli specifications
Modifiers:	3 pedals: una-corda, sustaining, and sostenuto
Dimensions:	L: 5 ft 1½ in (156cm); W: 4 ft 10½ in (149cm); W: 640 lbs (290kg)

Feurich

Julius Feurich Pianofortefabrik GmbH
An der Stemme 6
91710 Gunzenhausen
GERMANY

JULIUS GUSTAV FEURICH LEARNED HIS TRADE AT THE PLEYEL FACTORY IN PARIS, BEFORE RETURNING IN 1851 TO GERMANY TO SET UP HIS OWN FIRM IN LEIPZIG. WITH HIM HE BROUGHT A DETAILED KNOWLEDGE OF UPRIGHT PIANO BUILDING, HITHERTO UNKNOWN IN GERMANY. BY THE 1930S, A FEURICH GRAND WAS THE HOUSE INSTRUMENT IN MORE THAN 40 CONCERT HALLS WORLDWIDE.

Finding himself in the same city as Julius Blüthner, Feurich came to an arrangement that he would produce only upright pianos and Blüthner would make only grands. This cozy agreement lasted only four years before competitive pressure led both companies to produce both types of piano.

Feurich grew steadily, making good-quality pianos through the beginning of the twentieth century. When war broke out in 1914, Feurich's 360 employees were producing 1,000 uprights and 600 grand pianos a year. During the 1920s, production declined but the company's representative, Carl Müller, still bought the ailing Euterpe piano firm and the W. Hoffmann Company in Berlin. After the war, during which the Leipzig factory had been destroyed, Müller started up production of all three makes in Berlin. In 1949, Julius Feurich, great-grandson of the founder, built a new factory in Langlau, helped by Müller. This remains the site of the Euterpe factory. In 1958 the companies were nationalized, and the group grew steadily under the banner of the Euterpe Piano Company, reaching its peak in 1979, when 276 employees produced 2,500 upright and 250 grand pianos a year.

In July 1991 the Bechstein Group bought a majority shareholding in the Euterpe Piano Company. Feurich remained autonomous and, finding a factory just 3 miles (5km) away, spent much of the 1990s gradually increasing production.

A Feurich poster from the early 20th century depicting an angel holding a lyre, the instrument featured in the company's logo.

Today, with a steady output of upright and grand pianos from the Gunzenhausen factory, Feurich is planning the production of a concert grand modeled on their beautiful instruments of the 1920s and 1930s.

grace notes

Julius Feurich

Julius Feurich, the descendant of an old piano-making family, was one of the first piano manufacturers in Germany to make the upright piano. Today, the company presents three models: the F116, the F118, and the F123, to which a sostenuto pedal can be fitted as an optional extra.

OUTPUT FEURICH PIANO PRODUCTION 1860 – 2000

YEAR

DATES & SERIAL NUMBERS

1860 - 400		**1950** - 51300	
1870 - 1200		**1960** - 55150	
1880 - 3900		**1970** - 62401	
1890 - 8400		**1980** - 70000	
1900 - 13900		**1990** - 74000	
1910 - 23800		**2000** - 76200	
1920 - 35100			
1930 - 46500			
1940 - 49600			

FEURICH

Model: F197

Casework: ebony, polished
Compass: AAA-c5, 88 notes
Action: Renner to Feurich specifications
Modifiers: 3 pedals: una-corda, sustaining, and sostenuto
Dimensions: L: 6 ft 6 in (197cm); W: 4 ft 11½ in (151cm); W: 792 lbs (360kg)

Model: F118

Casework: cherry, polished
Compass: AAA-c5, 88 notes
Action: Renner to Feurich specifications
Modifiers: 3 pedals: half-blow, sustaining, and celeste/moderator
Dimensions: H: 46½ in (118cm); W: 58½ in (148cm); D: 22½ in (58cm); W: 418 lbs (190kg)

Model: F116

Casework: ebony, polished
Compass: AAA-c5, 88 notes
Action: Renner to Feurich specifications
Modifiers: 3 pedals: half-blow, sustaining, and celeste/moderator
Dimensions: H: 45½ in (116cm); W: 57½ in (146cm); D: 22½ in (57cm); W: 396 lbs (180kg)

August Förster

August Förster GmbH
Jahnstrasse 8
D-02708 Löbau
GERMANY

FOUNDED IN 1859, AUGUST FÖRSTER HAD CREATED REVOLUTIONARY CONSTRUCTIONS LIKE THE QUARTER-TONE GRAND PIANO AND THE ELEKTROCORD BY THE TIME OF THE SECOND WORLD WAR. TODAY, AUGUST FÖRSTER PIANOS ARE RENOWNED FOR THEIR UNCOMPROMISING ATTENTION TO DETAIL.

Friedrich August Förster was born in Oberseifersdorf, Germany, in 1829. He started his working life as an apprentice cabinetmaker, repairing musical instruments in his spare time. As his passion flourished, he moved to Löbau to study piano making with Hieke and Karl Eule. In 1854 he passed his exams as a piano maker, but it was not until five years later that Förster set up his own small workshop, where he produced his first piano. In 1862 he established a factory site in the suburbs of Löbau where, numerous modifications and alterations later, the factory is still sited today.

August Förster died in 1897, leaving the firm to his son, Cäsar, who would live only until 1915. He in turn bequeathed the firm to his sons Gerhard and Manfred and—as strangely typical in piano history—each son had different attributes to aid the growth of their firm. In this case, Manfred was the businessman and Gerhard the ingenious maker responsible for revolutionary constructions. Between 1924 and 1931, he built several quarter-tone pianos to accommodate music composed by the Czech Alois Haba. Later he built an experimental electric piano called the Elektrochord, based on the design patented by Oscar Vierling in 1933.

Today the factory is owned and run by Wolfgang Förster, fourth generation of the founding family.

maker's marks

- *The characteristic tone of an August Förster piano is warm and mellow, with a robust, resonant bass.*

- *August Förster currently produce six models of upright piano from 4 feet, 6 inches (116cm) high to 4 feet, 9 inches (125cm) high, and five models of grand piano ranging from 5 feet, 7 inches (170cm) to 9 feet (275cm) long.*

- *Giacomo Puccini composed most of his operas using his August Förster piano.*

- *Essentially a conventional grand piano, the Elektrochord used two strings per note, except for the bottom eight notes. Only one string is struck by the hammer; the other string, which is shorter and set at a much lower tension, is allowed to vibrate in sympathy. Electrostatic pickups placed on different parts of this string can be set both vertically and horizontally to achieve a wide range of tones and attack characteristics. As an optional extra the Elektrochord could be fitted with a radio or gramophone.*

grace notes

August Förster

Friedrich August Förster studied his craft and subsequently built a factory in Löbau in Saxony, the very heart of the German piano industry since Gottfried Silbermann had created his first instruments there.

* Löbau

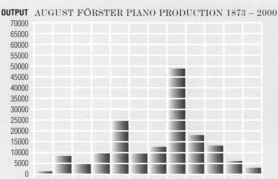

OUTPUT AUGUST FÖRSTER PIANO PRODUCTION 1873 – 2000

YEAR: 1873 1880 1898 1904 1910 1924 1929 1937 1960 1970 1980 1990 2000

DATES & SERIAL NUMBERS

Year	Serial	Year	Serial
1873	900	**1937**	73000
1880	1700	**1960**	122500
1898	10000	**1970**	140500
1904	15000	**1980**	154000
1910	25000	**1990**	160000
1924	50000	**2000**	162600
1929	60000		

Model: 190 Classik

Casework: white, polished
Compass: AAA-c5, 88 notes
Action: Renner to August Förster specifications
Modifiers: 3 pedals: una-corda, sustaining, and sostenuto
Dimensions: L: 6 ft 4 in (190cm); W: 849 lbs (385kg)

Model: 125G

Casework: black with medallion, polished
Compass: AAA-c5, 88 notes
Action: Renner to August Förster specifications
Modifiers: 3 pedals: half-blow, sustaining, and celeste/moderator
Dimensions: H: 49 in (125cm); W: 61 in (153cm); D: 23 in (58cm); W: 584 lbs (265kg)

Model: 116 Super E

Casework: cherry with inlay
Compass: AAA-c5, 88 notes
Action: Renner to August Förster specifications
Modifiers: 3 pedals: half-blow, sustaining, and celeste/moderator
Dimensions: H: 46 in (116cm); W: 61 in (153cm); D: 23 in (58cm); W: 485 lbs (220kg)

Grotrian-Steinweg

Pianofortefabrikanten Grotrian-Steinweg
Grotrian-Steinweg Strasse 2
Postfach 5833
W-3300 Braunschweig
GERMANY

STILL ONE OF GERMANY'S MOST DISTINGUISHED PIANO MARKS, GROTRIAN-STEINWEG HAD ITS BEGINNINGS IN THE PARTNERSHIP OF GEORG FRIEDRICH KARL GROTRIAN AND HEINRICH STEINWEG, FOUNDER OF THE STEINWAY DYNASTY. THEY BUILT THEIR FIRST PIANO TOGETHER IN 1835 AFTER A DESIGN OF GROTRIAN'S.

Grotrian's business interests took him to Moscow, where he established a successful retail concern. When he returned over a decade later to his native Germany, he founded a new piano-making partnership with Heinrich's son, Carl Friedrich Theodor Steinweg. The pair moved production to Braunschweig and forged a successful business making quality pianos.

Heinrich Steinweg, meantime, had emigrated to America, changed his name to Steinway, and established his own company. In 1865, Heinrich died and Theodor Steinweg sold his shares and

Model: 165/32

Casework: black, polished
Compass: AAA-c5, 88 notes
Action: Renner to Grotrian-Steinweg specifications
Modifiers: 3 pedals: una-corda, sustaining, and sustenuto
Dimensions: L: 5 ft 5 in (165cm);
W: 4 ft 11 in (150cm)

emigrated to America to run the now flourishing Steinway firm. Friedrich Grotrian died just two years later and the firm was handed to his son, Wilhelm, who together with the other shareholders, A. Helfferich and H. Schulz, produced pianos under various different names, including the Steinweg brand. The company grew steadily, so that by 1920 it employed 1,000 people and produced 1,600 instruments a year. Since the death

grace notes

Georg Friedrich Karl Grotrian

The first square piano made by Grotrian-Steinweg is in the collection of musical instruments owned by the city of Braunschweig. Clara Schumann regarded Grotrian-Steinweg pianos very highly and in 1995 they built a grand piano (number 150,000) with casing similar to the one she owned.

• Braunschweig

OUTPUT GROTRIAN-STEINWEG PIANO PRODUCTION 1860 – 1865

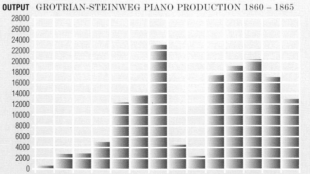

YEAR

DATES & SERIAL NUMBERS

1865 - 560		**1950** - 67900
1870 - 1137		**1960** - 85682
1880 - 4175		**1970** - 104665
1890 - 7228		**1980** - 124707
1900 - 12131		**1990** - 141600
1910 - 24171		**2001** - 154571
1920 - 38076		
1930 - 61235		
1940 - 65499		

Model: 114 V

Casework: burr walnut, polished
Compass: AAA-c5, 88 notes
Action: Renner to Grotrian-Steinweg specifications
Modifiers: 3 pedals: half-blow, sustaining, and celeste/moderator
Dimensions: H: 5 ft 5 in (165cm); W: 57½ in (146cm); D: 21¾ in (55cm)

Model: 108M

Casework: yew with open grain
Compass: AAA-c5, 88 notes
Action: Renner to Grotrian-Steinweg specifications
Modifiers: 3 pedals: half-blow, sustaining, and celeste/moderator
Dimensions: H: 42½ in (108cm); W: 57½ in (146cm); D: 20½ in (52cm)

maker's marks

• Nearly half Grotrian-Steinweg's present employees are piano builders and a special apprentice program ensures that the firm's high standard of workmanship will continue into the future.

• The ingenious "Duo-Concert Grand" combines two grand pianos together with one lid. The two grands are connected with removable rim parts and a soundboard fillet can be fitted to fill the space between both pianos. The grands can easily be separated and used as solo instruments each with its own lid.

• Star back construction design on upright models ensures that all the counterforces that withstand the strings' tension run through one central point; this is beneficial to the tuning stability of the instrument.

of their father in 1917, Willi and Kurt Grotrian had been in control of the firm, and armed with their father's advice to "build good pianos and the rest will take care of itself" they maintained the high-quality craftsmanship for which their company was renowned.

In 1919 the company name was formally changed to Grotrian-Steinweg and, despite legal wrangling over their name with the Steinway company, production increased to 3,000 instruments in 1927. By 1931, the Great Depression had taken effect and production slumped to only 700 instruments a year. After the closure of the factory during the war years, it took until 1948 for Grotrian-Steinweg to resume piano production—a time not only spent rebuilding the bomb-damaged factory, but also piecing together their traditional piano-making methods.

By 1954, re-established as a maker of fine pianos, the company set up the Grotrian-Steinweg competition to support young pianists. In 1974, the new factory on Grotrian-Steinweg Strasse was finished, boasting the most up-to-date facilities. It is from here that the firm is controlled by a sixth-generation Grotrian, Knut, aided by his son Jobst.

Rud. Ibach & Sohn GmbH & Co. KG
Postfach 405
Mittelstrasse 34
5830 Schwelm, Westfalia
GERMANY

Main brand: Rud. Ibach Sohn
Other brands: Roth & Junius, Schiedmayer

Ibach

FOUNDED IN 1794 BY JOHANNES ADOLPH IBACH, TODAY THE COMPANY IS RUN BY A SIXTH-GENERATION IBACH, MAKING THE COMPANY THE OLDEST FAMILY-OWNED, INDEPENDENT MAKER OF PIANOS IN EXISTENCE. THE FIRM BEGAN IN AN AGE WHEN BOTH USING METAL IN THE PIANO'S STRUCTURE AND THE CONCEPT OF ADVERTISING ONE'S GOODS WERE CONSIDERED TO BE AGAINST THE ETHICS OF THE CRAFT.

Initially studying organ building with several of Germany's most prominent makers, Johannes Adolph Ibach saw the promise of the developing piano and soon his attention was entirely focused on this exciting new instrument. In 1794, he set up a factory—not in the traditional heart of piano-making in Saxony, but in Beyenburg, near Düsseldorf—and despite the economic depression caused by the Napoleonic wars, business grew steadily.

Johannes's eldest son Carl Rudolf became a partner in 1834 and the name was revised to Rud. Ibach Sohn. Keeping up with the development of the grand, and producing an upright version as early as 1838, their reputation grew rapidly, and Carl Rudolf attended many European trade exhibitions and fairs.

In 1863, Peter Adolph Rudolf Ibach became the third-generation Ibach to manage the firm and, under his leadership, it developed, necessitating an enlarged and modernized factory. Extensively improving the tone of his pianos, P. A. Rudolf was respected by the leading composers and musicians of the time, including Richard Wagner, who thought of him as the musician's "friendly tone engineer."

Wishing to create more interesting piano cases, P. A. Rudolf set competitions for leading architects and designers, and to this day Rud. Ibach & Sohn still design and make pianos with extraordinary cases.

While P. A. Rudolf was expanding the commercial side of the company, his brother Walter was traveling the world learning new ideas from the world's top piano builders. After an absence of ten years, he returned to Germany and helped his sister-in-law, Hulda, to run the company after Peter's death in 1892.

By the beginning of the twentieth century, Ibach were producing pianos in three factories (in Schwelm, Barmen, and Berlin), now led by a fourth-generation member of the family, Rudolf. The company was firmly established as a mature maker and their pianos were favored by musicians and composers alike.

However, the economic crisis of the 1930s saw Ibach's piano production severely cut to a twelfth of their output at the beginning of the century. The 1940s brought no relief, with the company's factories, concert halls, and archives largely destroyed during the Second World War.

grace notes

RUD. IBACH SOHN

Johannes Adolph Ibach

Formerly a textile factory, Rud. Ibach's present site in Schwelm was bought by the Ibach family in the 1880s to produce upright pianos. It soon had the most advanced technology in the region and, despite needing to be rebuilt after the Second World War, it is still Ibach's headquarters.

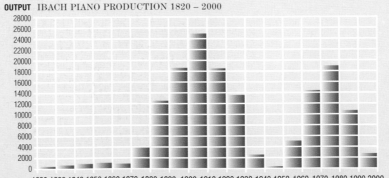

OUTPUT IBACH PIANO PRODUCTION 1820 – 2000

DATES & SERIAL NUMBERS	
1820 - 464	**1930** - 96000
1830 - 701	**1940** - 98300
1840 - 1189	**1950** - 98500
1850 - 1906	**1960** - 103800
1860 - 2900	**1970** - 117901
1870 - 3800	**1980** - 136675
1880 - 7800	**1990** - 147437
1890 - 20100	**2000** - 150076
1900 - 38600	
1910 - 63600	
1920 - 82100	

Model: Classicism

Casework: mahogany, polished; with pyramid mahogany inlay
Compass: AAA-c5, 88 notes
Action: Renner to Ibach specifications
Modifiers: 3 pedals: una-corda, sustaining, and sostenuto
Dimensions: L: 7 ft 2½ in (220cm);
W: 5 ft 1½ in (156cm);
W: 816 lbs (370kg)

The beleaguered company did not resume piano production until 1952, when fifth-generation Adolf Ibach and his wife, Margrit, worked hard to maintain the high quality of the largely handcrafted instruments. Respected for their quality craftsmanship, Ibach resumed their position as one of Germany's finest piano makers. The factory in Schwelm was rebuilt and became the company's headquarters, and a global network of dealers was established.

Model: Richard Wagner

Casework: black, polished
Compass: AAA-c5, 88 notes
Action: Renner to Ibach specifications
Modifiers: 3 pedals: una-corda, sustaining, and sostenuto
Dimensions: L: 7 ft 10½ in (240cm);
W: 5 ft 1½ in (156cm);
W: 948 lbs (430kg)

Today, under the guidance of Rolf Ibach, this well-respected piano company continues their tradition for artistic case designs and has employed leading architects such as Richard Meier to design piano cases. In 1994, a production run of three historical designs by architects such as Bruno Paul and Peter Behrens was introduced to celebrate 200 years of piano making. With the Ibach family still at the helm of the business, Rud. Ibach Sohn can look forward to a successful third century.

Model: H-128

Casework: burr walnut with inlay, polished; designed by Peter Behrens
Compass: AAA-c5, 88 notes
Action: Renner to Ibach specifications
Modifiers: 2 pedals: half-blow, and sustaining
Dimensions: H: 50½in (128cm); W: 54¼ in (138cm); D: 25¼ (64cm)

maker's marks

• *Ibach characterize their sound as being firm and transparent in the bass section, rich and warm in the tenor, and with a pearl-like singing tone in the treble, which is maintained at all volumes.*

• *Producing a variety of upright and grand pianos, all Ibach instruments are made predominantly by hand.*

• *As well as producing a standard series of pianos, Ibach maintain their tradition of designing extraordinary cases.*

• *In the 1880s, Ibach built pianos incorporating the Janko keyboard—a patented keyboard layout that enabled the player to cover a wider span of notes with each hand.*

Kawai

Kawai Musical Instrument Manufacturing Company Ltd
200 Terajima-Cho, Hamamatsu
JAPAN

Names used: Kawai, Diapson, Schiedmayer. Also makes pianos for other distributors under the names of Boston and Schulz & Sons.

ESTABLISHED IN 1927, KAWAI IS NOW THE SECOND LARGEST PIANO MAKER IN THE WORLD AFTER YAMAHA. FOUNDED BY KOICHI KAWAI, WHO AT THE AGE OF TWELVE WORKED WITH TORAKUSU YAMAHA TO BUILD HIS FIRST PIANO, KAWAI WAS THE FIRST JAPANESE PIANO COMPANY TO BUILD ITS OWN ACTIONS.

Koichi Kawai worked for Yamaha from 1897 to 1927, when he left to set up on his own. His first piano was a 64-note upright selling for just 350 yen. A year later, he produced his first grand piano. The difficulties he overcame in these early years were enormous, since he not only faced a lack of qualified craftsmen and a shortage of good-quality materials, but also had to cope with an underdeveloped network of dealers. During the 1930s, now under the name Kawai Musical Instrument Manufacturing Company, output increased from barely 250 pianos a year to 1,000, but the factory was completely destroyed in the Second World War, leaving the future in doubt.

Through a combination of hard work, optimism, and the inclusion of music in the school curriculum, the factory was re-established, and in 1949 production started on both uprights and grands. By 1953 output had risen to 1,500 pianos a year and the company employed 500 people. Such was the influence of Kawai in Japan that Koichi received the prestigious Blue Ribbon Medal from the emperor, the first time that a person working in the musical instrument industry had received such an award.

Koichi's son, Shigeru Kawai, took over the firm on his father's death in 1955 and re-equipped the factory for modern production techniques to increase output. Aggressive sales techniques were used, such as contacting new parents to extol the benefits of a musical education, in particular the piano, and he built a nationwide network of music schools and an academy of music to train new teachers. In succeeding years, he also expanded the company's manufacturing base from one factory to fourteen, including one in the U.S. opened in 1989. By 1960 Kawai employed nearly 2,000 door-to-door salesmen and over 300,000 people in the Kawai Music Schools. The Kawai America Corporation was formed in 1963 to sell pianos and electric organs within the U.S.; Kawai Europe, Kawai Canada, Kawai Australia, and Kawai Asia followed.

In 1980 a 300,000-square-foot factory was built, capable of producing sixty grand pianos a day. In 1989 the company

KAWAI
P I A N O S

grace notes

Koichi Kawai

In 1991, under the guidance of Koichi Kawai's grandson, Hirotaka, Kawai Musical Instrument Manufacturing Company entered into a joint venture with Steinway Musical Properties to produce a new line of pianos called the Boston. The development took six years to complete using sophisticated computer technology to test the new designs and materials.

• Hamamatsu

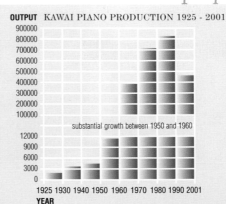

OUTPUT KAWAI PIANO PRODUCTION 1925 - 2001

substantial growth between 1950 and 1960

DATES & SERIAL NUMBERS

1925 - 4200	**1970** - 425121
1930 - 6000	**1980** - 1126366
1940 - 9600	**1990** - 1950000
1950 - 14200	**2001** - 2410000
1960 - 26000	

Model: GM-10

Casework: black, high gloss polyester
Compass: AAA-c5, 88 notes
Action: Kawai ultra responsive action
Modifiers: 3 pedals: una-corda, sustaining, and sostenuto
Dimensions: L: 4 ft 11 in (150cm);
W: 4 ft 11 in (150cm)

maker's marks

• *Kawai pianos have been designated official instruments of the Arthur Rubinstein International Piano Master Competition and the Chopin International Piano Competition.*

• *Through the use of modern technology and extensive sales networks, Kawai has become the second largest producer of pianos in the world.*

• *At the Shigeru Kawai Research and Development Laboratory, master piano makers use handcraft skills to explore new methods and materials used in the production of Kawai pianos.*

presidency was passed to Shigeru's son, Hirotaka Kawai, who has since invested millions of dollars to introduce robotic technology into the production process. In the last ten years, production sites have been established outside Japan, in the U.S., and Malaysia.

Determined to find a stronger and more stable material for action parts, Kawai pioneered the use of the polymer composite acrylonitrile butadiene styrene, from which their action parts are made today.

Model: K-50

Casework: walnut, polish
Compass: AAA-c5, 88 notes
Action: Kawai ultra responsive action
Modifiers: 3 pedals: half-blow, sustaining, and celeste/moderator
Dimensions: H: 49¼ in (125cm); W: 60¼ in (153cm); D: 23¼ in (59cm)

Model: CP150 (digital)

Casework: simulated rosewood
Compass: AAA-c5, 88 notes
Action: Kawai enhanced AWA grand action
Modifiers: 3 pedals: una-corda, sustaining, and sostenuto
Dimensions: H: 44 in (112cm); W: 55½ in (141cm); D: 24½ in (62cm)

Kemble

Kemble and Company Ltd
Mount Avenue
Bletchley
Milton Keynes MK1 1JE
ENGLAND

DURING THE 1890S, IN AN AGE WHEN NO ENGLISH HOME WAS CONSIDERED PROPERLY FURNISHED WITHOUT A PIANO, ROBERT KEMBLE BEGAN IMPORTING PIANOS FROM GERMANY. AT ABOUT THE SAME TIME A SMALL REED ORGAN MANUFACTURER CALLED YAMAHA STARTED PRODUCTION IN JAPAN. EVENTUALLY THE TWO COMPANIES WOULD MERGE TO BECOME THE LARGEST PIANO MAKER IN WESTERN EUROPE.

Kemble's import venture was a success and by 1920 the company had begun to produce its own pianos out of a workshop in Stoke Newington, London. Up until the First World War, this was London's piano district and it is said that Robert Kemble found his employees by looking for front windows with piano felt as curtains. On finding one he would ask whether any of the residents had worked in the piano trade before the war. Any who had were offered a job. Working together with his wife's cousin, Victor Jacobs, Kemble prospered despite the harsh economic climate of the 1920s and 1930s. In 1935 Kemble launched three new models: the Jubilee (named to commemorate the Jubilee of King George V that year), the Cubist, and the Minx. The demand for these

instruments, particularly the tiny Minx, stretched capacity to the limit.

Kemble changed its production in 1939 to help the war effort—making bomber doors—but piano production resumed soon after the war. In 1967 Kemble bought the rights to the names Cramer and Brinsmead, and the following year moved out of London to Bletchley in Milton Keynes, where upright pianos are still produced. The year before, Kemble Ltd had been set up to distribute electric organs for the Yamaha Corporation. What began as a distribution deal ended in a buy-in: by 1971 Yamaha had become a minority shareholder in Kemble Ltd.

In the early 1980s Kemble came within a whisker of closing, but at the last minute won the biggest contract to build

pianos in the U.K. industry, making the Dietman range of pianos for Ibach. In 1984 Kemble found itself in difficulties once again and once more Yamaha heavily invested in the business, this time taking majority control. By 1986 Kemble was producing pianos under the Yamaha name for the European market and a large investment was made to increase production dramatically. In 1992 Kemble achieved the Queen's Award for exports, which had more than doubled in a three-year period. Output hit its high point in 1999, when nearly 7,000 pianos were made, and remains steady today.

grace notes

Robert Kemble

Now sited in one of the most advanced piano-producing plants in Europe, Kemble's foresight in 1968 in moving from the traditional piano-building district of London to the new town of Milton Keynes in Buckinghamshire aided the spectacular growth of the company, now Western Europe's largest piano manufacturer.

Milton Keynes

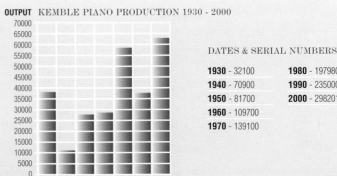

OUTPUT KEMBLE PIANO PRODUCTION 1930 - 2000

YEAR

DATES & SERIAL NUMBERS

1930 - 32100	**1980** - 197980
1940 - 70900	**1990** - 235000
1950 - 81700	**2000** - 298201
1960 - 109700	
1970 - 139100	

Model: K121Z

Casework: Georgian mahogany luster
Compass: AAA-c5, 88 notes
Action: Yamaha to Kemble specifications
Modifiers: 3 pedals: half-blow, sustaining, and celeste/moderator
Dimensions: H: 48 in (121cm); W: 60¼ in (153cm); D: 24 in (61cm)

maker's marks

• *Kemble's pianos are known for a rich, mellow, European sound.*

• *Bavarian spruce from sustainable forests is used for the soundboards. Keyboards are made from spruce for stability in different climatic conditions.*

• *The case of the Quantum 131 was designed by Conran & Partners, a distinguished British design firm.*

• *With over 70 percent of the staff remaining at Kemble for fifteen years or more, a wealth of experience is handed down through the factory from one generation to the next.*

• *In the 1930s, Kemble produced an upright piano called the Minx. Standing only three feet (90cm) tall, it housed an action below the keyboard that was lifted rather than pushed by the keys. As an additional extra, a modulator was fitted to reduce the volume of the strings.*

Model: Quantum

Casework: black, polyester
Compass: AAA-c5, 88 notes
Action: Yamaha to Kemble specifications
Modifiers: 3 pedals: una-corda half-blow, sustaining, and sostenuto
Dimensions: H: 52 in (131cm); W: 60¼ in (153cm); D: 25 in (64cm)

Model: The Classic

Casework: mahogany, satin
Compass: AAA-a4, 85 notes
Action: Yamaha to Kemble specifications
Modifiers: 3 pedals: half-blow, sustaining, and celeste/moderator
Dimensions: H: 42¾ in (109cm); W: 51¼ in (130cm); D: 19 in (48cm)

Knight

British Piano Manufacturing Company Ltd
Woodchester Mills
Woodchester, Stroud
Glos. GL5 5NW
ENGLAND

THE GREAT DEPRESSION OF THE 1930S DEALT A BODY BLOW TO AN INDUSTRY ALREADY AILING FROM THE ADVENT OF RADIO, CINEMA, AND THE GRAMOPHONE. ALFRED KNIGHT SHOWED ENORMOUS SELF-BELIEF WHEN HE SET UP HIS COMPANY IN LONDON IN 1935.

Knight had worked for various piano firms, and was himself a gifted pianist who delighted in demonstrating his own instruments. His enthusiasm paid off: by the end of the decade the Knight company was producing 1,000 pianos a year.

During the Second World War, the company continued to make pianos under government contract. Fitted with metal trim for protection, and specially built to withstand beer spills, nine Knight pianos are reputed to have gone ashore immediately after the Normandy Landings in 1944.

After the war, Knight had a distinct advantage over other makers in that its piano production had never stopped. Alfred Knight worked tirelessly to build export contacts and still demonstrated his own pianos to a professional standard with flair and humor. In 1955 he moved the company to a much bigger factory in Loughton, Essex, and later that decade led a takeover of British Piano Actions. Alfred personally began to redesign the piano action using the newly developed plastics of the day. He achieved great success using nylon impregnated with graphite, and glass fiber, for frictionless jacks and flanges, and developed a non-staining white plastic key top for natural key coverings.

Upon Alfred's death the company was left in the control of his daughter's family. Since 1991, Knight pianos have been produced to their original specifications by Whelpdale, Maxwell & Codd, now part of British Piano Manufacturing Ltd.

maker's marks

- *Knight upright pianos offer a warm and singing tone with an exceptionally even treble section.*

- *The Knight iron frame offers twice the strength of those in an average piano. It is a full-perimeter frame built on a girder principle that is secured to a four-post beech back. The pin block is fitted in a pocket cast into the frame for exceptional tuning stability.*

- *There is no treble stress bar in the K10 model. Several resisting bars are cast in the bottom left-hand corner of the piano to resist the strings' tension, eliminating the possibility of weak-sounding notes.*

- *Hard fiber plate bushings are used to support the tuning pins to enhance tuning stability.*

- *The bass strings are covered with extra heavy pure copper, giving a total weight of 7 lbs (3kgs) a set.*

Model: K10

Casework:	cherry, satin
Compass:	AAA-c5, 88 notes
Action:	Renner to Knight specifications
Modifiers:	3 pedals: half-blow, sustaining, and celeste/moderator
Dimensions:	H: 43¾ in (112cm); W: 55 in (140cm); D: 21½ in (54.5cm)

KNIGHT

grace notes

Founded in 2000, the British Piano Manufacturing Company produces Knight pianos to their original specifications from the heart of the Cotswold hills in Gloucestershire. Piano making has been carried out at the historic Woodchester Mills plant since 1911, when the Bentley Piano Company moved there from London.

Stroud

OUTPUT KNIGHT PIANO PRODUCTION 1936 – 2000

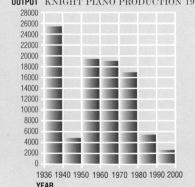

YEAR	1936	1940	1950	1960	1970	1980	1990	2000

DATES & SERIAL NUMBERS

Year	Serial
1936	1001
1940	3588
1950	8420
1960	28245
1970	47888
1980	65000
1990	70970
2000	73250

Leipziger Pianofortefabrik

Pianofortefabrik Leipzig GmbH & Co.KG
Ludwig-Hupfeld Strasse 16
D-04178 Leipzig
GERMANY

Names used: Rönisch, Hupfeld

FOUNDED IN 1845 BY THE IMPOVERISHED CARL RÖNISCH, THE FIRM WOULD BECOME A PIONEER IN EXPORTING GERMAN PIANOS TO EVERY CORNER OF THE GLOBE.

Carl Rönisch was born in Silesia in 1814. At the age of ten he began a five-year apprenticeship in a machine shop, during which he became interested in the piano. After three years studying the art of piano-building, Rönisch began making pianos under his own name in Dresden in 1845. In 1857, he produced Germany's first baby grand, and became Official Purveyor to the Court after delivering three grand pianos to the king of Saxony. By 1862, Rönisch was exporting pianos to Russia, Sweden, England, Spain, and Portugal.

Carl died in 1892 aged 78, leaving the business to his sons, Albert and Hermann, who sought to expand. In 1898 they set up a branch in St. Petersburg and in 1902 entered into a cooperation agreement with Ludwig Hupfeld, a manufacturer of player pianos. The company grew rapidly; exports reached record levels and by now Rönisch was producing 3,000 instruments annually.

But in 1918, in the wake of a family tragedy and the impact of the First World War, Hermann sold the company outright to Ludwig Hupfeld AG.

Rönisch prospered between the wars, but the company's Dresden factory was destroyed in bombing raids in 1945, and production was moved to Hupfeld's Leipzig factory. The following year Leipziger Pianofortefabrik was born, and by 1986 annual output stood at 8,600. Following German Reunification in 1990, the production process was reorganized and the range redesigned. Carl A. Pfeiffer bought Rönisch in 1997, and established Pianofortefabrik Leipzig GmbH, a new home where the creativity and quality of the Rönisch name lives on.

maker's marks

• *Hupfeld's Phonoliszt-Violina, made by Rönisch and Hupfeld in 1910, is an automatic musical instrument that incorporates a full eighty-eight-note piano and three violins, all played by means of rolls.*

• *Pianofortefabrik Leipzig GmbH & Co. KG still make pianos faithful to the tradition and philosophy of their founder, Carl Rönisch: "fine tone quality through a rock-solid, durable construction."*

Model: 123 KP

Casework:	black gloss, flame mahogany panels
Compass:	AAA-c5, 88 notes
Action:	Renner to Rönisch specifications
Modifiers:	3 pedals: half-blow, sustaining, and celeste/moderator
Dimensions:	H: 48½ in (123cm); W: 59 in (150cm); D: 23¼ in (59cm); W: 491 lbs (223kg)

grace notes

RÖNISCH

Carl Rönisch

By the time Carl Rönisch died in 1892, he employed 250 workers and had an annual output of some 1,500 pianos, many of which were exported overseas. In his lifetime, he became Royal Saxonian Councillor of Commerce, and his company was known as Official Purveyor to the Courts of the King of Saxony, and the Courts of Spain and Russia; the company was also Imperial Purveyor to the Emperor of Austria-Hungary.

• Leipzig

OUTPUT LEIPZIGER PIANO PRODUCTION 1855 – 2000

substantial growth from 1961

70000
60000
50000
30000
27000
24000
21000
18000
15000
12000
9000
6000
3000
0

1855 1860 1870 1880 1890 1900 1910 1920 1930 1940 1950 1961 1976 1980 1990 2000
YEAR

DATES & SERIAL NUMBERS

1855 - 420	**1940** - 76400
1860 - 960	**1950** - 77100
1870 - 3200	**1961** - 86000
1880 - 7900	**1976** - 150000
1890 - 18500	**1980** - 175000
1900 - 30000	**1990** - 200000
1910 - 50800	**2000** - 209960
1920 - 67500	
1930 - 76000	

The Mason & Hamlin Companies
35 Duncan Street, Haverhill
MA 01830
UNITED STATES

Mason & Hamlin

Owned by: Kirk and Gary Burgett of PianoDisc.
Names used: Falcone, Knabe, Mason & Hamlin,
Sohmer, and George Steck

MASON & HAMLIN REMAINED STEINWAY AND SONS' MOST SERIOUS AMERICAN COMPETITOR UNTIL THE 1920S. SOLD AS "THE WORLD'S COSTLIEST PIANOS," THE INSTRUMENTS WERE INDEED OF THE FINEST QUALITY. IT WAS LACK OF STABLE OWNERSHIP THAT WOULD CAUSE THIS ONCE ILLUSTRIOUS FIRM TO WANE.

Founded in 1854 by Henry Mason, a businessman and amateur musician, and Emmons Hamlin, inventor of the reed organ, the company soon gained renown for its organ harmonium and cabinet organ. The first Mason & Hamlin piano appeared relatively late on the scene, in 1881, but from the start it exuded quality. Further improvements were made over the years and in 1895, the founders employed the services of the distinguished German piano designer Richard W. Gertz, who improved the company's scale designs and incorporated in 1905 a patented tension resonator. For a while Mason & Hamlin grand pianos were fitted with a peculiar tuning system, which used machine screws instead of wrest pins and a pin block. This interesting device was discontinued in 1905 before it was fully developed.

From 1911, when Mason & Hamlin became part of the Cable Nelson Company, the firm began to slide, losing its former status with a series of changes of ownership that would eventually leave it as part of the Aeolian American Corporation in 1932.

In 1985, after the demise of Aeolian, Mason & Hamlin was acquired by the Sohmer Company, which was in turn acquired by Falcone Piano Company in 1989. In 1995, Mason & Hamlin Companies (including Knabe, Falcone, and Sohmer), which had emerged after a buyout in 1991, filed for bankruptcy and was rescued by PianoDisc. Under new and committed ownership, every part of the company has been revitalized and, in 2002, Mason & Hamlin pianos are near-perfect reproductions of the very best early twentieth-century models.

maker's marks

• *Mason & Hamlin pianos have a wide tone palette with a rich bass, clean tenor, and bell-like treble.*

• *In 1900, Richard Gertz, while working for Mason & Hamlin, obtained a patent for a tension resonator, which consisted of a series of adjustable metal bars set out radially from a central point beneath the piano and connecting with the rim, the idea being to regulate the pressure in the arch of the soundboard against the strings and assist their vibration over the entire board. The idea was incorporated on all Mason & Hamlin grand pianos. Now termed the crown retention system, it is still used on Mason & Hamlin grand pianos today.*

• *A peculiar stringing design was incorporated on the grand pianos until 1905. It employed a metal flange and a machine screw to adjust the string tension, rather than the wrest pin inserted into the wrest plank. The string was threaded onto a hook and as the screw was turned with a small T-hammer the string would be tuned. The system had many advantages over the traditional method, as the screw would not twist or stick like a wrest pin and required little effort to turn it. The accuracy was good but it required much more turning to bring the string to the desired point. A combination of this slowness and the prejudice of tuners (who had to adjust their technique to turning the screw the opposite way than with a wrest pin) led to this valuable idea being dropped.*

grace notes

The present owners of Mason & Hamlin, brothers Kirk and Gary Burgett, built their PianoDisc company from scratch into a US$20 million leader in the electronic reproducing piano market. Their move in 1996—widely seen as a gamble—to rescue the much under-realized American make of Mason & Hamlin has proved to be a huge success.

Haverhill •

Mason & Hamlin

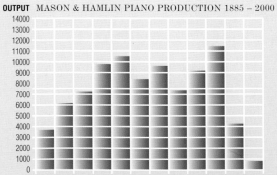

OUTPUT MASON & HAMLIN PIANO PRODUCTION 1885 – 2000

(bar chart, OUTPUT axis 0–14000, YEAR axis 1885 1890 1900 1910 1920 1930 1940 1950 1960 1970 1980 1990 2000)

DATES & SERIAL NUMBERS

1885 - 1893		**1950** - 57800
1890 - 5700		**1960** - 65200
1900 - 11800		**1970** - 74263
1910 - 19100		**1980** - 85853
1920 - 29000		**1990** - 90000
1930 - 39600		**2000** - 90988
1940 - 48000		

Model: Artist Grand Model A

Casework:	black, polished
Compass:	AAA-c5, 88 notes
Action:	Renner to Mason & Hamlin specification
Modifiers:	3 pedals: una-corda, sustaining, and sostenuto
Dimensions:	L: 6 ft 11¾ in (213cm); W: 5 ft 2½ in (159cm); W: 1,020 lbs (463kg)

Model: Monticello

Casework:	mahogany, polished
Compass:	AAA-c5, 88 notes
Action:	Renner to Mason & Hamlin specifications
Modifiers:	3 pedals: una-corda, sustaining, and sostenuto
Dimensions:	L: 7 ft (213.5cm); W: 5 ft 2½ in (159cm); W: 570 lbs (258kg)

MASON &B HAMLIN

Model: Professional Studio 50

Casework:	black polyester
Compass:	AAA-c5, 88 notes
Action:	Renner to Mason & Hamlin specifications
Modifiers:	3 pedals: half-blow, sustaining, and celeste/moderator
Dimensions:	H: 50 in (127cm); W: 37¾ in (96cm); D: 23⅛ in (59cm); W: 570 lbs (258kg)

Petrof

Petrof Pianos Musicexport
Václavske nam. 18
11227 Prague
CZECH REPUBLIC

Names used: Petrof, Weinbach, Scholze, Rosler, and Fibich.

FOUNDED IN 1864 BY ANTONIN PETROF 60 MILES (100KM) EAST OF PRAGUE, THIS FIRM OF PIANO MAKERS WAS FAMILY OWNED FOR THREE GENERATIONS, KEEPING ABREAST OF TECHNICAL INNOVATIONS AND EARNING PRIZES AT EXHIBITIONS. TODAY, DESPITE A CENTURY OF POLITICAL CHANGE, IT HAS MAINTAINED ITS POSITION AS THE CZECH REPUBLIC'S BEST-KNOWN MAKER.

Antonin Petrof, a trained carpenter, moved to Vienna in 1857 at the age of nineteen, to become apprentice to his piano-making uncle, Johann Heitzmann. He worked with various Austrian makers, returning in 1864 to his native Hradec Králové, where he set up his own factory, initially making small numbers of Viennese action pianos.

A keen traveler, Petrof picked up on the latest technical developments and incorporated them into his own designs, so that by 1875 he was using a cast-iron frame and a repetition action modified from the English grand action. In 1880, he started producing upright pianos as well as grand models and by the time of his death in 1915 Petrof had sold 35,500 pianos.

Antonin's three sons and three grandsons led the firm successfully through the two world wars and the Great Depression. Nationalized in 1948, Petrof in 1965 became part of the Industrial and Commercial Group-Czechoslovakia Musical Instruments Musicexport, under whose umbrella the firm has continued to flourish.

New factories were built, first in 1970 to increase production of upright pianos, and then in 1989 a second plant to concentrate on the grand piano market. By 1990 serial numbers had reached 450,000.

Petrof currently produces around 12,000 uprights and 1,750 grand pianos a year, and employs 1,000 people. Tovarna nà piano, established in 1997, united with Petrof in 2001, marking the climax of a privatization process that began in 1991.

A poster from the 1930s advertising Petrof pianos.

grace notes

Antonin Petrof

The city of Hradec Králové has a long musical tradition and it was here that Antonin Petrof began an enterprise that has survived through a century of turbulent political change. Consistently keeping up with the latest innovations in an ever-changing trade, Antonin was the first piano maker in the Austro-Hungarian Empire to use a full iron frame and a repetition action in his pianos.

Prague

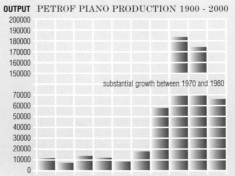

OUTPUT PETROF PIANO PRODUCTION 1900 - 2000

substantial growth between 1970 and 1980

YEAR

DATES & SERIAL NUMBERS

1900 -13000	**1960** - 87200
1910 - 24000	**1970** - 146900
1920 - 33400	**1980** - 330000
1930 - 46500	**1990** - 504500
1940 - 58000	**2000** - 570000
1950 - 67280	

Model: P111M

Casework: black, high polish
Compass: AAA-c5, 88 notes
Action: Renner to Petrof specifications
Modifiers: 3 pedals: una-corda, sustaining, and sostenuto
Dimensions: L: 6 ft 3 in (152.5cm); W: 5 ft (193cm); W: 763 lbs (347kg)

Model: P126IV Elegance

Casework: black, high polish
Compass: AAA-c5, 88 notes
Action: Renner to Petrof specifications
Modifiers: 3 pedals: half-blow, sustaining, and celeste/moderator
Dimensions: H: 49 in (125cm); D: 23 in (58.5cm); W: 460 lbs (209kg)

maker's marks

• *Sturdily built instruments cherished for their singing tone, Petrof pianos are found in La Scala in Milan, the Sydney Opera House, and the Vatican.*

• *Petrof maintains an educational facility that trains new craftsmen, enrolling up to 200 apprentices at a time.*

Model: P105V

Casework: black, high polish
Compass: AAA-c5, 88 notes
Action: Detoa
Modifiers: 3 pedals: half-blow, sustaining, and celeste/moderator
Dimensions: H: 42½ in (108cm); D: 21½ in (55cm); W: 408 lbs (185kg)

Pleyel

Manufacture Pleyel
30319 Alès Cedex
FRANCE

Also produces Gaveau and Rameau pianos

IN 1807, AT THE AGE OF FIFTY, IGNAZ PLEYEL FOUNDED A PIANO FIRM THAT WOULD BECOME AN IMPORTANT PART OF THE WORLD'S MUSICAL HERITAGE. HIS DELICATE-SOUNDING PIANOS WERE SOUGHT AFTER FOR THEIR ABILITY TO REPRODUCE THE MOST SUBTLE NUANCES. IT WAS CHOPIN WHO SAID, "WHEN I FEEL THE MUSIC FLOWING AND I AM STRONG ENOUGH TO STRIKE MY OWN SOUND, I MUST HAVE A PLEYEL."

A celebrated musician, and composer of symphonies and operas, Ignaz Pleyel was impassioned by instrument making, and his desire to create a piano to suit the needs of the new composers led him to found his now-famous firm in Paris. The first piano he made, in 1807, was a small, vertically strung upright, based on the cottage pianos widely seen in London.

As the firm grew in eminence, Ignaz took his eldest son, Camille, into the business. This turned out to be an excellent move: having studied the piano as a performer, Camille assumed a key role, contacting piano makers and performers in England and France to canvas their opinions and exchange ideas. Production increased, to the chagrin of some Pleyel users: in 1839 Liszt quoted

Rossini as saying, "Pleyel is making too many pianos. He no longer has the time to take care over them."

In 1855 the firm passed to Camille's son-in-law, Auguste Wolff, and pianos were produced under the name of Pleyel, Wolff, & Cie. By 1865 Pleyel had produced some 36,000 pianos, approximately the same number as Erard, which had been in existence twenty-seven years longer. In 1887 the company passed to Wolff's son-in-law Gustave Lyon and under the name of Pleyel, Lyon & Cie the firm expanded into the production of other musical instruments, including harps, timpani, and harpsichords. Piano production continued, however, and included a player piano called the Pleyela, and a double grand piano, with two keyboards facing each other

in one case. By 1910, with an annual production of about 3,000 pianos, Pleyel had reached its peak and dominated the French quality piano market.

In 1934 Pleyel acquired the firm of Antoine Bord. In 1961, facing financial difficulties, the firm merged with the combined firms of Erard and Gaveau. This conglomerate was acquired in 1971 by the Schimmel Company, which produced a small number of Pleyel pianos each year. Then in 1994, the Rameau company bought the names of Pleyel and Gaveau, and two years later Pleyel took control once more, opening a state-of-the-art production and R&D unit in Alès in the South of France, where they continue to make superb pianos faithful to the Pleyel tradition.

grace notes

*Ignaz
Pleyel*

Ignaz Pleyel was a student and friend of Haydn. Before manufacturing his first piano in Paris in 1807, he had composed forty-one symphonies, seventy quartets, and several quintets and operas, and was rated highly both as a musician and as a composer.

* Alès

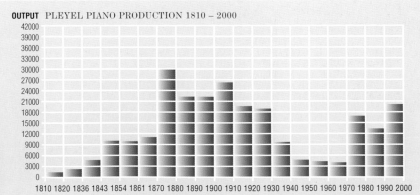

OUTPUT PLEYEL PIANO PRODUCTION 1810 – 2000

YEAR: 1810 1820 1836 1843 1854 1861 1870 1880 1890 1900 1910 1920 1930 1940 1950 1960 1970 1980 1990 2000

DATES & SERIAL NUMBERS

Year	Serial	Year	Serial
1810	760	**1920**	168850
1820	2100	**1930**	188000
1836	5010	**1940**	197314
1843	10000	**1950**	202000
1854	2000	**1960**	206545
1861	30000	**1970**	210700
1870	47500	**1980**	227800
1880	77500	**1990**	241000
1890	100000	**2000**	261800
1900	122500		
1910	149000		

Model: P190

Casework:	cherry, satin
Compass:	AAA-c5, 88 notes
Action:	Renner to Pleyel specifications
Modifiers:	3 pedals: una-corda, sustaining, and sostenuto
Dimensions:	L: 6 ft 3 in (190cm); W: 4 ft 11 in (150cm)

Model: P131

Casework:	mahogany, polished
Compass:	AAA-c5, 88 notes
Action:	Renner to Pleyel specifications
Modifiers:	3 pedals: half-blow, sustaining, and celeste/moderator
Dimensions:	H: 51½ in (131cm); W: 58½ in (149cm); D: 24¾ in (63cm)

Model: Académie

Casework:	black, polished
Compass:	AAA-c5, 88 notes
Action:	Renner to Pleyel specifications
Modifiers:	3 pedals: half-blow, sustaining, and celeste/moderator
Dimensions:	H: 45 in (114cm); W: 57 in (145cm); D: 21½ in (55cm)

Samick Piano Company

Names used: Samick, Hyundai, Kohler & Campbell, D.H. Baldwin, Bernhard Steiner, Otto Altenburg, and private label brands. Names no longer used: Horugel, Stegler, Schumann.

ONE OF FOUR PIANO MAKERS IN KOREA, SAMICK HAS A HISTORY THAT SPANS JUST THIRTY-FOUR YEARS, IN WHICH TIME IT HAS GROWN A BUSINESS FROM UNPROMISING ROOTS IN THE WAKE OF THE KOREAN WAR TO BECOME ONE OF THE LARGEST PIANO MANUFACTURERS IN THE WORLD TODAY.

Founded in 1958 by chairman Hyo Ick Lee, the company swung into full production of upright pianos under the brand name Horugel. This name would be used until the 1970s, when the Samick brand was introduced. A leading light in its domestic market, Samick became, in 1964, the first Korean company to export pianos, sending ten uprights to Hong Kong. Output of uprights steadily grew and, spurred on by the Prize of Piano Development awarded by the Korean Ministry of Trade and Industry in 1970, Samick became the first

Model: WFG 172

Casework:	Burbinga, high polish
Compass:	AAA-c5, 88 notes
Action:	Samick
Modifiers:	3 pedals: una-corda, sustaining, and sostenuto
Dimensions:	L: 5 ft 7¾ in (172cm); W: 4 ft 10 in (148cm); W: 702 lbs (318kg)

grace notes

Despite their short history, Samick are today the world's largest producers of grand pianos and have been awarded the Korean Standard of Excellence for their world series pianos.

• Incheon

DATES & SERIAL NUMBERS

1960 - 28017
1970 - 29109
1980 - 33444
1990 - HIKO 0001*
2001 - KJKA 0001*

* a change in the numbering system

Model: WSU 118F

Casework: cherry, high polish
Compass: AAA-c5, 88 notes
Action: Samick
Modifiers: 3 pedals: half-blow, sustaining, and celeste/moderator
Dimensions: H: 46½ in (118cm); W: 59 in (150cm); D: 25¼ in (64cm); W: 503 lbs (228kg)

Korean manufacturer of grand pianos.

The following years were to be spent securing a position on the world stage, and resources were focused on expanding the company's exports. Samick opened a branch in West Germany in 1980 and later entered a joint venture with the American Baldwin Piano and Organ Company.

The company has worked tirelessly since its founding to expand its production facilities. By the 1990s, after several changes in factories, the company could boast separate plants for upright, grand, and digital piano production, all incorporating the latest developments in machinery. In 1996 Samick opened a factory in Indonesia incorporating its own wood processing plant, where both uprights and grands are now built. With a new line of pianos for the millennium—and after just forty-four years producing musical instruments—Samick have come a long way in a short time, and look set to play a significant role in the future.

maker's marks

• *Samick describe their pianos as having a full and robust sound with crystal clear highs.*

• *The scale design for the Samick grand piano range was calculated by the eminent German scale designer Klaus Fenner, engaged for technical support in 1983.*

• *Samick offer an unusually large choice of nine different lengths in their grand piano range, from 55⅛ in (140cm) to 108 in (275cm) long.*

Model: WSU 131MD

Casework: black, polyester
Compass: AAA-c5, 88 notes
Action: Samick
Modifiers: 3 pedals: half-blow, sustaining, and sostenuto
Dimensions: H: 51½ in (131cm); W: 60⅗ in (154cm); D: 25⅗ in (65cm); W: 586 lbs (266kg)

Sauter

Carl Sauter Pianofortefabrik
Max Planck Strasse
D-78545 Spaichingen
GERMANY

FOUNDED IN 1819, SAUTER IS NOT ONLY ONE OF THE OLDEST PIANO-MAKING FIRMS IN GERMANY, BUT ITS HISTORY ALSO REFLECTS ONE OF THE LONGEST SINGLE-FAMILY-OWNERSHIP CONTINUUMS IN THE ENTIRE PIANO INDUSTRY.

The story starts in Vienna, Austria, where the young Johann Grimm did a six-year apprenticeship in piano building under the supervision of Johann Andreas Streicher, the city's leading maker of the time. In 1819, his education complete, Grimm returned to his home town of Spaichingen in southern Germany to set up a workshop with his adopted son, Carl Sauter. Johann and Carl completed six square pianos between them before realizing that the future lay in expanding their capacity, and they assembled a team of a dozen local craftsman to share the workload.

On Carl's death in 1863, the by now thriving company was left to a Johann, member of the next generation of Sauters. Not content to rest on the family laurels, and taking full advantage of the advances in transport, he traveled the world, gathering new ideas in piano building and

Model: 185 Delta

Casework:	black, polished
Compass:	AAA-c5, 88 notes
Action:	Renner to Sauter specifications
Modifiers:	3 pedals: una-corda, sustaining, and sostenuto
Dimensions:	H: 6 ft 1 in (185cm); W: 5 ft (152cm); W: 650 lbs (295kg)

SAUTER

grace notes

In 2002, keen to launch a new series of instruments and to promote microtonal music, Sauter completed an order of sixteenth-tone pianos for the Paris Conservatory. Sauter have been associated with this music form since the 1950s, when they were originally commissioned to build a microtonal piano for composer Julián Carrillo Trujillo. This instrument was exhibited in 1957 at the Brussels World Exhibition.

Spaichingen

OUTPUT SAUTER PIANO PRODUCTION 1840 – 2000

Bar chart with y-axis (OUTPUT) marked from 0 to 28000 in increments of 2000, and x-axis (YEAR) with values: 1840 1860 1870 1880 1890 1900 1910 1948 1960 1970 1980 1990 2000

DATES & SERIAL NUMBERS

1840	- 900	**1960**	- 22100
1860	- 1624	**1970**	- 46200
1870	- 2500	**1980**	- 73600
1880	- 3300	**1990**	- 97400
1890	- 4100	**2000**	- 108304
1900	- 5000		
1910	- 6002		
1948	- 11150		

Model: 112 Carus

Casework:	ash, satin black
Compass:	AAA-c5, 88 notes
Action:	Renner to Sauter R2 specifications
Modifiers:	2 pedals: half-blow and sustaining
Dimensions:	H: 44 in (122cm); W: 57¼ in (145cm); 23¼ in (59cm); W: 397 lbs (180kg)

bringing them back to the factory to be tested and adopted. Johann's research undoubtedly encouraged his successor, Carl Sauter II, to modernize the manufacturing processes in the family firm, and his successor, Hans Sauter, worked to sell the instruments worldwide with a highly effective sales and marketing policy.

The company's reputation was firmly established by the time Carl Sauter III took charge in the 1960s. But he was dissatisfied with the notable differences in repetition speeds between the upright and grand actions, and he led the development of an improved action, known as the R2,

for the upright range. A new factory was opened in 1984, in which machines were installed to speed production, but the company insists that many parts are still made by hand in the traditional way.

Carl Sauter's son, Ulrich, is now a prominent member of the firm, ensuring that the family tradition lives on into a new century, and 2001 has already seen the unveiling of a new Sauter concert grand after years of development.

maker's marks

• Sauter developed the "2 Double Escapement Action" for upright pianos to even out the differences in touch between an upright piano action and that of a grand. The action includes an extra jack spring to aid repetition.

• A grand piano was made by Sauter for the Paris Conservatory to help a pianist perform music written for a prepared piano. It was decorated with inlaid lines on the dampers and colored lines on the soundboard to identify the keyboard layout on the strung back and also to indicate where to touch the strings to produce harmonics. This piano has now been integrated into the Sauter line.

Model: 122 Domino

Casework:	maple, satin
Compass:	AAA-c5, 88 notes
Action:	Renner to Sauter R2 specifications
Modifiers:	3 pedals: half-blow, sustaining, and celeste/moderator
Dimensions:	H: 44 in (122cm); W: 57¼ in (145cm); D: 23¾ in (60.5cm); W: 440 lbs (200kg)

Schimmel

Wilhelm Schimmel Pianofortefabrik GmbH
Postfach 4860
D-3300 Braunschweig
GERMANY

WRITTEN IN 1914, THIS ENDORSEMENT OF SCHIMMEL PIANOS WOULD STILL HOLD TRUE TODAY: "THE TONE CAPTIVATED OUR ATTENTION AND, IN ITS SONORITY AS WELL AS DELICACY AND BEAUTY OF TONE, IT IS NO WAY WHATSOEVER INFERIOR TO THE BEST UPRIGHTS OF THE SELECT FEW TOP SELLING BRANDS."

The company that became one of Western Europe's largest piano manufacturers was founded in the small Leipzig workshop of Wilhelm Schimmel on May 2, 1885.

Schimmel, an apprenticed cabinetmaker who made violins in his spare time, had learned piano building at the eminent Stichel Pianofortefabrik in Leipzig. Once working for himself, he put his skills to good use: by 1897 the company had expanded, outgrowing the factory in Leipzig-Reudnitz that it had occupied since 1891, and moving to larger premises in Leipzig-Stotteritz. Schimmel had also become the Court builder for the Grand Duchy of Saxe-Weimar and, by 1909, for the King of Romania.

In 1914 the firm made its ten-thousandth piano, but further progress was hampered first by the First World War and subsequently by the economic difficulties that plagued Germany through the 1920s. In 1927, management passed to Wilhelm Arno Schimmel. He relocated production to Braunschweig, where, due to the market's collapse, Schimmel joined forces with a cooperative of German piano makers, Deutsche Piano Werke AG. This was not a success, and in 1931 Schimmel left DPW and renamed the firm Wilhelm Schimmel Pianofortefabrik GmbH.

The Schimmel factory maintained production throughout the Second World War with Arno Schimmel active in realizing his many ideas, which included work on a very small upright piano. In 1944 the factory was destroyed by fire and the rebuilding took four years, but in 1948 Schimmel was once again exhibiting at trade fairs. Despite the difficult times for the German piano industry, the company made its mark in the 1950s, producing pianos with startling designs, such as the Plexiglass grand piano.

Nikolaus Wilhelm Schimmel's succession to the company's leadership in 1961 saw the traditions of this fine German house pass on seamlessly to the third generation. A new factory was built in 1966 and a decision was taken to erect a new plant containing a concert hall and exhibition area; this grand project was finally completed in 1980. In that year, Schimmel made 10,000 pianos in its new facility, 1,000 of which bore the names Erard, Gaveau, or Pleyel (which they made under license between 1970 and 1993).

In addition to its emphasis on quality and traditional skills, Schimmel has continued to innovate, and in 2001 premiered a sophisticated new range of pianos to delight players and piano technicians alike.

grace notes

*Wilhelm
Schimmel*

Leipzig was the piano-manufacturing capital of nineteenth-century Germany, and it was in Leipzig-Reudnitz that Wilhelm Schimmel built his first factory. Wide acclaim soon followed for his advanced scale designs and highly developed actions. The Schimmel company is now headquartered in Braunschweig.

Braunschweig

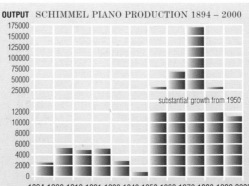

OUTPUT SCHIMMEL PIANO PRODUCTION 1894 – 2000

substantial growth from 1950

1894 1900 1910 1921 1930 1940 1950 1960 1970 1980 1990 2000
YEAR

DATES & SERIAL NUMBERS

1894 - 1000	**1960** - 50000
1900 - 3500	**1970** - 118200
1910 - 9000	**1980** - 292000
1921 - 13900	**1990** - 319400
1930 - 19350	**2000** - 330000
1940 - 22100	
1950 - 22900	

Model: CC 213 DE

Casework: bubinga high gloss
Compass: AAA-c5, 88 notes
Action: Renner to Schimmel specifications
Modifiers: 3 pedals: una-corda, sustaining, and sostenuto
Dimensions: L: 7 ft (213cm); W: 4 ft 11¾ in (151cm); W: 822 lbs (373kg)

Model: Classic Exquisit 122KE

Casework: cherry, semi-filled satin finish
Compass: AAA-c5, 88 notes
Action: Renner to Schimmel specifications
Modifiers: 3 pedals: half-blow, sustaining, and celeste/moderator
Dimensions: H: 48 in (122cm); W: 59 in (150cm); D: 23¼ in (59cm); W: 452 lbs (205kg)

SCHIMMEL
PIANOS

Model: Traditional Noblesse 120TN

Casework: ebony, gloss
Compass: AAA-c5, 88 notes
Action: Renner to Schimmel specifications
Modifiers: 3 pedals: half-blow, sustaining, and celeste/moderator
Dimensions: H: 47¼ in (120cm); W: 59 in (150cm); D: 23¼ in (59cm); W: 452 lbs (205kg)

maker's marks

• Schimmel have always tried to reflect contemporary taste in their piano designs. In the 1930s, to suit a popular desire for small instruments, Schimmel made a grand piano only 47 inches (120cm) deep. In the 1950s, Schimmel led the way in innovative case designs, building in 1951 the first see-through grand piano, the Plexiglas.

• For the twenty-first century, Schimmel have completed groundbreaking research on the acoustic properties of the piano strung back by computer modeling. With help from a local university, Schimmel's design team has managed to produce a sophisticated new range of instruments.

Seiler

Ed. Seiler Pianofortefabrik
Schwarzacher Strasse 40
871 Kitzingen
GERMANY

CABINETMAKER AND MUSICIAN EDUARD SEILER FOUNDED HIS
EPONYMOUS PIANO COMPANY IN 1849. HIS AIM WAS TO PRODUCE
UPRIGHT AND GRAND PIANOS THAT NOT ONLY WITHSTOOD THE
DEMANDS OF THE PROFESSIONAL BUT WOULD ALSO "PROVIDE AN EASY
ACCESS TO MUSIC FOR THE CULTURALLY VERSED MIDDLE CLASSES."

From small beginnings Seiler's rise was quick: by 1870 he had built 1,000 pianos, and this figure would double over the next two years. His reputation was enhanced in 1872, when he won the gold medal in Moscow for outstanding craftsmanship in his pianos.

Following the death of his father in 1875, Johannes Seiler took over the business. Employing 120 piano builders, the company continued to build good-quality instruments that won prizes at trade fairs across the globe and in 1898 Seiler produced its 25,000th instrument. By 1923, when Johannes' son-in-law Anton Dutz took over the company, it employed 435 people and produced 3,000 pianos a year, making it the largest piano factory in the east of Germany.

After the Second World War, the factory in Liegnitz was occupied and the family fled to Denmark, where production started in Copenhagen in 1951 under the direction of Steffen Seiler. The pianos were again made in Germany in 1957, at first under license. Then in 1962 a new factory was bought in Kitzingen, Germany, where Seiler is based today. As production increased, so did the need for space, and the workshop expanded in 1977 to include a concert hall and a training workshop.

The company is still owned by members of the Seiler family, Ursula and Manuela, who are dedicated to preserving this make's individual sound. Over the last five years, Seiler have re-analyzed their range of pianos to improve the quality of sound and the manufacturing process.

maker's marks

• Seiler pianos have an unmistakable transparent sound.

• Upright pianos include a patented Super Magnet Repetition Action, which replaces the traditional spring action repetition with two magnets that can provide repetition even in the lower third of the key's movement.

• Seiler's Membrator System (a specially tapered soundboard) and Tonal Volume Stabilizer (equalized tension across the bridges) increase the resonance of the soundboard and the volume of sound.

• In the 1980s Seiler produced a grand piano known as the Showmaster SM180. This unusual instrument functions as a normal piano but can easily be modified to accept contact pickups on its traditional soundboard.

grace notes

Eduard Seiler

The foundation of outstanding quality and craftsmanship that was laid by Eduard Seiler was a firm base on which Johann Seiler and Anton Dutz could expand the company. And the inventiveness of Steffen Seiler, who patented a steady stream of ideas including the "super magnet repetition action," has been continued by Ursula, who has led the company through the most recent process of re-analyzing.

Kitzingen

OUTPUT SEILER PIANO PRODUCTION 1870 – 2000

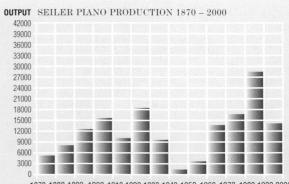

YEAR

DATES & SERIAL NUMBERS

Year	Serial	Year	Serial
1870	2000	**1952**	82700
1880	7291	**1960**	86100
1890	15335	**1973**	100005
1900	27799	**1980**	116880
1910	43419	**1990**	145200
1920	53671	**2000**	160000
1930	71725		
1940	81100		

Model: 206 Professional

Casework:	black polished
Compass:	AAA-c5, 88 notes
Action:	Renner to Seiler 175 specifications
Modifiers:	3 pedals: una-corda, sustaining, and sostenuto
Dimensions:	L: 6 ft 9 in (206cm); W: 4 ft 9½ in (146cm); W: 349 lbs (385kg)

Model: 180 Chippendale

Casework:	walnut, satin finish
Compass:	AAA-c5, 88 notes
Action:	Renner to Seiler 175 specifications
Modifiers:	3 pedals: una-corda, sustaining, and sostenuto
Dimensions:	L: 5 ft 11 in (180cm); W: 4 ft 9½ in(146cm); W: 705 lbs (320kg)

Model: 122 Vienna

Casework:	black polished, oval panel, and pilaster strips in burr wood
Compass:	AAA-c5, 88 notes
Action:	Renner to Seiler APK specifications
Modifiers:	3 pedals: half-blow, sustaining, and celeste/moderator
Dimensions:	H: 48 in (122cm); W: 58¾ in (149cm); D: 23¾ in (60cm); W: 496 lbs (225kg)

SEILER
1849
— Flügel und Pianos —

Steingræber & Söhne

Steingræber & Söhne
Friedrichstrasse 2
Postfach 110117
8580 Bayreuth
GERMANY

SMALL BUT PERFECTLY FORMED, STEINGRÆBER & SÖHNE IS POSSIBLY THE MOST UNUSUAL PIANO COMPANY IN THE WORLD. STILL RUN BY DESCENDANTS OF THE FOUNDING FAMILY, THE FIRM HAS MANAGED TO MAINTAIN A FRESH APPROACH TO PIANO DESIGN AND MANUFACTURE THROUGHOUT ITS 150 YEARS.

The firm was founded in 1852 by the 29-year-old Eduard Steingræber. There was a tradition of harpsichord making in the family, and this was given added impetus when the young Eduard met Streicher of Vienna on his travels. Steingraeber's own reputation as a quality maker grew quickly, and in 1874 he was asked by Richard Wagner to build a piano with a carillon for use in the temple scenes of Wagner's work *Parsifal*. In 1892, Eduard's sons Johann and Burkhard became partners and in 1910 Johann moved to Berlin, where he became a leading harpsichord maker.

Heinrich Hermann, Burkhard's son-in-law, became head of the firm in 1920 and his nephew Heinrich Schmidt took the reins in 1951. The Schmidt-Steingræber family still runs the company today. In 2002 Steingræber & Söhne unveiled a new concert grand, in celebration of their 150-year jubilee, with the serial number 44000.

Model: Chamber concert grand 205

Casework:	polished ebony
Compass:	AAA-c5, 88 notes
Action:	Renner to Steingræber & Söhne specifications
Modifiers:	3 pedals: una-corda, sustaining, and sostenuto
Dimensions:	L: 6 ft 8¾ in (138cm); W: 5 ft ¼ in (152cm); W: 860 lbs (390kg)

grace notes

The firm that Eduard Steingræber founded in Bayreuth quickly established itself as the best known and most revered piano manufacturer in Bavaria. Today, Steingræber & Söhne still produces hand-made pianos from this historic site.

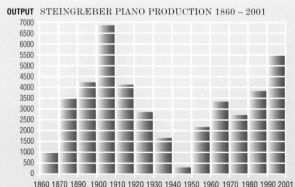

OUTPUT STEINGRÆBER PIANO PRODUCTION 1860 – 2001

YEAR

DATES & SERIAL NUMBERS

1860 - 1000	**1950** - 25800
1970 - 2000	**1960** - 28000
1890 - 5500	**1970** - 31420
1900 - 9750	**1980** - 34180
1910 - 16700	**1990** - 38000
1920 - 20800	**2001** - 43500
1930 - 23750	
1940 - 25450	

Model: Barock model 138

Casework: walnut with burred walnut panels, interrupted by relief carving

Compass: AAA-c5, 88 notes

Action: Renner to Steingræber & Söhne specifications

Modifiers: 2 pedals: half-blow, and sustaining

Dimensions: H: 54¼ in (138cm); W: 60 in (152cm); D: 26¼ in (67cm); W: 575 lbs (261kg)

Steingræber & Söhne

Perfektion seit 1852

Model: Eukalyptus

Casework: black polish with eucalyptus panels

Compass: AAA-c5, 88 notes

Action: Renner and Yamaha to Steingræber & Söhne specifications

Modifiers: 3 pedals: half-blow, sustaining, and sostenuto

Dimensions: H: 51¼ in (130cm); W: 58¼ in (148cm); D: 24¾ in (63cm); W: 498 lbs (226kg)

maker's marks

• *Steingræber & Söhne make custom-made pianos, including ecologically friendly instruments. The firm specializes in using only organic materials such as natural paints and glues in the case, and the keys are covered with cattle bone. The makers are also able to build a new instrument into existing casework, if it is no longer feasible to repair an old model.*

• *The company also makes pianos that can be used by players who do not have the use of their legs. The sustain and soft effects are operated by levers positioned on the instrument wherever the player finds it most comfortable to operate them.*

• *Steingræber & Söhne makes what is believed to be the tallest commercially available upright, Model 138, at 4½ feet (138cm).*

• *A patented repetition lever is added to the Steingræber & Söhne upright piano action to allow the jack to escape without encountering any friction, giving it a quicker repeat strike.*

Steinway & Sons

Steinway and Sons, Inc
1 Steinway Place
Long Island City
NY 11105
UNITED STATES
Owned by: Steinway Musical Properties, Inc.

STEINWAY PIANOS HAVE BEEN IMITATED FOR OVER A CENTURY, BUT THEY REMAIN UNIQUE AND INIMITABLE. MOST OF TODAY'S PIANO MAKERS WOULD BE OVERJOYED TO HEAR THEIR INSTRUMENTS DESCRIBED AS "AS GOOD AS A STEINWAY."

It is said that Heinrich Engelhard Steinweg, drafted to fight at Waterloo, made a zither on which he played patriotic songs. On leaving the army, he worked in an organ-builders' shop, where he learned the art of instrument making. In 1825 he made his first piano in his kitchen; in 1839 he exhibited two square pianos and one grand at the Brunswick Fair, and won the gold medal. To fulfill his growing orders, he took his three sons, Theodore, Charles, and Heinrich, into the business.

The revolution that tore through Germany between 1848 and 1849 saw the family split: Charles Steinweg landed in New York in 1849 and sent back word of the amazing possibilities in the New World, urging the rest of the family to follow him. Theodore stayed behind to wind down the German business, while the others left for New York. On arrival, they changed their name to Steinway, and took up employment in various piano factories.

They formed the family firm in March 1853 and their beautifully built pianos soon gained a following. Steinway then stunned the piano world by exhibiting an overstrung square piano with a full iron frame at the great fair of the American Institute of 1855. Huge success ensued, and a massive factory was built on New York's 53rd Street and Fourth Avenue.

That same year, Theodore moved from Seesen to Braunschweig, where he too was building a successful business in partnership with Georg Grotrian (*see p.78*). On the death of his brothers he sold his share in the German business, today called Grotrian-Steinweg, and moved to join his father in New York. Theodore now had at his disposal unlimited capital, experienced workmen, and the most modern factory to realize his dream of creating a grand piano that employed a string tension never before attempted. He studied metallurgy to find a proper alloy, and researched the chemistry

The tone regulating or "voicing" of a grand, from a 1948 Steinway & Sons catalog illustrated by Susanne Suba.

STEINWAY & SONS

grace notes

Heinrich Engelhard Steinway

In 1903, a Steinway grand piano, serial number 100000, was presented to the White House as a gift to the American people (it is now exhibited at the Smithsonian Institute's National Museum of American History). It was replaced in 1938 by a second Steinway, serial number 300000, made in a mahogany case and supported on three sculpted eagles. This second Steinway remains in the East Room of the White House.

Long Island City •

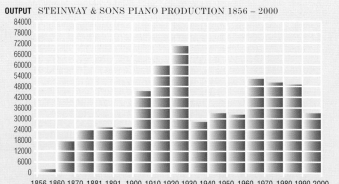

OUTPUT STEINWAY & SONS PIANO PRODUCTION 1856 – 2000

YEAR

DATES & SERIAL NUMBERS

1856 - 1000	**1940** - 300000
1860 - 3000	**1950** - 332600
1870 - 21000	**1960** - 365000
1881 - 45000	**1970** - 418000
1891 - 70000	**1980** - 468500
1900 - 95000	**1990** - 516600
1910 - 140000	**2000** - 549600
1920 - 200000	
1930 - 271000	

Model: Living Room Grand L

Casework:	mahogany, polished
Compass:	AAA-c5, 88 notes
Action:	Renner to Steinway specifications in Germany; made by Steinway in the United States
Modifiers:	3 pedals: una-corda, sustaining, and sostenuto
Dimensions:	L: 5 ft 10 in (179cm); W: 4 ft 8 in (146.5cm); W: 617 lbs (280kg)

of glues, varnishes, and other raw materials. He even returned to Germany, to meet Helmholtz and hear his ideas on the physics of music and vibrating strings.

Theodore's crowning achievement was the Centennial concert grand of 1876, with duplex scale, bent rim case, cupola iron frame to hold the strings at hitherto unimaginable tensions, and an action strengthened to lift the enlarged hammers. When he died in 1889, he left behind forty-five patents and a grand piano design that could scarcely be improved upon.

William Steinway, Henry's youngest son, was employed to market the pianos. He established Steinway Hall in New York in 1871, and in London in 1876. In 1880 a Hamburg factory was opened to make pianos for the growing European market. That same year, he bought a 400-acre site on Long Island, and by 1910—sixteen years after his death—the American Steinway factory was complete.

Steinway was badly affected by the Great Depression, and production fell a

staggering 220,000 pianos from 1927 to 1931. During the Second World War, the firm was commissioned to make aircraft parts and 3,000 small portable upright pianos for the forces (G.I. pianos). In Germany the factory was taken over by the government to make dummy aeroplanes.

The Steinway family sold the firm to C.B.S. in 1972. In 1985 it was sold to Steinway Musical Properties, Inc., who brought in engineers from non-piano-making backgrounds to find the right balance between modern engineering and traditional handcrafted methods, in an effort to streamline the manufacturing process. This has not resulted in any evident modifications to the design of the pianos.

maker's marks

• *Theodore Steinway engineered the modern overstrung scale, developing the grand piano's rim, frame, and hammer design to create a more powerful sound.*

• *The "duplex scale" was patented in 1872, a feature that adds harmonic color to the sound of a piano by bringing out overtones. The design incorporates two extra lengths of string that are allowed to vibrate in sympathy with the speaking length's fundamental vibration. One is positioned between the front duplex bar and the capo d'astro, the other between the soundboard bridge and a duplex bar mounted on the frame.*

• *In 1936 a diaphragmatic soundboard design was patented. This was to allow the soundboard to respond throughout the scale and vibrate more freely. The diaphragmatic soundboard is made thicker in the center and tapers toward its edge, where it is fitted to the inner rim of the grand piano.*

Model: Traditional K-52

Casework:	walnut, polished
Compass:	AAA-c5, 88 notes
Action:	Renner to Steinway specifications for Hamburg models; made by Steinway for New York models
Modifiers:	3 pedals: half-blow, sustaining, and celeste/moderator
Dimensions:	H: 52 in (132cm); W: 60 in (152.5cm); D: 26.8 in (68cm); W: 672 lbs (305kg)

Stuart & Sons

Stuart & Sons
Piano Australia Pty Ltd
9 Rangers Road
Neutral Bay
Sydney, NSW 2089
AUSTRALIA

PIANO DESIGN HAS REMAINED FUNDAMENTALLY UNCHANGED FOR THE LAST HUNDRED YEARS. WITH THE BIG COMPANIES TIED TO THEIR OWN PARAMETERS, WAYNE STUART FIRMLY BELIEVES THAT IT IS UP TO THE INDIVIDUAL TECHNICIAN TO INSTIGATE THE PIANO'S FUTURE EVOLUTION.

Wayne Stuart studied his craft in Europe and Japan, setting up his own company in 1995. Since then, he has developed a new concept in piano building in Australia. His cabinet designs are made from a variety of Australian woods, producing a strikingly different appearance when compared to the traditional piano finishes; and all his instruments come fitted with four pedals: una-corda, sustain, sostenuto, and half-blow stop. But it is for his tone generation design that Stuart is considered a visionary by the trade. He believes that by employing agraffes as the coupling device on the long wooden bridge—instead of the traditional sidegraft pins—the vibrating strings' decay rate is lengthened and tuning stability improved.

All Stuart pianos are custom-made by Piano Australia Pty Ltd, who also manage the sales and service. With each handmade piano taking about a year to complete, output is small, and most of the instruments are built to order.

maker's marks

- *Stuart & Sons pianos are designed with extra notes at each end of the keyboard compass, creating a full eight octaves (F21.8268 to f5587.6517 hertz) that enhances the tone of the regular end notes of the piano keyboard, AAA and c5.*

- *Stuart & Sons currently make three models of piano: a 114-inch (290cm) concert grand, as well as a 86½-in (220cm) grand and a 51½-in (130cm) upright piano.*

Model: Stuart Grand

Casework:	veneered in Birdseye Huon Pine bordered in Lace She Oak and Ebony
Compass:	FFF-f6, 88 notes
Action:	keyboards and action frames made by Stuart & Sons
Modifiers:	4 pedals: una-corda, half-blow, sustaining, and sostenuto
Dimensions:	L: 114 in (290cm); W: 65¾ in (167cm)

grace notes

Since the arrival of the first piano in Australia in 1788—belonging to surgeon George Worgan—the instrument has been treated as a valuable possession. However, few Australian manufacturers survived the two world wars and the Great Depression, and by the 1970s a combination of cheap imports and rising labor costs closed down the remaining few. The industry has been rejuvenated by Wayne Stuart's designs, and his involvement in establishing Piano Australia Pty Ltd has given new life to piano manufacturing in his native country.

• Sydney

STUART & SONS

The British Piano Manufacturing Company Ltd
Woodchester Mills
Woodchester
Stroud
Glos. GL5 5NW
ENGLAND

Welmar

Welmar Pianos

AT THE END OF THE FIRST WORLD WAR, BLÜTHNER'S ENGLISH AGENTS, WHELPDALE AND MAXWELL, FACED A SERIOUS PROBLEM: ALTHOUGH THE BLÜTHNER FACTORY HAD SURVIVED THE WAR AND PRODUCTION HAD RESTARTED, WIDESPREAD POPULAR ANTIPATHY AGAINST ALL THINGS GERMAN CAUSED SALES TO PLUMMET. SO THEY DECIDED TO MANUFACTURE THEIR OWN PIANO.

maker's marks

• *The Welmar's outstanding characteristic is its full, rounded, and musical tone, the result of Jack Codd's apprenticeship at Blüthner in Germany.*

The London firm of Squire & Longson was offered a contract to manufacture the pianos—to be named Welmar—at their factory in Camberwell.

The London factory was destroyed by fire in 1929, and after it was rebuilt a continued decline in business caused the respected Squire & Longson company to fold, its name being bought by Kemble. The Welmar Company, still owned by Whelpdale, Maxwell & Codd, moved to a new factory in Clapham, and took with them key figures from the Squire & Longson company. They made two grand piano models: a 4 foot, 6 inch (137cm) and a 6 foot (183cm) model. With the experience of Jack Codd, who had completed his apprenticeship in the

Model: 114 Regency

Casework: pyramid mahogany
Compass: AAA-c5, 88 notes
Action: Renner to Welmar specifications
Modifiers: 3 pedals: half-blow, sustaining, and celeste/moderator
Dimensions: H: 3 ft 8 in (112cm); W: 4 ft 8 in (143cm); D: 1 ft 10 in (56cm); W: 419 lbs (190kg)

Blüthner factory in Leipzig, they concentrated on producing pianos with the Blüthner tone.

In 1939, with the outbreak of war, the British government forced piano production to be amalgamated. Production for the British firms of

Marshall & Rose, Rogers, and the illustrious Broadwood was moved to the Welmar factory in Clapham.

Production of Welmar upright pianos continued at the London factory until 2000, when the Whelpdale, Maxwell & Codd group—making pianos with the names Welmar, Knight, Bentley, Broadwood, and Marshall & Rose —merged with the Woodchester Piano Company to form the British Piano Manufacturing Company. Today all these pianos are produced in one of the most famous piano factories in England, Woodchester Mills near Stroud.

grace notes

It was in the Welmar factory in Clapham, South London, that Ingbert Blüthner, the great-grandson of the famous Leipzig firm's founder, served an apprenticeship in the 1930s. The site was the last piano factory in London until it closed in 2000, when production moved to the west of England.

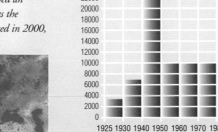

• Stroud

WELMAR

OUTPUT WELMAR PIANO PRODUCTION 1925 – 2000

DATES & SERIAL NUMBERS	
1925	- 13000
1930	- 16500
1940	- 23500
1950	- 50000
1960	- 60000
1970	- 70000
1980	- 80000
1990	- 108000
2000	- 111000

(Bar chart, vertical axis 0–28000; horizontal axis YEAR: 1925 1930 1940 1950 1960 1970 1980 1990 2000)

Yamaha Corporation

Yamaha Corporation
P. O. Box 3
Hamamatsu 430-8651
JAPAN

Names used: Yamaha and Everett

ALTHOUGH THE FIRST JAPANESE PIANO, A SQUARE OF UNKNOWN ORIGIN, WAS EXHIBITED AT THE PARIS EXPOSITION OF 1878, IT WAS ONLY FROM 1899 THAT A CONTINUOUS LINE OF PIANO PRODUCTION COULD BE TRACED IN JAPAN. WHEN SUCH A LINE DID EMERGE, IT WAS DRAWN BY TORAKUSU YAMAHA, MECHANICAL ENGINEER, AND FOUNDER OF WHAT WAS DESTINED TO BECOME THE WORLD'S LARGEST MANUFACTURER OF PIANOS.

Torakusu Yamaha was born in 1851, and at the age of seventeen studied horology under a British engineer in Nagasaki. Although he did not have the capital to set up his own watchmaking company, these mechanical skills were eventually to aid him in another direction. He found work in Hamamatsu as a mechanical engineer and in 1887 was asked by the local school to fix an American reed organ. Amazed at the workings of the instrument, he decided to build his own, and set up the Yamaha Organ Manufacturing Company in 1889. In 1897, with a capital of 30,000 yen, his firm was incorporated under the name Nippon Gakki Co. Ltd., of which Torakusu Yamaha would be president. Official consideration was being given to piano production, and Yamaha, under a commission from the Japanese Ministry of Education, received a grant to research the latest technology, visiting American firms. In 1901 Yamaha produced its first upright and within a year its first grand piano. By 1907 the company, by now in extensive factories in Hamamatsu, was making some 600 pianos a year as well as 8,000 reed organs and 13,000 violins and its capital rose to 600,000 yen. Torakusu died in 1916, by which time the company had won many awards for its pianos and was building its own piano actions.

The company survived the turbulent 1920s and 1930s, and during the war was commissioned to make aircraft parts. Piano production restarted in 1947 and from there the company grew rapidly. In 1954 Yamaha initiated the foundations of its own music school and in 1960 started exporting instruments to the United States.

In 1973 Yamaha acquired the American brand Everett Piano Co. and the Everett plant in South Haven, Michigan, where both Yamaha and Everett pianos would be made for the U.S. market. In 1986 this plant was closed and U.S. piano production was moved to Thomaston in Georgia.

In 1987, to celebrate its centennial, Nippon Gakki changed its name to the Yamaha Corporation. Today it is the largest musical instrument manufacturer in the world, producing about 130,000 pianos a year.

grace notes

❋ YAMAHA

Torakusu Yamaha

Since the debut of the Yamaha concert grand fifty years ago, Yamaha pianos have gained increasing respect from performers of all musical genres and have been regularly selected for music festivals and competitions around the world. In addition to factories in Hamamatsu, Japan, Yamaha has overseas production subsidiaries and joint ventures in China, Taiwan, Indonesia, England, and the U.S.A.

• Hamamatsu

OUTPUT YAMAHA PIANO PRODUCTION 1920 – 2000

substantial growth from 1960

1920 1930 1940 1950 1960 1970 1980 1990 2000
YEAR

DATES & SERIAL NUMBERS

1920 - 2100		**1970** - 980000	
1930 - 10163		**1980** - 3030000	
1940 - 31900		**1990** - 4820000	
1950 - 44200		**2000** - 5860000	
1960 - 122000			

Model: C7

Casework: polished ebony
Compass: AAA-c5, 88 notes
Action: Yamaha
Modifiers: 3 pedals: una-corda; sustaining, and sostenuto
Dimensions: L: 6 ft 7 in (227cm); W: 5 ft 1 in (155cm); W: 900 lbs (409kg)

Model: V118

Casework: polished white
Compass: AAA-c5, 88 notes
Action: Yamaha
Modifiers: 3 pedals: half-blow, sustaining, and celeste/moderator
Dimensions: H: 46½ in (118cm); W: 59¾ in (152cm); D: 22¾ in (58cm); W: 473 lbs (215kg)

Model: MPX1Z (digital)

Casework: open pore American walnut
Compass: AAA-c5, 88 notes.
Action: Yamaha
Modifiers: 3 pedals: half-blow, sustaining, and silent operation
Dimensions: H: 47¾ in (121cm); W: 60¼ in (153cm); D: 24 in (61cm); W: 552 lbs (251kg)

maker's marks

• *Pioneers of the Disclavier in 1986, Yamaha have since been at the cutting edge of digital/acoustic instruments. Celebrating the change in millennium and its own centenary, Yamaha built a limited-edition piano that could demonstrate the potential technology for the future, the Disclavier PRO-2000.*

• *The Yamaha grand action is built on aluminum alloy rails that are unaffected by changes in temperature or humidity.*

Young Chang

Young Chang Akki Co., Ltd
178-55, Gajwa-Dong
Seo-ku, Incheon
SOUTH KOREA

Names used: Young Chang, Wagner (no longer used). Also make pianos under the names Wurlitzer and Weber.

IN LITTLE OVER THIRTY YEARS YOUNG CHANG HAS EMERGED AS ONE OF THE WORLD'S LARGEST PIANO-PRODUCING COMPANIES. FORMED IN 1956 IN WAR-TORN SOUTH KOREA BY THE THREE KIM BROTHERS, THE COMPANY HAS BECOME A MAJOR PRODUCER OF EVERY TYPE AND MODEL OF PIANO.

Although the war that ravaged South Korea had only ended in 1953, the speed at which the economy was being rebuilt and the symbol of music as a cultural refinement laid a platform that gave new impetus to musical instrument makers.

Piano manufacturing was set in motion by three brothers who each had different gifts to offer their new firm. Jai-Young Kim was a trained accountant; Jai-Sup Kim, an engineer; and Jai-Chang Kim, an accomplished pianist and technician.

The company started a relationship with Yamaha, at first importing Yamaha pianos, but when high import duties made this unprofitable, Young Chang began importing half-finished pianos from the Japanese factory and completing them in house. In return, Yamaha helped Young Chang tool their factory, an association that ended in 1975 with Young Chang's

Model: PG-208

Casework:	ebony polish
Compass:	AAA-c5, 88 notes
Action:	Young Chang
Modifiers:	3 pedals: half-blow, sustaining, and sostenuto
Dimensions:	L: 6 ft 10 in (186cm); W: 4 ft 11 in (125cm); W: 836 lbs (379kg)

grace notes

With its rich cultural heritage of traditional Korean music, the import of and education in Western music, and the subsequent experimental fusion of the two, South Korea in 1956 offered a firm musical foundation for the Kim brothers to succeed in creating Young Chang.

• Incheon

DATES & SERIAL NUMBERS

Uprights		Grands	
1978 - 7800000		**1978** - 7800000	
1980 - 8000000		**1980** - 8000000	
1985 - 0147000*		**1985** - 016000*	
1990 - 1537386		**1990** - 0053945	
1995 - 2113092		**1995** - 0093299	
2001 - 2496752		**2001** - 0135688	

* a change in the numbering system

Model: PF-110

Casework: traditional mahogany, hand-rubbed lacquer
Compass: AAAc-5, 88 notes
Action: Young Chang
Modifiers: 3 pedals: half-blow, sustaining, and celeste/moderator
Dimensions: H: 43½ in (110cm); W: 56½ in (143.5cm); D: 24 in (61cm); W: 461 lbs (209kg)

decision to become a player on the world market. A fire destroyed the factory in 1976, but the company quickly relocated to Incheon.

In 1984 grand pianos were brought to the production line for the first time and by 1989 an article published in the *Piano Technicians' Journal* made after a visit by Yat-Lam Hong reported that the Young Chang factory in Seoul had the most

advanced production systems available. Young Chang has a workforce of over 5,000 staff and makes over 100,000 pianos a year. In the mid-1990s, Young Chang expanded, building an additional factory in China. In 2001, a collaboration with Steinway Musical Properties saw Young Chang start production of the Steinway-designed Essex range of pianos.

maker's marks

• *In under fifty years since first manufacturing pianos, Young Chang has become one of the world leaders in the piano industry. It has a workforce of over 5,000 staff and makes over 100,000 pianos a year.*

• *The Pramberga range of pianos are designed by third-generation master piano builder, Joseph Pramberga.*

YOUNG ⓒ CHANG

Model: PE-102

Casework: mahogany red polish
Compass: AAA-c5, 88 notes
Action: Young Chang
Modifiers: 3 pedals: half-blow, sustaining, and celeste/moderator
Dimensions: H: 43 in (109cm); W: 56 in (142cm); D: 20 in (51cm); W: 441 lbs (200kg)

other piano makers

A NUMBER OF HIGHLY REGARDED PIANO MANUFACTURERS DID NOT SURVIVE
THE SOCIAL AND ECONOMIC UPHEAVALS OF THE TWENTIETH CENTURY.
HOWEVER, SOME OF THE LUCKIER ONES HAVE BEEN ACQUIRED BY OTHER
COMPANIES, AND THEIR BRAND NAMES ARE STILL ALIVE TODAY.

Aeolian

The Aeolian name came from the word *aeolian* used to describe a musical instrument whose sound is activated by wind. Founded in 1883 by William B. Tremaine, the company was to dominate the player piano market for many years.

The company made its name producing the Pianola, a pneumatic player piano developed in 1897 by Edwin Votey, but it was the introduction of the Duo-Art reproducing piano that kick-started the growth of the Aeolian empire. The Duo-Art was a sophisticated mechanism that read paper rolls so accurately it could reproduce every nuance and dynamic of the recorded performer, and gained the company enough status to open a concert hall in New York—Aeolian Hall—and acquire many illustrious trade names, including Chickering, Mason and Hamlin, and Knabe. However, production of these highly regarded names was not enough to save the Aeolian company. By 1983, suffering a financial crisis brought on by the combination of a recession and a run of very poor instruments, the company was sold to the former president of Steinway, Peter Perez. Perez worked hard to market the company's chief assets—the names Chickering, Mason and Hamlin, and Knabe—and was able to turn around the company's image, but the continued production of poor instruments led to the final demise of this well-known make. They went out of production in 1985.

Bentley

Although the first Bentley pianos appeared in showrooms in 1930, the man behind this popular English make, Douglas Grover, was already a third-generation piano maker. Grover and Grover Pianos dated back to 1830 and produced as many as 500 instruments a year. In 1906 Douglas Grover took over the family tradition. In 1911 he bravely moved his business away from London, to a disused cotton mill in the Cotswold Hills, and it became known as the Stroud Piano Company. The Woodchester Mill was a perfect relocation: a five-story mill in a picturesque setting, which had stood on the site since 1605 and had been visited by King George III in 1788.

Production expanded through the 1920s, and in 1930 Douglas Grover and his son Richard launched a new upright piano, the Studio, to be sold under the new Bentley name. This piano proved an immediate success and four years later a 4-foot 6-inch (116cm) grand piano was added to the range. Production stood at 3,000 pianos a year, but disaster struck in 1938 when a fire destroyed the mill with most of the plant and machinery. Within one week Bentley had occupied a smaller factory across the road. Nine months later, with help from the rest of the piano-making industry in England, the former production level had been regained.

After the Second World War, Bentley became virtually self-sufficient, making

DATES & SERIAL NUMBERS: AEOLIAN

1903 - 1900	**1920** - 63000
1910 - 23000	**1930** - 91000

DATES & SERIAL NUMBERS: CHICKERING

1850 - 10000	**1900** - 93000	**1950** - 195000
1860 - 22000	**1910** - 115000	**1960** - 212750
1870 - 35500	**1920** - 132500	**1970** - 230300
1880 - 55500	**1930** - 148400	**1980** - 245989
1890 - 78500	**1940** - 167200	

DATES & SERIAL NUMBERS: KNABE

1850 - 4100	**1900** - 47000	**1950** - 144620
1860 - 7400	**1910** - 68000	**1960** - 162750
1870 - 13000	**1920** - 88000	**1970** - 179259
1880 - 20000	**1930** - 107300	**1980** - 194164
1890 - 33000	**1940** - 124000	

DATES & SERIAL NUMBERS: MASON & HAMLIN

1885 - 1893	**1920** - 29000	**1960** - 65200
1890 - 5700	**1930** - 39600	**1970** - 74263
1900 - 11800	**1940** - 48000	**1980** - 85853
1910 - 19100	**1950** - 57800	

actions and keyboards, soundboards, pin blocks, and bass strings, and the complete production of pianos was exported to support national interest, for which Richard Grover received the MBE in 1969. In 1962, after being trained in Germany, David Grover—great-grandson of Douglas—joined the company, and in 1963 a new design called the Compact replaced the well-loved Studio range. This too proved to be a popular model and through the 1980s Bentley consolidated itself as a European maker by diversifying its model range. In 1989 fire again struck the Bentley factory and destroyed 40 percent of the production area; again, the factory was rebuilt on its historic site. In 1993 Whelpdale Maxwell & Codd, Ltd., acquired the Bentley Piano Company, and production was moved to their factory in South London.

British Piano Manufacturing, Ltd., formed in 2000, today produce Bentley pianos to their original specification in the former Bentley factory in the Cotswold Hills.

Boston

Owned by Steinway Musical Properties, Inc. Pianos made by Kawai Musical Instrument Mfg. Co. Ltd, Hamamatsu, Japan.

The Boston Piano Company was formed in 1991 in a collaboration between Steinway & Sons and Kawai, with the aim of producing a top-quality instrument at a mid-range price. Drawing on the experience of Steinway, development of the piano took six years to complete, using sophisticated computer technology to test the designs and materials.

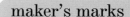

maker's marks

- *Boston grand pianos are wider, particularly in the tail, than other grand pianos of the same size. This allows for a larger soundboard area and therefore a bigger sound.*
- *Duplex scaling adds a harmonic richness to the instruments' inherent tone.*
- *The scale design is calculated at a low tension for a long sustain.*

Boston's polished mahogany grand—model GP-163—has a Kawai action, three pedals, and is 5 feet 4 inches (163cm) long.

Erard

"Sebastien Erard by his ingenious inventions elevated the piano to a plane whereby it became the favorite instrument for the expression of the tone poems of all the great composers," observed Alfred Dolge. Erard made his first square pianos in Paris, France, in 1777. Originally from Strasbourg, he moved to Paris as a young man, where he began making harpsichords of amazingly high quality. Despite the protest from Parisian harpsichord makers,

This beautiful mahogany 1903 Erard grand has two pedals—una-corda and sustaining— gate legs, and a lyre-shaped lyre.

maker's marks

- *In 1808, Erard invented both the agraffe, and his first repetition action, le mécanisme à l'étrier, which enabled a note to be repeated without letting the key return to its fully returned position. This action was improved in 1821 and forms the basis of the modern grand action.*

- *In 1838, Erard patented the harmonic bar to provide a rigid support to the treble strings; this was the inspiration for the capo d'astro bar used on many modern pianos.*

- *Erard's pianos were reputed to have a heavy touch, but their tone was powerful and clear, making it ideal for concert use. This clear tone was often unforgiving for the amateur pianist but adored by advanced musicians as it enabled them to create their own sound.*

- *The concert grand first produced in the mid-1870s had a keyboard compass of ninety notes, from GGG to c5. Its dynamic range was exceptional, and produced considerable power but still kept the clarity and range of color that had become the Erard sound.*

- *Gabriel Fauré and Maurice Ravel owned Erard pianos and Claude Debussy was well acquainted with them.*

who thought piano production would harm their own careers, Erard obtained a license from Louis XVI to produce pianos. In 1789 the French Revolution destroyed his business. Erard moved his operation to London in 1792, and did not return to Paris until 1796.

In the early 1800s he began improving the design of the grand piano, with many of his patents achieving widespread use, such as individual hammer flanges, agraffes, a repetition action, and, in 1838, the harmonic bar. Throughout the nineteenth century, Erard constantly experimented with pianos, encompassing much work on soundboard design, hammer sizes, and strike positions, and other tonal experiments that endowed his instruments with immense musical quality.

On Sebastien's death in 1831, his nephew Pierre took over the firm, and ensured that Erard pianos were used by anyone of social or musical renown. With pianos in the possession of Queen Victoria, Mendelssohn, and Liszt, to name but a few, it seemed clear to affluent and musical people in Europe that Erard pianos were the best available. In the 1870s, Erard produced arguably the most sophisticated concert grand, which was capable of

considerable power and sonority, with the clarity and range of color to which Erard users had been accustomed.

Erard's history after 1914 is one of decline. Not only did the company feel the effect of two world wars and the Great Depression, but German and American pianos also presented a new ideal in piano making. Their "fatter" sound was more forgiving to the amateur pianist than the clear sound of the Erard, and when the French market was opened to foreign

DATES & SERIAL NUMBERS: ERARD

1800 - 1640		**1910** - 97500	
1810 - 3805		**1920** - 108000	
1820 - 5200		**1930** - 120000	
1830 - 9000		**1940** - 126200	
1840 - 15000		**1950** - 128300	
1850 - 22000		**1960** - 131815	
1860 - 32000		**1970** - 133129	
1870 - 43000		**1980** - 135600	
1880 - 53000		**1988** - 136260	
1890 - 63000			
1900 - 80000			

competition, Erard failed. Erard pianos were produced under various different names throughout the twentieth century, such as Erard et Cie, Guichard et Cie, and Erard et Blondel, and in 1960 the company merged with Gaveau. Another great French maker, Pleyel, joined this consortium in 1961. In 1971 the Schimmel Company acquired the rights to the Erard name, together with Gaveau and Pleyel.

Everett Piano Company

Pianos made by Dongbei Piano Company, China, Artfiled Piano Ltd., China, and Macao Piano Company, China.

In the latter half of the nineteenth century Boston was renowned for being a piano-making center of the highest order. It was here in 1883 that a musical instrument retailer, John Church Company, started producing small quantities of upright and grand pianos under the name of Everett.

maker's marks

• *Starting work for Everett Piano Company in 1899, John Anderson designed and made what some consider the most beautiful concert grand ever made. With only two cross bars interrupting the strike point of the hammers, an even scale design, and beautiful flowing lines of the case and iron frame, the piano offers an ideal sought by many advanced piano designers and makers.*

Initially making commercial pianos, the company changed policy when Frank L. Lee became president and they began to earn a reputation for pianos of the very best quality.

Although it took many years for the Everett Piano Company to become recognized as a quality piano maker, by the dawn of the new century—with the assistance of Swedish designer John Anderson—Everett pianos were the choice of many leading virtuosos of the time. The firm believed wholly in the quality of their product and remained a relatively small company, which would in time hinder their place in the increasingly competitive market.

In 1926 the Cable Nelson Company acquired the Everett Piano Company, but despite a flirtation with making player pianos, the problems engulfing the late 1920s through the 1930s led to a further decline in production and sales. After the Second World War the company saw a growth in sales. The Everett studio upright became a popular choice, particularly within schools, and in 1956 to meet growing demands a new factory was built in South Haven.

The Hammond Organ Company, who wanted to start trading in the piano market, bought the company in 1962, but when there was found to be little profit in the piano trade, Everett was sold on to a group of investors called the United Industrial Syndicate. In 1973 Everett was sold to the Yamaha Corporation. They modernized the South Haven plant to produce both Everett and Yamaha upright pianos. Production at the Everett factory ceased in 1986, when Yamaha moved its U.S. piano plant to Georgia. The Everett name was licensed to the Baldwin factory until 1989. Since 1995, Wrightwood Enterprises, Inc., has used the Everett name, and Dongbei Piano Company in China now makes their pianos.

Falcone Piano Company

Owned by PianoDisc.

The company was set up in 1984 by an Italian-born piano technician, Santi Falcone, whose aim was to produce an affordable grand piano of the highest quality that would compete with the world's finest makes. His experimentation began in 1978, when he sold his successful chain of retail stores to initiate a piano-making project. Attracting investors and technicians from Boston, he made his first piano, a 6-foot (183-cm) grand, by 1982; this was superseded the next year with the completion of a 9-foot (274-cm) concert grand. In 1984, the company employed eleven technicians and produced just two pianos a month; this gradually increased to five pianos a month with forty technicians in 1987. The growth in production came with the acquisition of an old shoe factory in Massachusetts, where the top floor was converted to a concert hall. In 1989 the Falcone Piano Company acquired Sohmer & Company which already owned the prestigious Mason and Hamlin name.

Santi Falcone sold his business in 1991 to businessman Bernard Greer and the Falcone name was incorporated into the Mason and Hamlin Companies. Production was terminated in 1994, when Mason and Hamlin went into liquidation. The owners of PianoDisc now own the Falcone brand as part of Mason and Hamlin, which they bought in 1996. As yet there are no plans to restart production of this enterprising brand.

maker's marks

• *The sound quality of Falcone pianos is judged by many well-known jazz and classically trained pianists to be rich and even over its entire compass at every dynamic.*

• *Falcone specialized in making three lengths of grand piano: 9 foot, 7 foot 4 inches, and 6 foot 1 inch. The firm believed that any piano smaller than this would compromise the sound quality of its handmade instruments.*

• *Falcone patented a soundboard calibrator, a soundboard-tuning device that alters the tone color of the soundboard.*

Gaveau

Pianos now made by Pleyel.

Founded in Paris in 1847 by Joseph Gabriel Gaveau, this French firm was to gain an excellent reputation for high-quality harpsichords, and in particular small upright pianos.

By 1907, when Gaveau was passed to the founder's son, Etienne, the firm was producing and selling over 1,000 pianos a year. Etienne Gaveau expanded the factory and had a 1,100-seat concert hall, Salle Gaveau, built in Rue la Boetie in Paris.

Between the 1910s and 1940s, the severe economic climate meant that Gaveau, now joined by his sons Marcel and André, had to diversify to compete with their main competitor, Pleyel. Production started of small unfretted clavichords and spinets, made possible by the short-term hiring of Arnold Dolmetsch, who designed these instruments for Gaveau between 1911 and 1914. On Dolmetsch's return to England, Gaveau returned to producing upright pianos only.

DATES & SERIAL NUMBERS: GAVEAU	
1855 - 1450	**1930** - 88400
1860 - 2000	**1940** - 95100
1870 - 7000	**1950** - 102000
1880 - 10000	**1960** - 110380
1890 - 21000	**1970** - 115622
1900 - 33800	**1980** - 121600
1910 - 51500	**1988** - 122500
1920 - 66100	

maker's marks

• *In 1924 Gaveau made a piano designed by Emile-Jacques Ruhlmann, an important French furniture designer, for inclusion in his pavilion at the Exposition Internationale des Arts Décoratifs et Industriels Modernes in Paris 1925. It is believed that six instruments were made to this design.*

• *In the 1930s Gaveau made a mini-piano with a dropped action called le menuet.*

In 1960 Gaveau joined forces with Erard and a year later with their great rival Pleyel. But the financial instability continued, and in 1971 this conglomerate was taken over by the Schimmel Company in Germany. The contract with Schimmel ended in 1994, and production of this well-loved French make returned to France. Since 1996 Gaveau has been produced at the Pleyel factory in the south of France.

Irmler

Leading virtuosos and composers such as Mendelssohn played their concerts on Irmler grand pianos and the company's distinguished awards and appointments to royal courts across Europe led them to be ranked among Germany's best makers.

Johann Christian Gottlieb Irmler studied piano-making with the masters of Vienna. On his return to Germany in 1818, he set up his own firm making very good grand, square, and upright pianos in Leipzig, then the cultural capital of Europe. Starting from a small shop, by the time of his death in 1857 his pianos were

A 49-inch (123-cm)-high upright piano by Irmler (model Europe M12) with a sleek ebony polish and burl walnut oval inlay.

sold around the world. His sons Otto and Oswald were been trained in the art of piano-making and assumed control of the Irmler factory upon his death.

Irmler had achieved a good profitable export business, particularly to North America, and they also had a steady home market. However, as other German makers were invading their home territories, Irmler quickly had to develop more aggressive tactics in selling their pianos and keep apace with the most advanced ideas of the time. In 1861 they introduced steam-driven works in their factory. Later that same year Otto died, leaving the running of the factory to his younger brother, Oswald. The success that followed marked Irmler as one of Germany's finest makers

of pianos and by the turn of the century they had been honored by the courts of the emperor of Austria and the kings of Württemberg, Sweden, and Romania.

Oswald died in 1905, leaving the firm in the very capable hands of his sons, Emil and Otto. Irmler carried on producing pianos independently until the 1950s. Today they are made in Asian and European factories under the name Irmler Europe and imported into the United States by German Piano Imports.

DATES & SERIAL NUMBERS: IRMLER	
1850 - 5100	**1920** - 23000
1860 - 5500	**1930** - 26000
1870 - 6500	**1940** - 28000
1880 - 7500	**1950** - 30900
1890 - 8500	**1953** - 41000
1900 - 13250	
1910 - 19000	

Kimball

No longer produces pianos.
Names used: Kimball, Conn, Jasper-American, W. W. Kimball, Hinze, Harrison, Schuerman, DeVoe & Sons, Whittaker, Becker, La Petite, Krakauer, Whitney, Whitmore.

Evolving from a small retail dealer to one of the world's largest piano manufacturers, Kimball is the result of the shrewdness and hard work of its founder, William Wallace Kimball. With no musical background but a great insight into the market changes of the 1850s, William Wallace Kimball traded a piece of land in Iowa for four square pianos made by Grovesteen and Truslow, and set up a retail outlet in Chicago in 1857.

In 1864 he took up sales rooms in the prestigious Crosby Opera House, where he sold low-priced reed organs and pianos produced by East Coast makers such as Chickering and Hale. Kimball worked with such energy that he soon became the largest piano dealer in the west and the business continued to prosper until the Chicago fire of 1871, in which the company suffered the loss of all its stock and showrooms. The esteem that Kimball had achieved led to Joseph Hale himself telegraphing on the day of the fire, announcing "You can draw on me at once

DATES & SERIAL NUMBERS: KIMBALL		
1870 - 14000	**1920** - 322000	**1970** - 764200
1880 - 28000	**1930** - 383000	**1980** - B65951
1890 - 8500	**1940** - 438000	**1990** - R00001
1900 - 71000	**1950** - 517000	**1995** - R20401
1910 - 211000	**1960** - 604000	

for $100,000." Kimball was forced to set up business in his home and by 1880 had grossed in excess of one million dollars.

By the 1880s Kimball had started the production of reed organs and after the opening of a 96,000-square-foot factory in 1882, production soon achieved a staggering 15,000 instruments a year. In 1887 an extension was built onto the existing organ factory, in which production of pianos was to start in 1888. In the first year, five hundred less-than-satisfactory pianos were produced, but after the employment of ex-Steinway and Bechstein technicians, the instruments immediately rose in quality. They were sold aggressively, not only by the many showrooms but also by forty on-the-road salesmen, employed by Kimball to seek business in the remotest corners of North America.

William Wallace Kimball died in 1904, leaving his company to a succession of family members. The company was to peak in 1910, producing pianos for the medium-priced market, but by 1959 the company was on the point of insolvency, caused at first by the Great Depression of the 1930s and then by a series of over-optimistic decisions made by the then president W. W. Kimball, Jr.

In 1959 the Jasper Corporation, a manufacturer of office furniture, bought the company and later changed its name to Kimball International. Its staff had no previous experience of producing pianos, and this showed, with over half of all the pianos produced being returned to the factory. Production techniques did improve and were further aided by the acquisition of the great Austrian piano makers Bösendorfer in 1966 and the American firm Krakauer in 1980.

Until 1996 Kimball International continued to produce large quantities of low-priced instruments. In 1995 Kimball stopped making grand pianos and production of uprights stopped the following year. Bösendorfer still operates autonomously.

Knabe

Pianos now made by Young Chang.

Founded in Baltimore in 1839, Knabe was to become one of the most distinguished American piano makers. The tone quality of their pianos—which were initially advertised under the slogan "Pianos of quality for genteel people of means"—was greatly admired by leading virtuosos like d'Albert and Saint-Saëns, and wherever they were exhibited, they were invariably awarded prizes for high workmanship and superior construction.

Originally an apprentice cabinet- and piano-maker from Prussia, Valentine Knabe emigrated to America in 1833, where he found work with the piano maker Henry Hartye. In 1839, after learning the new language and business techniques, he set up a partnership with Henry Gæhle, producing pianos under the name of Knabe and Gæhle. In 1854 Knabe bought out his partner and started to manufacture pianos with his sons, William and Ernest. By the time of Valentine's death in 1864, Knabe and Company had established itself as a maker of fine pianos, and the company continued to flourish under the control of his sons.

By 1870 some 500 pianos were produced each year; with the redevelopment of the firm's factory, this production leaped to 2,000 by 1890. During the last quarter of the nineteenth century Knabe pianos were greatly admired and new showrooms were set up in New York and Washington. The Japanese government selected Knabe pianos to be used in all their schools and among many artists enlisted to play their pianos was Rubinstein. For the opening of the Carnegie Hall in 1891, Knabe sponsored the appearance of Tchaikovsky as guest conductor.

maker's marks

• *Albert Einstein, a devoted music lover, owned a Knabe piano, as did Francis Scott Key (composer of "The Star-Spangled Banner").*

• *A Knabe piano was the official choice of the Metropolitan Opera House in New York for over forty years.*

After the sudden deaths of the Knabe brothers in 1889 and 1894, Valentine's grandsons ran the company until 1908, when the company was absorbed into the American Piano Company. After one year William Jr. and Ernest Jr. left the conglomerate to found the short-lived Knabe Brothers Company in Ohio. This company produced pianos until 1914, retaining the tone characteristic associated with the family name. Despite the takeover and the formation of the Knabe Brothers Company, Knabe continued to sell their pianos and by 1916 production had reached 3,000 pianos a year. The American Piano Company became part of the Aeolian Corporation in 1932, and continued to produce upright and grand pianos until Aeolian's collapse in 1985, when the Knabe name, equipment, patterns, and unfinished pianos were all sold to Sohmer & Co. Today the Young Chang company produces pianos bearing the Wm. Knabe name in its Korean factory and KB Knabe in its Chinese plant.

Schiedmayer & Söhne

Name now used by Kawai.

A reputable clavichord maker, Balthasar Schiedmayer is reported to have made his first grand piano in 1735 at Erlangen in Germany. Little is known of his further accomplishments but they must have been considerable, since his son

Johann carried on his father's tradition after his death in 1781 and became piano-maker to the elector of Brandenburg. Johann moved to Nuremberg, where he achieved considerable success, and his son Johann, after settling in Stuttgart, laid the foundations for one of Germany's most distinguished firms.

A progressive firm, Schiedmayer built upright pianos as early as 1842 and, under the adapted name to include Johann's eldest sons Adolf and Herman, Schiedmayer & Söhne won the gold medal at the World's Fair in London in 1851. His youngest sons, Julius and Paul, devoted themselves to making harmoniums of excellent quality under the name J. & P. Schiedmayer. In 1860, with a diminishing market in harmoniums, they were forced to make pianos under the name Schiedmayer Pianofortefabrik.

To the end of the century both Schiedmayer firms would continue to build on their success of their forefathers, independently achieving recognition for their fine instruments.

In 1969 the two branches merged and produced small upright and grand pianos.

Today Kawai make a range of pianos with the Schiedmayer name.

Boasting an ebony polished case, an intricate fretted music desk, and una-corda and sustaining pedals, Schiedmayer's "Stuttgart" grand piano was available at the beginning of the twentieth century.

DATES & SERIAL NUMBERS: SCHIEDMAYER & SÖHNE

1880 - 11000	**1920** - 35321	**1961** - 54135
1890 - 15150	**1930** - 45037	**1970** - 124870
1900 - 20005	**1940** - 49600	**1980** - 126640
1910 - 28611	**1950** - 53100	

DATES & SERIAL NUMBERS: J. & P. SCHIEDMAYER

1880 - 14300	**1920** - 351800	**1960** - 67005
1890 - 22400	**1930** - 60200	**1969** - 69623
1900 - 231000	**1940** - 64000	
1910 - 43000	**1950** - 64200	

MAINTENANCE

An invaluable guide
to selecting a new or
second-hand piano, with
detailed step-by-step
photographs showing how
a piano's condition can be
maintained, and—in extreme
cases—reconditioned,
restored, and rebuilt.

Choosing a piano

FOR MANY, PIANO SHOPS HAVE AN AIR OF MAGIC ABOUT THEM: ROW UPON ROW OF BEAUTIFULLY FINISHED PIANOS, KEYBOARDS SHINING, INVITING THE PASSERBY TO STOP AND SAMPLE THEIR UNIQUE SOUND. BUT WITH SO MANY MAKES, MODELS, AND STYLES TO CHOOSE FROM, SELECTING A PIANO—WHETHER YOUR FIRST OR A REPLACEMENT FOR A BELOVED OLD FRIEND—CAN BE AN INTIMIDATING EXPERIENCE. PERHAPS MORE SO THAN MANY A MAJOR PURCHASE, BUYING A PIANO IS A SIGNIFICANT UNDERTAKING, REQUIRING CAREFUL RESEARCH AND CONSIDERATION.

Few things are more frustrating for the pianist—from beginner through to seasoned professional— than an instrument that does not accurately reflect the intentions of their fingers. Much of the incentive for learning to play lies in the piano's inherent tone and response, and in the modern age, when so many other activities compete for precious leisure time, a poor-quality piano offers the would-be musician scant motivation to devote hours of practice to the art. It is always advisable to buy, if not the best-quality instrument affordable, then at least one that is a little better in quality than the demands that are likely to be made of it.

A cheap, second-hand piano, though visually beautiful, may in reality be discouragingly bad in musical terms and thus not the bargain it first appears. Its tone may be false and dead, and its touch can often be quite uneven and difficult to control. Such problems not only put the value of any piano lessons in jeopardy, but also result in high maintenance costs, as unsatisfactory notes require repairing and regulating, and the old unstable structures need more frequent tuning. If the cost of a good-quality new or second-hand instrument simply cannot be met, then many dealers offer rental programs, that—for a monthly fee—will supply good-quality instruments for hire. This type of plan often permit the discounted purchase of the instrument at intervals throughout the rental.

Rococo painter Jean-Honoré Fragonard's The Music Lesson *depicts an eighteenth-century lady hard at work at the piano.*

selecting a new piano

Aesthetically a piano has only to fit the purchaser's own taste, but in most cases a piano with a conservative finish and styling will hold its value far better and be more sought after in resale than an unconventional or flamboyant-looking instrument. Although the cabinet has no effect on the touch or tone, it can reveal the care with which the piano has been made. Inspect the quality of the finish, particularly on nonexposed areas, to assess the detail and level of the craftsmanship. The piano should be made to last, so check that all the panels are veneered on both sides, an essential element of construction to ensure the stability of the casework parts.

upright or grand

Although in most cases the available space and the price differential will probably render the choice between an upright and a grand piano self-evident, both styles offer very different qualities to suit the individual pianist's need. The grand piano has a superior action and its horizontal plane suits accompanying and performance work, but the upright piano can hold other advantages for many buyers.

size, fit, and aesthetics

Grand and upright pianos come in all shapes and sizes, but in general, the larger the piano is, the fuller its tone and the broader its dynamic spectrum. More often than not the choice between the height of an upright and the length of a grand depends on the room within which the instrument is to be situated. When working out the available space, take into account the comfort of the practicing pianist and the positioning of the piano within the room for its future care, as drafts and heat sources can seriously damage the piano structure. A piano also needs space around it to sing, so try not to cramp too large a piano in

Many buyers choose an upright piano for its space-saving qualities (above), yet the longer string length and superior action of a grand justify the extra investment (below).

advantages

UPRIGHT PIANOS

• *Upright pianos are generally lower in price.*

• *An upright piano will take up far less floor area than a grand. An average upright piano occupies a floor area of just 5 feet by 2 feet (150cm by 60cm), compared to the area taken by a medium-sized grand, 5 feet by 6 feet (150cm by 180cm).*

• *A celeste or mute effect is featured on most upright pianos, usually employed via the middle pedal.*

• *Taller models of upright pianos, over 4 feet (120cm), have longer bass strings and a larger soundboard area than most grands smaller than 5 feet 3 inches (160cm). They should produce a richer, sustained bass tone.*

GRAND PIANOS

• *The grand action design allows a note to be repeated when the key has only returned halfway, generating a much faster repetition. Together with a longer key length the action is much more responsive, allowing greater dynamic control. Many companies individually weight their grand keyboards to offset the mass of the hammer heads.*

• *Grand pianos over 5 feet 3 inches (160cm) employ longer string lengths and a larger soundboard area, so have a greater dynamic range than most uprights.*

• *Apart from being to many people an attractive piece of furniture, the horizontal plane of a grand piano does not obscure the pianist's vision, particularly important when accompanying, and the fully opening top enables different levels of sound. The grand piano's music desk is also in a far better position.*

• *The una-corda effect is standard on all grand pianos, which creates a unique change in tone. The middle pedal almost always operates a sostenuto pedal, a selective damping effect.*

too tight a space—a concert grand that sounds great in a showroom may sound less impressive in an average dining room.

Although the height of the keyboard and other important dimensions are now standard, it is important to ensure that the adult pianist and the piano fit. Using an adjustable stool, set its height so that the pianist's forearms in the playing position are roughly parallel to the floor. The pianist's legs should be comfortably positioned under the keyboard and the feet should be able to depress the pedals with the heel remaining on the floor and with the ankle flexing in a comfortable arc throughout the session. If the legs feel trapped under the keyboard or the feet have to leave the floor in order to press the pedals, then the piano does not fit.

The choice of keyboard compass between eighty-five and eighty-eight notes is of little consequence to most intermediate pianists, but beware of pianos that only incorporate a six-octave (72-note) compass, as these can be extremely limiting.

acoustic or electric

With far-reaching improvements to digital technology, most electric pianos now include sampled sounds of the best acoustic pianos and feature a mechanical action of some description. But the sound created by a real vibrating string and wooden soundboard achieves a character of tone that is individual to that instrument and this effect simply cannot be replicated with absolute authenticity by digital means. Although some electric pianos offer an excellent compromise between sound and portability, many pianists and technicians still consider them to be a different musical instrument.

All acoustic pianos can now be fitted with various forms of digital technology, combining the advantages of both types of instrument. Most include accompaniment sounds, teaching aids, and a silent operation, so that headphones can be used.

touch and tone

While the hallmarks of a good piano include a responsive and even touch that can be controlled across the dynamic range, and a tonally balanced sound throughout the instrument's compass, the ideal touch and sound are very much a matter of individual preference.

An electric or digital piano may be preferable to an acoustic piano for recording or accompaniment purposes—and because it is more portable— although few possess the same qualities or draw as an acoustic piano.

An acceptable tone can range from the mellow, thick haze of one piano to the bright, metallic ring of another; there is no right or wrong sound. To be able to judge a piano's true tone, the instrument must be accurately tuned, since poor tuning not only confuses the ear but can also mask many defects in a piano's construction, including false strings and misaligned hammers. Most technicians will advise pianists to follow their instinct and choose a piano that feels and sounds right for them, as this first impression will undoubtedly encourage future practice and musical ideas. When trying out a piano, play quietly and slowly, and listen to how the tone develops under long, sustained passages. Most new pianos sound fine when played at loud volumes, particularly when the pianist is used to an older instrument that needs replacing. Although it is always wise to check if a particular instrument's tone distorts at a given volume, it is when the playing is at its most tender that the true tone, sustain, and balance of an instrument can be most accurately judged. If any part of a piano's tone sounds unbalanced from end to end, uneven from note to note, or just uncomfortable to the ear, then the instrument should be rejected.

Be aware that a room's acoustics vary greatly depending on its size, construction, décor, and floor covering, and this will have a considerable effect on any piano's volume and tone. So expect a piano to sound brighter in a room that has exposed hard surfaces and to sound softer in a room containing many soft furnishings.

The touch should be comfortable to play and responsive, without it feeling too loose or too stiff. A piano's keyboard is weighted progressively more lightly from bass to treble but the graduations from key to key should be imperceptible. A keyboard should offer some resistance to the fingers, since if the touch is too light the action will be very difficult to control, but if the action feels sluggish or imprecise then it is not doing its job and another piano should be chosen. Even a relatively inexperienced pianist can tell if the touch of a particular piano offers an uncomfortable resistance to the fingers, although sometimes this is psychologically due to the overwhelming and sometimes surprising volume of a new instrument.

The pedals of a new piano should always be tested. Check that

In the 1930s, Harrods' piano showroom occupied the entire floor of the famous London store. Today, at any one time, there are up to fifty pianos on display.

the sustain pedal allows subtle pedaling and accurate damping of large chords. Most pedal complaints can be relatively easily regulated by a technician and even a small adjustment can make a huge difference to the quality of pedaling. Finally, be sure that the middle pedal offers the type of effect that you want.

durability

High price does not always indicate high quality, and even the cheapest piano can look amazingly good. Factors dictating a piano's durability include the quality of materials used and the details of its construction, but even so, a piano's true life expectancy is greatly influenced by how it is maintained by its owner. The best approach is to ask the dealer and technician for advice on the quality of any particular instrument. With help from manufacturers' specifications, and their in-depth technical knowledge, they are in the best position to judge how well a piano has been put together.

All pianos come with warranties from the manufacturer, and some stores extend these further. Allow the firm to arrange transport details and discuss the instrument's first tuning, as this is often included in the purchase price.

special considerations in selecting a second-hand piano

Although many pianos have no antique value beyond their musical one, the pianos made by the best makers of the 1920s are still considered by some to be superior to any that can be bought today for a similar price. Certainly second-hand pianos are cheaper than comparable new instruments and although a degree of compromise for case and size is required, many fine instruments can still be obtained. Most piano dealers and workshops stock a selection of second-hand instruments that have been partially reconditioned or fully rebuilt, and the warranty supplied with these instruments can help give peace of mind. Yet with the advice of a trusted piano technician, the most economical way of buying a second-hand piano is by private treaty. Of course, the costs of the technician's assessment, of moving, and of tuning need to be considered, but generally with patience and flexibility a suitable instrument can be found at a fraction of the cost of a new piano. Although the same criteria for selecting a new piano apply in choosing a used piano, the process must begin with a full, qualified evaluation of its condition.

In all circumstances it is a better investment to pay an experienced technician to evaluate a piano before it is bought,

The length of the bass strings is crucial to the quality of their tone, and a cross-strung upright piano back can accommodate longer bass strings than a shorter case.

rather than find later that the piano cannot be serviced. Because the condition of the instrument's structure and strung back plays so critical a role in its ability to hold accurate tuning, a fault within either can prove very costly, if not altogether uneconomic, to repair, with terminal consequences for the piano's future safe musical use.

assessing the piano

A technician armed with a check sheet and a wealth of previous experience inspecting instruments of similar ages can quickly assess the piano's entire structural condition. This should include a visual inspection of the iron frame, and a test of the resistance of the wrest pins. Although it can hint at an instrument's condition, the appearance of the soundboard alone is not usually sufficient to determine whether a piano represents a good buy. The strung back of any piano can be successfully rebuilt in the workshop, but the process is an expensive one and so is most often reserved for high-quality instruments that justify the investment. Many workshops will choose not to rebuild a piano unless they can fully guarantee its returning quality.

The technician should also accurately assess the action, keyboard, and trapwork, evaluating not only the condition of

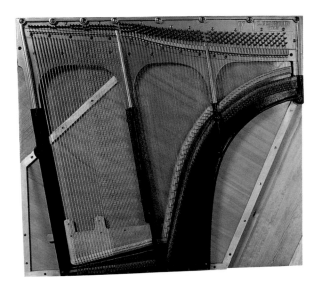

Commonly found on the second-hand market, a straight-strung upright piano needs to be a lot taller than a cross-strung piano if it is to have the same bass string length.

individual parts after maybe decades of playing, but also their preservation from damage by damp, moths, or woodworm. Not only the condition of the hammer and damper felts should be checked but also the security of the action rails and the movement of the action centers. Action problems have a critical effect on the touch and tone of an instrument, and while some can be remedied quite simply and cheaply, others may prove expensive to cure.

It is important that a piano's keyboard should be clean and free of any distinguishing marks, chips, or cracks, as these can be visually distracting, uncomfortable, and even sharp to the touch.

The condition of the case, although not a factor in musical performance, can speak volumes about a piano's previous use and treatment. Domestic accidents occur, but often result in damage very different from that caused by frequent moving and exposure to unsympathetic users. Such apparently superficial damage can lead a technician to carry out specific structural checks.

Only after a thorough assessment can a piano's true value be established, and although most used instruments require a service, for some their life can be renewed only in a piano workshop.

instruments to avoid

this type of action is recognized by the wooden damper rail fitted at the top

damper wires connecting the whippen to the over-damper head—their appearance inspired the name "birdcage action"

• *Unfortunately, however quaint an intriguing design or rare piano can be, pianos fitted with obsolete actions or unique stringing styles, or made with unusual materials, should on the whole be avoided by most pianists, since replacement parts may be difficult to obtain and hence serious maintenance problems may result. In fact, many upright pianos of the late nineteenth and early twentieth centuries, including some made by the most illustrious makers, can pose a potential risk.*

• *Old upright pianos with dampers that work above the hammer head, rather than belows, known as "birdcage" actions, should be avoided, because their inefficient design cannot be accurately serviced, leaving the damping of the strings poor. Many technicians also advise against buying "minipianos" of the mid 1930s; although their Bauhaus designs are collectible, their short keys and pulling action create an unusual touch and their tone is not complete.*

The front view of the inside of a cross-strung, over-damped piano, around 1900. The vertical wires connecting the dampers to the piano action resemble a birdcage. This type of piano should be avoided.

Front view of the inside of a modern cross-strung, under-damped upright piano. This design, quite typical since the 1920s, is worth considering as a second-hand buy, after evaluation by an expert.

the Restorer's art

MANY PEOPLE BUY THEIR FIRST PIANO ON THE SECOND-HAND MARKET, WHERE GOOD-QUALITY
USED INSTRUMENTS ARE WIDELY AVAILABLE IN VARIOUS STATES OF DISREPAIR. MANY OF THESE
INSTRUMENTS PERFORM AT A LEVEL FAR BELOW THEIR POTENTIAL, AND REQUIRE SOME DEGREE
OF REFETTLING TO BRING THEM TO PLAYABLE CONDITION. THE WORST ARE BEYOND REPAIR.

*The condition of the hammers determines
the sharpness and accuracy of the piano's tone. If
they are badly worn (above right), they may need
to be restored or rebuilt (above left).*

Unlike a violin, a piano can only deteriorate with age; with its massive string tension of up to 20 tons and thousands of moving parts, many of which are continually rubbed or hammered, it is no surprise that the action should become less responsive and the tone lose dynamic range with the passing years. Regular adjustment can correct these problems in the short term; but after extended and heavy use, strings lose their resonance and leathers and felts wear thin, resulting in wobbly keys, poor repetition, and noisy connections within the action and trapwork. Routine maintenance such as tuning, regulating, and voicing reach the limit of their effectiveness when the hammer heads are too marked to produce a sharp, clear tone, and the other action parts too worn to operate free from friction and noise. Wooden soundboards, bridges, and pin blocks or wrest planks may begin to split, causing tuning instability and a further loss of tone. Most pianos can be played for many years without the need for major repairs, but when tuning, regulating, and voicing can no longer achieve their goal, the piano must have drastic surgery.

The nature and extent of any reconditioning work may depend on factors other than the piano's condition. An instrument's monetary value is often more closely linked to its make and model number than its musical worth, so spending vast sums rebuilding a piano by a lesser-known maker may not make financial sense. But there are other ways to value a piano: in its potential to be a fine instrument with a tone color of its own, and with a beautifully weighted and controlled touch, for example. It may also have sentimental value.

The age of the piano must also be taken into account before embarking on any work. Many old-fashioned pianos were designed and built in such a way that they will never produce the touch or tone color of more recent models. Some instruments may be so old that care should be taken to preserve them for historical reasons. The future demands to be made on the piano also need to be assessed. Bearing in mind the cost, age, and user's requirements, a good technician can offer three alternative options to rejuvenate an old or worn piano: restoration, rebuilding, or reconditioning.

The strings—although partly rusted, pitted, and tarnished—appear to be original and the wrest pins are capable of holding their tension. Their removal will obviate their future use, so thought should be given to whether they should be replaced, lightly cleaned, or left alone.

restoration

One definition of restoration is "to put back into nearly the original form," and this technique is reserved for pianos of historic interest and technical curiosities. Working with such instruments requires an enormous amount of thought, care, patience, and skill. Some pianos have survived relatively whole after hundreds of years of playing, neglect, abuse, climate change, and war. That many survive today with strings, hammers, and keyboards intact is testimony to the skill and craftsmanship of their makers.

Many of the original fortepiano makers' building techniques are now forgotten and their tools lost; there seemed little need at that time to document individual processes, and many were thought to be trade secrets, so were kept closely guarded within a workshop. Certainly, when working on such instruments, it is difficult to duplicate any of the original work to the same high standards, particularly without the use of today's labor-saving machine tools.

To restore an antique piano is not to create a modern piano; the restorer's objective is to enhance the instrument while retaining as much of the original as possible. When an instrument has been chosen for restoration, much extra work has to be considered. A thoughtful restorer will use water-based animal glues where possible, for they are easily and safely reversed. If any worn or missing wooden parts need to be replaced, they should be copied

The top of the piano is broken around the hinge, and this should be fixed to stop the other hinge from breaking. This is a relatively straight-forward woodwork repair; the main concern is to match the grain and color of the timber so that the repair cannot be seen.

Although the bridges are secure and not split, a crack has appeared in the soundboard and will need further investigation.

The broken hammer heads have survived within the bottom of the instrument so they can be remounted carefully using hot animal glue.

The keyboard felts, although dirty and hard, still function and their replacement largely depends on the level of restoration to the rest of the instrument.

A square piano by Thomas Thomkinson, around 1850 (above), with its keyboard and action removed (right). Although old and not used, this instrument is still structurally sound and its parts appear to be original. Whether this piano should be restored or rebuilt depends on its historical interest and its intended future use.

using the same type of wood, if possible of a similar age. Many restorers' workshops hold stocks of aged timber salvaged from previously dismantled antique instruments and furniture.

Much has been done recently to analyze strings taken from pianos of various ages, and exact replicas are now produced. These can be ordered from specialist suppliers so that strings made of the same composite can be used. A restorer will also analyze the felt, cloth, and baize coverings, and use not only the correct color and type of material but also try to match its weight and weave. Cloths and braids that are dirty but not worn may be cleaned with delicate soaps, thereby retaining as much of the original material as possible.

Any parts that are removed should be kept and cataloged, together with a report containing photographs, measurements, and an account of all the processes used. Special techniques are used on antique instrument cases to remove years of dirt and grime, leaving the original finish exposed. Bruises and other defects that mark the case are often left as a monument to an instrument's age.

Today there is great debate about the process of restoration. Restorers struggle with the desire for reversibility, as many restoration processes simply cannot be reversed. Another area for discussion concerns the numerous repairs and modifications that a 200-year-old instrument may already have had.

It can be argued that alterations made in the nineteenth century on an older instrument should also be kept during restoration, to become part of the instrument's history and a record of the type of work completed during that time.

Not all antique pianos can be restored to a fully playing condition, so thought should also be given to the resulting capabilities of an instrument. Restorers working for museums and other collections now have a difficult choice: is it better to preserve an instrument to be seen or to restore it to be played and heard? The answer is not necessarily straightforward. There is little doubt that all instruments are made to be played; however, due to the natural aging process of the materials used to make a piano, it is unlikely that even a fully restored instrument would sound exactly the same as it did when it was new. Bearing this in mind, it seems that the most sensible option is to preserve the old instrument just as it is and at the same time build an exact replica—one that can be played and heard, and will withstand the demands of touring.

After years of being continually rubbed and struck, a piano action will require some degree of maintenance. This grand action from a Bösendorfer piano of 1910 is too worn to be much improved by reconditioning or servicing. With (1) deeply grooved hammer heads, (2) flat rollers, (3) worn back checks, and (4) loose key tops, only a complete rebuild will recreate the accuracy of touch and tone that this action once offered.

rebuilding

Rebuilding a piano is designed to restore an instrument to its original condition, or better. It involves the complete disassembly of the piano into its smallest constituent parts; these are then individually cleaned, repaired, or entirely replaced with new, so that when the piano is reassembled it can be regulated and tuned to the closest tolerances. With over 10,000 parts such comprehensive work is very expensive, and is usually only deemed appropriate for high-quality and valued instruments.

before work starts

Any rebuild starts with an assessment by a technician to evaluate the instrument's design and build quality. This ensures that the piano's potential performance when rebuilt will both meet the owner's expectations and justify the cost involved. The assessment should also make it clear immediately whether it would be more cost-effective to replace the piano rather than rebuild it. Since the cost of a rebuild may equal or exceed the purchase price of a high quality piano in showroom condition, the evaluating technician must satisfy himself that the instrument once rebuilt will compare favorably with a new piano.

The technician then evaluates the current condition of the instrument to determine whether it has deteriorated so far that it is beyond repair. Pianos damaged by fire or flood are not generally repairable as they tend to suffer severe structural damage, some of which may develop years after the initial accident. Much the same is true of pianos that have been damaged during handling. The iron frame, although strong enough to resist the tension of the strings, is brittle and will easily crack if the piano is dropped. Although a repair is possible, it is both costly and risky as the repaired frame cannot be entirely guaranteed to withstand the returning string load.

Once a full assessment of the piano's condition and potential has been made it is moved to a workshop and work can begin. Detailed measurements are taken from the strung back before the strings are removed and the frame lifted out. The soundboard, bridges, and pin block or wrest plank can then be clearly reinspected, and repaired or replaced as deemed appropriate. The increased access also allows further inspection and any necessary

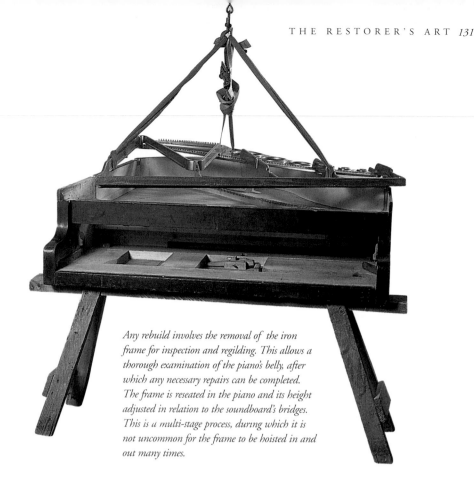

Any rebuild involves the removal of the iron frame for inspection and regilding. This allows a thorough examination of the piano's belly, after which any necessary repairs can be completed. The frame is reseated in the piano and its height adjusted in relation to the soundboard's bridges. This is a multi-stage process, during which it is not uncommon for the frame to be hoisted in and out many times.

repair of the strung back's supporting structure. The frame is regilded and then secured back in place, particular attention being paid to its height in relation to the bridges. The strings and wrest pins are replaced with new and the tension is returned as quickly as possible to the strung back in order not to distort the soundboard or its structure.

The action, keyboard, and damper mechanisms are completely disassembled and thoroughly rebuilt, with all the felt parts recovered, the springs replaced, and every center pin checked for the correct tolerance. New hammer heads are always fitted in the rebuilding of a piano, careful calculations being made to ensure that their dimensions will allow them to strike the strings accurately and produce their best tone. The trapwork is cleaned and lubricated and the case is refinished. All the hardware, such as the pedals and hinges, is polished or replated, and all the decals, felt trims, and rubber buttons are returned.

The instrument is then regulated and its keyboard reweighted to compensate for any changes in the hammer weight. Finally the piano is tuned several times to stabilize the new strings, and voiced so that it produces its most pleasing and appropriate sound.

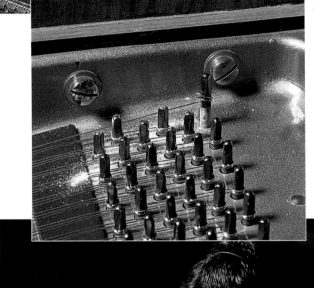

restringing a grand piano

Once the iron frame has been reseated, the piano can be restrung. Using the appropriate gauge music wire to replace the old strings, the diameter of the new wrest pins is increased, usually by just one or two gauges larger than the set that has been removed. It is important both for ease of tuning and for the protection of the wrest plank that the size of the wrest pins is consistent over the entire compass.

The sequence illustrated shows the last string being fitted on a grand piano at John Broadwood & Sons. The strings on this maker's pianos are individually tied to their own hitch pin by means of an eye.

1. Once the eye is secured on the relevant hitch pin, the gauged wire is threaded through the agraffe, cut to length, and tightly wrapped around the wrest pin to create three or sometimes four coils. Gloves are worn to protect the strings and wrest pins from contact with sweat and grease.

2. To help lubricate the tuning action a small amount of Viennese chalk is applied to the fine thread of the wrest pin.

3. The wrest pin is then positioned above the wrest pin hole.

4–6. Using a punch to protect the top of the pin and with the underside of the wrest plank fully supported by an adjustable jack, a minimum of heavy hammer blows are struck, leaving the wrest pin slightly higher than its final height.

7. Once the wire's feed around the bridge pins has been checked, the string is pulled to a low tension. To improve tuning stability the coils around the wrest pin are lifted so that they hold tightly together. The wrest pin is then tapped down to its final height, the number and closeness of the coils are inspected, and the strings are seated securely on the hitch plate and bridge. The surrounding area is then cleaned of wire debris and spilt chalk before the strings are tuned to their full tension. The speed and technique of the first tuning is essential to keep the increase in string pressure as even as possible over the soundboard. Taking approximately seven minutes, the strings' first tuning is called a "chip up."

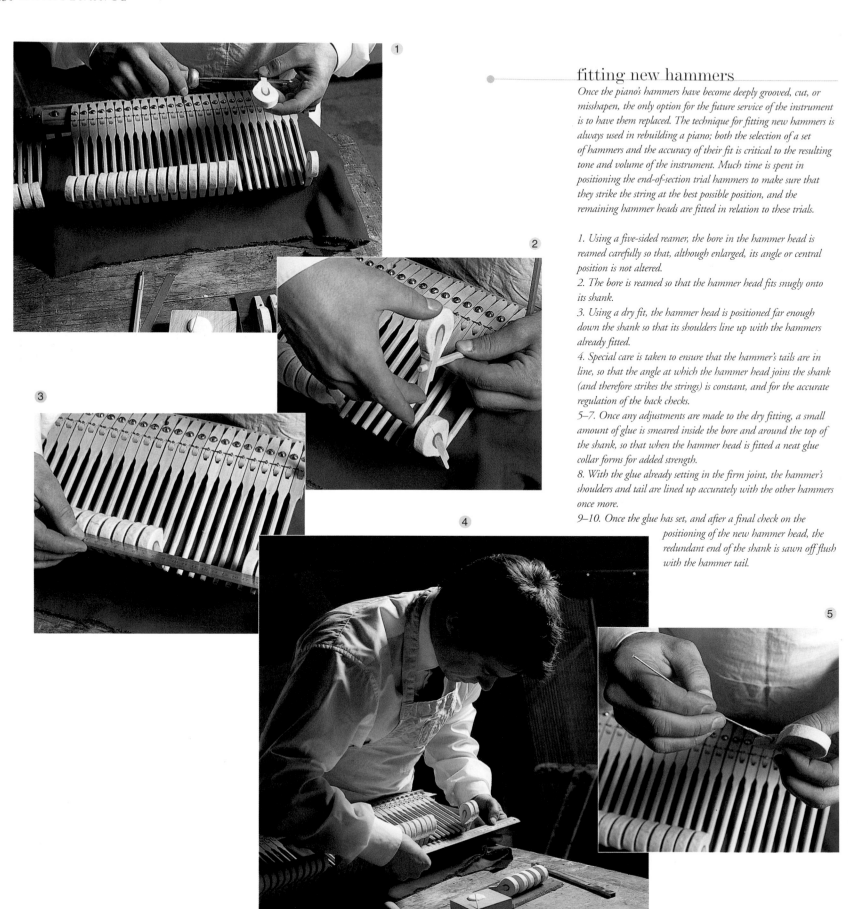

fitting new hammers

Once the piano's hammers have become deeply grooved, cut, or misshapen, the only option for the future service of the instrument is to have them replaced. The technique for fitting new hammers is always used in rebuilding a piano; both the selection of a set of hammers and the accuracy of their fit is critical to the resulting tone and volume of the instrument. Much time is spent in positioning the end-of-section trial hammers to make sure that they strike the string at the best possible position, and the remaining hammer heads are fitted in relation to these trials.

1. Using a five-sided reamer, the bore in the hammer head is reamed carefully so that, although enlarged, its angle or central position is not altered.
2. The bore is reamed so that the hammer head fits snugly onto its shank.
3. Using a dry fit, the hammer head is positioned far enough down the shank so that its shoulders line up with the hammers already fitted.
4. Special care is taken to ensure that the hammer's tails are in line, so that the angle at which the hammer head joins the shank (and therefore strikes the strings) is constant, and for the accurate regulation of the back checks.
5–7. Once any adjustments are made to the dry fitting, a small amount of glue is smeared inside the bore and around the top of the shank, so that when the hammer head is fitted a neat glue collar forms for added strength.
8. With the glue already setting in the firm joint, the hammer's shoulders and tail are lined up accurately with the other hammers once more.
9–10. Once the glue has set, and after a final check on the positioning of the new hammer head, the redundant end of the shank is sawn off flush with the hammer tail.

weighting the keyboard

To counter the possibility that the weight of a new set of hammers will be slightly different from the ones replaced, the keyboard needs to be reweighted. Adjusting the position and quantity of lead weight inside the piano's keys affects both the force with which the pianist has to press on the keys (down-weight) and the speed at which the keys return to rest (up-weight). The adjustment is only carried out once the action and keyboard have been fully regulated and does not take into account the weight of the dampers.

1. Small brass weights are used to measure both the down-weight (usually in the region of 1.76 oz or 50 grams) and the up-weight (usually 0.70 oz or 20 grams) of the individual keys. Various sizes of lead weight are loosely positioned on top of the key to adjust the readings.
2. Once the correct position of the lead weights is determined, the weights are fitted through the side of the key.

reconditioning

If for financial or technical reasons a complete rebuild is not deemed appropriate, a piano's performance may be greatly enhanced by reconditioning. This process aims to recreate a properly functioning piano at a reduced cost by dealing specifically with known problem areas within the action, keyboard, and strung back. In reconditioning, an instrument is not necessarily completely disassembled; instead, pieces may be cleaned (if necessary), repaired, and realigned, with only the essential minimum inclusion of new parts.

As with a rebuild, a complete and accurate assessment of the piano has to be carried out by a qualified technician to ensure that all of the instrument's actual or potential problems will be rectified by the work commissioned. For example, it would be pointless to improve a piano's action response if the instrument's strung back were not able to support the strings' tuning; likewise, if the damper felts were hard and the hammers cut and misshapen, fitting new bass strings would be of little advantage.

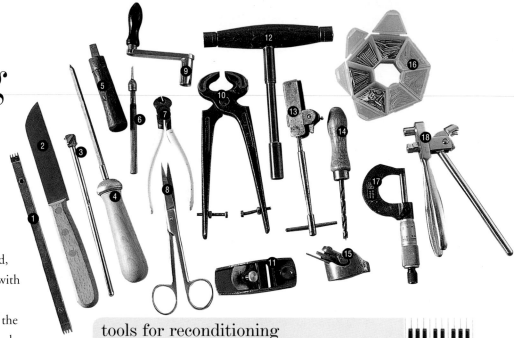

tools for reconditioning

1 string spacer	**9** stringing key	**15** small plane, curved base
2 felt knife	**10** hammer roller	**16** center pins of
3 offset screwdriver	removing pliers	various gauges
4 5-sided hammer reamer	**11** small flat plane	**17** micrometer
5 brass drift	**12** T-hammer	**18** hammer head remover
6 pin vice	**13** upright hammer shank	
7 flush top cutters	extractor	
8 sharp scissors	**14** hammer shank drill	

a delicate process

A typical reconditioning would include thorough cleaning of the whole instrument, with repairs to any damaged notes, followed by a thorough regulation, fine tuning, and voicing procedure. It might also include a certain amount of renovation within the action, as its performance might be impaired by a fault in just one area. A set of weak springs, a row of tight centers, or individual degraded felts would all affect a piano's repetition or touch weight. The hammers require special attention and, as part of a reconditioning, they are usually reshaped. As a result of their being continually struck against the strings, the hammers' noses become compressed and their form distorted, making the tone hard. A delicate process of removing the outer layers of felt on the hammer head produces a clean, fresh striking surface without changing the hammer's original shape. This does, however, alter the weight of the hammer head and this can make the touch of a piano too light, so only the minimum amount of felt should be removed. A set of hammers that are badly worn, misshapen, or cut by the strings should be replaced.

Partial restringing may be necessary to improve the evenness and fullness of tone. Bass strings lose their resonance with age and their windings become loose, creating buzzes; if the piano holds its tuning and the steel strings are in good condition, then it is appropriate to replace only the bass strings rather than carry out a complete restring. Likewise, the bass strings may sound fine and the treble section uneven, perhaps due to a number of replacement strings, in which case this section alone can be restrung.

A reconditioning will also typically include a touch-up of the piano's case, including the repair of minor chips and either dewaxing or overpolishing to revive the shine.

It is not always necessary to move the entire piano to a workshop to recondition it. Regulating, voicing, and small amounts of stringing can be efficiently completed in the home and the action and keyboard can be removed and transported alone if they require considerable repair work. A technician can decide whether it is appropriate to complete the required work on site or in a workshop.

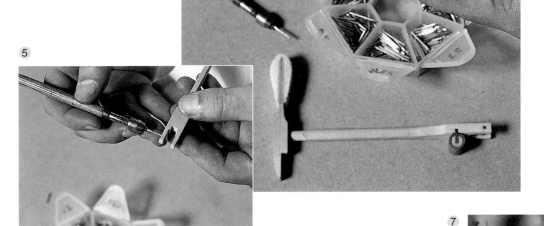

recentering an action part

The piano's moving action parts pivot on a center pin that runs through a cloth-lined bushing in the flange. General wear or extreme abuse can cause this delicate fit to become loose so that the movement of the action part cannot be accurately controlled by the key. Equally, if the action is exposed to damp conditions, the bushing may swell, making the part's movement sluggish. The technique of correcting the fit of the center pin is known as recentering.

1. The affected action part is carefully removed from the action.
2. Its center pin is semi-removed using parallel-action decentering pliers.
3. The pin is carefully pulled free and disposed of.
4. The gauge of the replacement center pin is determined so that it creates a tight fit within the wooden half of the joint, in this case the hammer flange.
5. The cloth bushings are individually reamed so that they offer the correct resistance to the chosen center pin, a subtle technique requiring patience and practice.
6. The new pin is then inserted into the carefully supported flange and part.
7. Its ends are cut flush to the sides of the flange.
8. The resistance of the part is tested before it is refitted to the action.

reshaping the hammers

Creating a fresh striking surface on lightly grooved but otherwise good hammers is a good place to start improving a piano's tone. Used in reconditioning, the technique is known as hammer reshaping and involves carefully removing the top layers of hammer felt to expose an unmarked surface beneath, leaving the profile of the hammer head unchanged, albeit slightly smaller. As the work produces a fine dust of irritating felt fibers, extraction is used and a dust mask worn.

1. A section of hammers is lifted.
2. A protective cloth is positioned over the action's underlying parts.
3. The section of hammers is returned to rest.
4. Each individual hammer is in turn lifted and supported on a wedge-shaped wooden block.
5. Using various strips of graded garnet paper the top layers of felt are filed away from the hammer's shoulders. It is important that the technician constantly re-adjusts the positioning and pressure of the fingers so that the profile of the hammer head is not altered.
6. Both shoulders of the hammer are treated by the same amount so that the hammer's profile remains symmetrical.

By working exclusively on the hammer's shoulders, the felt fibers across the nose fall away without the need for filing on this delicate area. Once reshaped, the hammers are then regulated, adjusted so that they strike their strings simultaneously, and finally voiced.

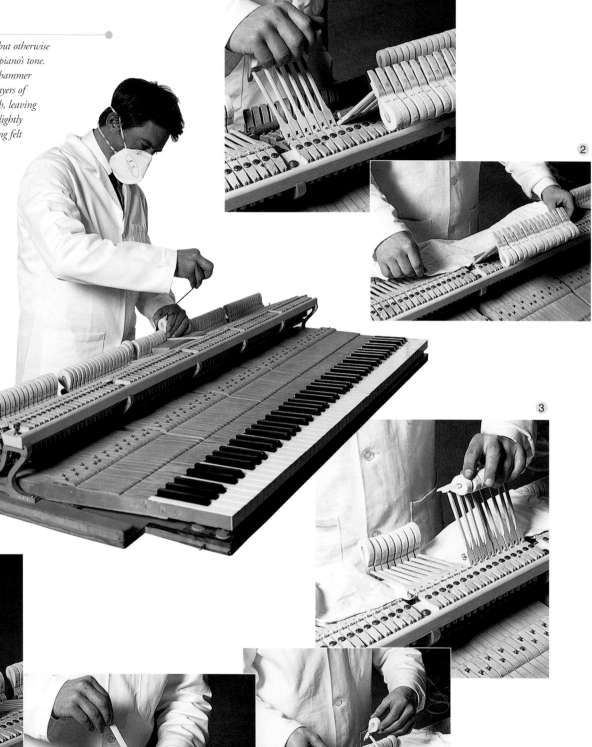

the piano workshop

A piano workshop is a truly wondrous and magical place for any lover of the piano. Emotions and imagination are stretched by the sight of so many pianos and their parts in various states of dismantling and reassembly, yet to walk around lifting the falls and finding so many different makers' names from bygone ages is both exciting and exhilarating. Unusual odors suffuse the air, of scraped spruce and hot animal glues, as well as the musty smell of hundred-year-old instruments. Most workshops are full of pianos partially or totally dismantled, their innards in different trays leaving just an empty shell that once produced—and will produce again—beautiful sounds and melodies. Grand pianos lie on their sides waiting for the time when they will be lifted onto their legs so that they can once more provide comfort and pleasure, and uprights stand boldly offering their keys to any passerby, almost daring them to play.

aladdin's cave

Your eyes will flicker constantly between the instruments themselves and the huge quantities of different materials kept in stock, available to use in any eventuality. A workshop would not be complete without drawers full of action springs, flanges, and all the other small individual parts that go into making such a complex mechanical instrument. Large sheets of various felts, cloths, and baize, all of different thickness and color, are stored protected from dust, waiting to be cut into strips and ultimately used in a mechanism capable of creating music. Meter upon meter of wire is kept—every coil different from the one next to it by just 0.025 of a millimeter in diameter—ready to be cut and then put under enormous tension to become, when struck, a vibrating string. Most workshops hold vast stores of pieces salvaged from previously discarded instruments, as unusual action parts and ivory key heads are always kept for possible future use.

A piano is both a musical instrument and a piece of furniture. It is made of wood, metal, and cloth, and houses a complex mechanical action, and so a workshop requires many types of tools. Some are simple woodworking tools that can be seen in most hardware stores, but many are specialist devices that have been

The case and fitting department of the Chappell & Company in London, around 1870.

designed and made to perform just one single function. The difference between instrument repairing and other forms of woodwork is the extreme level of tolerance that has to be achieved. The tools, then, have to be precise, and so the ones commonly used are of the type designed for pattern makers. Many technicians swear by old tools that have been acquired along the way, and not only for sentimental reasons: it is firmly believed that yesterday's tools were made using a far superior metal and finished to a much higher tolerance than those made today.

As in other spheres, machine tools are an invaluable and time-efficient aid for many processes, and the selection found in a workshop will depend on the type of work that the workshop offers. Most technicians would regard a bandsaw, a pillar drill, and a high-speed polisher as basic essential items, but to be able to offer wrest plank repairs, casework replacement, and finishing requires more specialized equipment.

Any work done on a piano will determine not only its future performance but also its value, so it is important that you choose the right technician to carry out any repairs. Any craftsman worth his salt should, for an agreed fee, carry out a full evaluation of the piano and be happy to talk openly about the instrument and its potential. Ask to see other instruments rebuilt in the workshop, and references from satisfied customers. Get a written quotation for the work to be done and the length of time it will take, together with the estimated cost and details of any guarantees included.

Caring for a piano

ALL MUSICAL INSTRUMENTS REQUIRE A HIGH STANDARD OF CARE AND A CERTAIN AMOUNT OF MAINTENANCE TO KEEP THEIR TONE SWEET AND THEIR MECHANISM IN THE FULLEST WORKING ORDER. THE PIANO, WITH ITS THOUSANDS OF INTERNAL MOVING PARTS, IS—DESPITE ITS HEAVY CONSTRUCTION—A RELATIVELY SENSITIVE INSTRUMENT.

As the piano is built largely of wood and felt it should come as no surprise that, without regular servicing and care, its touch and sound will deteriorate over time; yet many people expect a piano to perform well year after year with little or no attention. The amount of use and skilled maintenance a piano receives, and the climatic conditions in which the instrument is kept, determine not only how long a piano lasts but how well it performs. Every pianist can recognize a key that sticks or does not quickly repeat, but most will grow accustomed to an action that is not working efficiently and adapt their playing technique to compensate for it. Likewise, the piano's tone can change considerably over a period of time.

A piano tuner can readily evaluate the actual and potential condition of the instrument and its parts. Primarily required to tension the strings so that they vibrate in harmony, most tuners also regularly adjust or repair other minor developing faults before they become harmful to the action parts, keyboard, or strung back. They can also judge when a piano needs regulating and voicing, the results of which can dramatically transform the touch and tone of any piano, providing that its individual parts are structurally sound and are in good condition.

Purchasing a new piano is a considerable investment and, with the high expectations placed on the instrument's performance, it is essential for every pianist to know how to care for his or her piano.

The regular tuning of a piano is an essential part of its maintenance. During the late nineteenth century, piano tuning was considered to be a suitable way for a woman to earn a living.

humidity control

Temperature and, more acutely, humidity are critical elements in the care of any musical instrument and the more extreme their changes, the more damaging the results. Relative humidity is the amount of moisture contained in the air as a percentage of the maximum amount of moisture that the air is capable of holding. The air's moisture content varies with weather conditions and activities within the home, while the amount of moisture the air is capable of holding varies with the temperature. Wood is a hygroscopic material—that is, its cells readily absorb moisture from the surrounding air when relative humidity rises, and lose water when relative humidity falls. This brings about a dimension change across its grain as the wood expands and then contracts to accommodate the varying levels of moisture. The worst possible situation for a piano is one where it is exposed to hot, humid summers and dry, cold winters.

the soundboard

The soundboard, being the largest single area of wood and often coated with a thin finish, is particularly sensitive to climatic change. Despite being made of spruce—a wood placed in the most stable category of timbers—its dimensions still change up to ten times more across the grain than along the grain. Since the soundboard is made up of several planks glued together and fixed around its edge, this movement is restricted, and the only way it can relieve its expansion is upward, naturally increasing the soundboard's crown. When the atmosphere dries, the air retracts the moisture and the soundboard shrinks, so its crown flattens.

As the soundboard moves up and down so does the bridge, altering its resistance to the pressure of the strings. This causes a change in their tension and tuning is lost. Unfortunately, as the strings lie across the soundboard

Many problems can occur within the keyboard, action, strung back, and supporting structure of a piano if it is exposed to extreme changes in humidity. If the atmospheric conditions in which the instrument is kept are too dry, then splits may develop in the piano's soundboard (1) causing tuning instability and a deterioration in tone. Other problems occur when the piano is exposed to humid conditions. the keys and action parts may stick (2) as the wood expands, and the strings and wrest pins start to rust (3).

Humidity levels are measured with a hygrometer. Various types exist; this one gives an accurate temperature and relative humidity reading at the touch of a button.

and the pressure change is more acute in its middle, the tuning will not go sharp or flat evenly over the piano's compass. Small movements of the soundboard are natural in all makes and models of piano; the problems arise when those changes become extreme.

If the humidity is allowed to rise beyond safe levels, pressure ridges develop at the joints of the soundboard's individual planks and these will crush the delicate cells within the soft spruce. If the piano is subjected to excessive dryness, the soundboard shrinks to a point where it cracks along the grain of the timber. This is altogether more serious, since a split soundboard, as well as affecting a piano's tuning stability, causes its tone and sustain to deteriorate.

Although most evident in the soundboard, humidity changes affect all the piano's wooden parts. In older pianos, solid beech wrest planks can shrink and split causing the wrest pins to become too loose to be able to hold the string tension. Many of the problems found in an action and keyboard develop from excess humidity. If the keys swell they bind on the pins that guide their movement and become unable to return freely. Action parts too can become sluggish, due to a tightening of the center pin bushing.

If the piano encounters very damp conditions then more than just its wooden parts are at risk: the strings and tuning pins may rust and many of the numerous glue joints within the strung back, casework, and action begin to soften. Even the piano's tone is affected, because as the hammer felt absorbs moisture, it loses its hardness and so produces a softer, more mellow tone.

To avoid these problems a piano should be kept in conditions of controlled relative humidity. This should be a constant 42 percent, but never fall below 35 percent or rise above 65 percent; and temperature should ideally remain a constant 68°F (20°C).

A humidity stabilization system such as this is ideal if climatic change is less dramatic.

Hygrometers can be used to monitor the relative humidity within a room, and humidifiers and dehumidifiers used to counter atmospheric changes. In areas of lesser climatic variation the immediate vicinity around a piano can be adequately stabilized by the use of specialist devices such as the Dampp-Chaser system. These can be installed reasonably economically in both upright and grand pianos and should be fitted by a competent professional. Technicians no longer advise keeping a jar of water in the bottom of an upright piano, a rattle-inducing and possibly damaging exercise that has very little effect on the humidity within the entire piano.

humidity stabilization system

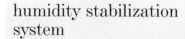

1 humidifier
2 dehumidifier
3 easy-fill watering tube
4 light panel
5 humidistat

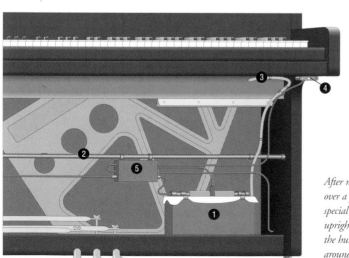

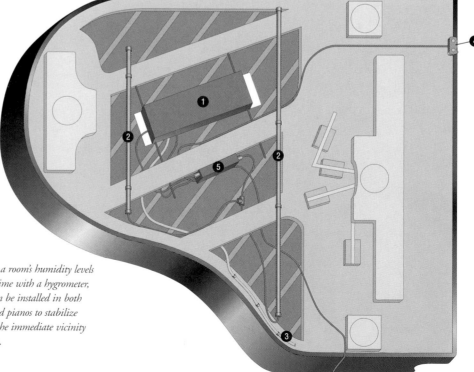

After monitoring a room's humidity levels over a period of time with a hygrometer, special systems can be installed in both upright and grand pianos to stabilize the humidity in the immediate vicinity around the piano.

where to place the piano

It is not easy to find the perfect location for your piano—somewhere pleasing both to the eye and to the ear, and at the same time out of harm's way. A separate music room is, of course, ideal but is not often attainable. Choose a room that offers a relatively constant temperature and humidity (this rules out the kitchen, hallway, and conservatory or sunroom), and that offers few distractions or restrictions for the practicing student. If possible, don't choose a room directly below a bathroom; if it should flood, the piano will be ruined. Once the room has been chosen, consideration must be given to the piano's location within it. The most suitable place is against an inside wall, away from drafty windows, doors, and exposure to direct sunlight, which will almost certainly cause the finish on the piano's case to fade. Care must also be taken to position the piano as far away from heat sources as possible. Never place a piano next to a radiator, heater, or fireplace; nor over cold or warm air ducts, or air-conditioning units.

Spare a thought for the room's acoustics; a piano suffocated by shelves and cabinets cannot sing its true tone, and having to move a piano out from underneath a shelf every time it needs tuning is not ideal for the instrument or your relationship with your tuner. Carpet and soft furnishings within a room will soften a piano's tone and the opposite is true if a room has many hard and flat surfaces. Don't expect a piano positioned in a room with carpet, curtains, or other soft furnishings to sound the same as it did in a stark showroom with exposed wooden floors.

Try to keep the top of the piano free of framed photos and other items that could vibrate when the piano is played. Nothing is more annoying than an accompanying rattle every time a particular note is played. Although to some a piano makes a lovely plant stand, resting a vase or pot on its top can spell disaster if it is overfilled or

This view of a New York public school in 1881 highlights one of the roles of a school piano, as accompaniment to the singing at morning assembly.

knocked over. Imagine the damage done by water pouring through the casework hinges, soaking everything inside, let alone the instrument's case. Care should also be taken with drinks around the piano. Hot cups will leave a white ring, called bloom, if rested on certain finishes; and most soft drinks will make a sticky mess if spilled over a keyboard or grand action. In extreme cases this can only be rectified by replacing the affected parts.

Be careful when handling small objects—paper clips, thumbtacks, and pencils—around the piano, as they would cause nonthreatening but nevertheless annoying problems if they fell inside.

To protect a floor covering from the piano's weight, castor cups can be used. Choose the largest diameter for protection, yet the thinnest depth—if the cups are too high they will raise the height of the piano, making the pedals uncomfortable to use.

With the exception of a piano with an ivory-covered keyboard, the fall and top should always be kept shut when the piano is not in use, to prevent dust from settling inside. Ivory, like wood, is a natural material and its great asset as a key cover is that it absorbs moisture from the pianist's hardworking fingers and so its surface remains dry. Once absorbed, the moisture needs to evaporate off into the air and failure to do this will cause the ivory to yellow.

Fit a thin castor cup with a large diameter underneath your piano's castors to help protect the floor covering. Castor cups are available in a myriad of different woods, colors, and sizes to suit the piano case or your décor.

moving a piano

All pianos, to a greater or lesser degree, fall out of tune as a result of being moved. A surefire way to inflict really serious damage on a piano, however, is to drop it. Not only is its casework and wooden structure likely to be badly affected, but the iron frame itself can crack, rendering the instrument untunable and often beyond repair.

This point cannot be overstressed: piano moving should always be done by experts. Avoid at all costs attempting to move your piano by yourself—if it should fall, more than the piano may suffer irreparable damage. Everyone knows that pianos are very heavy but few appreciate how that weight is distributed within the instrument, and understanding this ratio is the first technique in overcoming a piano's weight and bulk. The back of an upright is far heavier than the front and the treble end is often heavier than the bass. A small tilt backward when lifting an upright may send the piano crashing to the ground. An upright piano in a school or public place, or one that is often moved, should be fitted with castors that protrude at the back to stop this from occurring. In a grand, the keyboard end is heavier than the tail end and the treble end weighs more than the bass. Any piano should be able to be pushed across a flat floor, as long as its castors are in good condition and of an appropriate size. If it is to be moved any further, then it is essential to use a four-wheeled trolley, which is easier to push and turn, and absorbs much of the vibration from the traveling motion.

moving an upright piano
Moving an upright can be extremely dangerous for both the instrument and the people involved, as the piano's great weight is not evenly distributed throughout its bulk. For the greatest protection, an experienced piano mover will lift or tilt the piano from one end so that a heavy-duty, four-wheeled trolley can be slid beneath it. Once balanced, the upright piano can be moved with ease.

With its cumbersome shape, heavy weight, and high value, a grand piano requires an experienced mover. Moving grands on their side limits any bending forces on their legs, and facilitates placement in most rooms. Grand pianos that are too long for the available access can be hoisted through window openings by a crane, and specialized piano moving firms exist that are able to carry out this nerve-racking procedure.

moving a grand piano
1. After protecting the music desk, securing the fall, and removing the lyre, the piano is covered before being tightly tied to a protective "shoe."
2. The bass leg is removed—and marked for easy repositioning—and the piano is slowly lowered to rest on the bass end. While lowering the piano, great care is taken not to put any sideways stress on the remaining two legs.
3. The piano is lifted onto its long side and, after removing and checking the markings on the remaining two legs, a trolley is slid beneath it.

Once repositioned, the piano is brought back to a horizontal position using the same procedure, but in reverse. After making sure that the legs are fitted correctly and securely, the shoe is then removed, the fall and music desk unsecured, the lyre and backstays are refitted, and the pedals' operation checked.

tuning

Most musicians can tune their own instruments, but with a piano, the high tensions involved, the sheer number of strings, and the complex nature of the instrument combine to require the services of a highly trained and experienced technician.

Tuning is the adjustment of each individual string's tension so that they vibrate at the frequencies that give the correct pitch. A piano is a fixed-pitch instrument, which means the tuning intervals cannot be changed through the player's technique as they can with wind, brass, and unfretted stringed instruments. Since the 1850s, pianos have been tuned in equal temperament, a tuning system that ensures every interval played within any key will sound in harmony.

tuning tools

1 two different lengths and sizes of tuning heads
2 T-hammer
3 tuning crank
4 upright rubber wedge
5 "Papps" wedge
6 tuning forks
7 grand rubber wedge

This in effect means that all intervals within an octave are tuned fractionally sharp or flat so that the overall effect sounds pleasing. The octaves in the middle register of the piano are then tuned pure, gradually being stretched in the top treble and flatter in the extreme bass. This helps to balance the ends of the piano, as the higher harmonics heard in the bass strings sound much sharper than the actual notes in the upper register. So the piano tuner's job is actually to mistune a piano in order that it sounds pleasing in all keys. There are two possible ways to pursue this. Most experienced tuners use a tuning fork (invented by John Shore in 1712) to set either C40 (middle C) or A37 to the correct pitch and then work empirically by ear to

Rubber wedges are used to stop unwanted strings from vibrating so that only the strings being tuned actually sound.

A tuning crank is used to turn the wrest pins and so alter the strings' tension. Its fit is essential for tuning stability and the protection and longevity of the wrest pins, so a tool kit will contain many heads of different sizes and lengths. Although primarily turning the wrest pin while listening to the string's vibrations, a competent piano tuner is also aware that compensation has to be made for twisting stresses in the wrest pin itself and strings hanging on bearing surfaces.

The key is struck firmly so that the resulting hard hammer blow can aid the equalization of the string's tension over the bridges and entire sounding and nonsounding length.

equalize the rest of the piano. Some, however, use an electrical device that gives the desired pitch for each note. Whichever system is used, this is only half the job. Probably the toughest area of skill to master is in stabilizing a piano's tuning, so that the strings do not shift their position once finely set. It is awe-inspiring to think that there are something like 220 strings on a piano, with each one holding up to 200 pounds (90kg) of tension, running over two bridges and rubbing against sidegraft pins, not to mention the twisting and bending opportunities within the pin block itself; and that it only needs one to slip a fraction to destroy a piano's sound. To master piano tuning takes a great amount of patience, time, and good instruction and most technicians train at a college or in a workshop for four years before gaining the basic competence.

Finding a good tuner is essential for a piano's potential. It is always best to have a recommendation from a trusted source. Most countries now have recognized trade bodies whose members have to pass a stringent test, like the Piano Technicians Guild in the U.S. or the Piano Tuners Association in the U.K.

All pianos need tuning periodically and the frequency depends on the severity of climatic change, the age and condition of the instrument, and how it is to be used. It is important to keep a piano regularly tuned, because its pitch will drop flat if neglected, and it may take several tunings to achieve stability at the correct pitch. For anybody starting piano lessons, particularly children, it is essential to develop not only the finger coordination to press the right notes but also the ear to recognize pitch and the tone colors of a piano.

To keep a domestic instrument tuned to concert pitch and to maintain a degree of stability requires a minimum of two tunings a year. Pianos with new strings may need more, as these strings need to stretch out much of their elasticity before they become stable enough to hold a constant tension. A teacher's piano should be tuned more often, because it will receive much more varied use than a practice piano and will aid a student's ability to recognize pitch and tone. Concert and studio pianos are tuned before each use; this can be twice a day and a technician may be held on call until the session has finished, in case something goes wrong with the piano.

The tuning fork's small vibrations cannot be heard adequately when compared to the volume of the piano string. So, after the fork is set vibrating—usually by striking it against a relatively soft, forgiving surface—it is then placed against a larger sounding board, such as the underside of the keyboard, to amplify its volume.

pitch raising

A piano is designed to sound its best when it is tuned to concert pitch, and if the pitch is allowed to drop—as it naturally will if a piano is not regularly tuned—this will not only affect the tone of the piano but also compromise the pianist's ear training. The only way to achieve an accurate and stable tuning is to have all the strings already close to their proper pitch, since altering a string's tension by even a relatively small amount will put an additional load on the piano's strung back and so cause the pitch of previously tuned strings to change. If a piano is no closer than three beats to concert pitch, a tuner will have to perform a series of quick tunings to raise the tension of all the strings, so that the supporting structure can accommodate the new load before a fine tuning can commence. There is a risk of broken strings while pitch raising and a technician should advise you on how likely they are to break on a particular instrument and the cost of replacement.

regulation

All pianos require periodic servicing called regulation. This is the adjustment of the mechanical parts that make up the action, keyboard, and trapwork, to compensate for wear in the cloth, and dimensional changes in the wooden parts. Regulation ensures that a piano is capable of producing a uniform touch, fast repetition, and wide dynamic range. With over thirty-five points of adjustment per note in a grand piano and twenty-five in an upright, regulation is a skilled job that takes a considerable amount of time to complete.

when to regulate

A need for regulation may show itself in many ways. Inability to execute fast passages or legato touch may mean your piano needs regulating, rather than that you need to practice more, and bubbling or blocking hammers can destroy the tone of any instrument. Dampers may stop their strings from vibrating at differing times after release of the keys and pedal, causing difficulties in phrasing; and uneven key heights and touch weights affect the sensitivity needed by the fingers to control the speed of the piano hammer. An unregulated piano will not only perform poorly, but may have a shorter life span. Unnecessary and uneven wear develops as parts become misaligned and those that are meant to push start to punch; and hammers break if they are unable to escape the pianist's finger pressure before they hit the string.

How often a piano requires regulating depends on the conditions in which it is kept, as well as on how it is used and how often it is played. Most pianos require regulation within six months of purchase, either from new or after being rebuilt, because of compression of the cloth and felts, which absorb much of the shock between one action part and another. After this initial

regulating tools

1 Steinway set-off regulator
2 check regulator
3 key spacer
4 grand damper crank
5 grand jack regulator
6 upright set-off regulator
7 grand hammer flange spacer

8 capstan regulator
9 spring hook
10 regulation gauges
11 small screwdriver
12 small screwdriver
13 key-easing pliers
14 center-pin extractor

15 grand key-easing pliers
16 wire cranking pliers (side to side)
17 wire cranking pliers (forward and back)

work a domestic piano may only need regulating every five years. A piano that suffers extended and heavy use by a professional pianist should be regulated annually. Changes in humidity affect all of a piano's wooden parts, not just the action and keyboard, but it is the dimensional change in these parts that is most likely to degrade performance. As the wooden parts swell they exert pressure on the screws that hold them; as they dry they shrink, causing the screws to become loose. When this happens the action parts become noisy and fall out of alignment, resulting in uneven wear that future regulation cannot compensate for.

Most technicians make small adjustments to a piano's regulation every time it is tuned, but over time and with continued use, a piano will require a full regulation to maintain the responsive and even touch it had when it was new.

regulating methods

With over thirty-five points of adjustment per note in a grand piano's action, keyboard, and trapwork alone, the regulation process is lengthy. The pictures on this spread show the steps in regulating the escapement of grand piano hammers:

1. The hammers have to be spaced centrally—left and right to their corresponding strings—in order to maximize the life expectancy of the hammer felt, limit the strain put on the hammer's center pin, and ensure accurate regulation of the una-corda pedal later in the process.

2. Crucial to the clarity of the piano's tone, the hammer should stand vertical and strike all of the corresponding strings simultaneously. To adjust the vertical standing of the hammer head, the hammer shank is lightly heated, softening the wood's fibers so that the shank can be twisted and reset into a new position once the flame has been withdrawn.

3. Using a gauge of the right diameter placed below the strings, the hammer is very slowly pushed toward the gauge, which it should kiss lightly before falling away.

4–5. The adjustment is made on most grand piano actions by turning the set-off dolly, situated beneath the hammer rail, using a capstan regulator.

6. The escapement of the repetition lever is regulated with the action outside the piano by turning the small drop-screw. Using an adjustable rail, set it to the height of the piano's strings. A piano technician can accurately adjust this important requirement of the grand piano.

7. Once the drop screw has been adjusted, the repetition spring is regulated. On some grand piano actions, the strength of the spring can be adjusted by turning a small screw mounted in the repetition lever. The spring's strength is regulated so that it can hold the weight of the hammer head, lifting it slightly but not so much that its action can be felt by the pianist.

voicing

Tone is a crucial element of the piano's sound, and its evenness and beauty is essential to the expression of music. If tuning is the adjustment of the strings' tension to the correct harmonic pitch, then tone is the intensity and quality of the sound produced. Although the basic sound character of a piano is modeled within its design, an experienced technician can modify a piano's tone to the requirement of its owner by using a technique called voicing.

recognizing tone

Any number of adjectives can be used to describe a piano's tone. Metallic or wooden, harsh or soft, bright or mellow, all conjure up sound images; but whichever descriptions are used, the quality of tone is subjective. No rules prescribe how a piano should sound, other than that its tone should be even throughout and, of course, be musical. The instrument's role should be considered—a grand capable of filling a theater or cutting through an orchestra may be altogether too much in a living room—as should the type of music to be played: a rich and warm tone may enhance a Beethoven sonata more than it would a modern jazz improvisation. To this end, the piano should offer a tone that the pianist finds encouraging and pleasurable to play, as well as one that blends with the occasion.

Much of a piano's inherent tone derives from the design and construction of the strung back assembly, and this is the primary reason why all makes of piano sound so different. Certainly during the first half of the twentieth century, piano makers took great pride in producing pianos with an individual tone character. The classic warm, mellow tone of a Blüthner stood in stark contrast to the powerful, metallic ring of a Steinway or indeed the rich, hollow sound of a Bechstein.

Even today, makers "engineer in" their own trademark sound through various design modifications. Stringing scales are calculated to require different degrees of tension, soundboard dimensions are reworked to produce different response times, and various forms of sympathetic vibration are used to enhance the fullness of sound, including Steinway's duplex scaling and Blüthner's aliquot stringing. These all contribute to a make's inherent tone character, which cannot be altered by voicing.

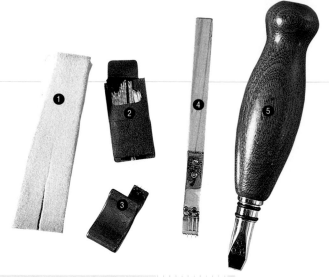

voicing tools

1 split felt wedge for damping individual strings
2 packet of sharp needles
3 short voicing tool holding many short needles, used for the pianissimo voicing of upright pianos
4 voicing tool fitted with three medium length needles, used for mezzo-forte voicing
5 heavy voicing tool fitted with a single long needle, used for fortissimo voicing

Beyond this, however, there are a number of factors that can be altered to enhance a piano's tone. A room's size and contents have an enormous effect on the way sound vibrations travel. Hard and shiny surfaces reflect sound vibrations, particularly the higher frequencies, resulting in brighter sounds, whereas fabrics, carpet, and other soft furnishings absorb sound energy, creating a warmer, more rounded sound. So by reorganizing a piano's environment, it is possible to change its tone.

The shape, positioning, and regulation of the hammer heads all have a significant effect on tone, as does the condition of the strings and bridges. As a piano ages, its original tone quality is gradually lost through use and deterioration, and an experienced technician can usually restore this.

how a piano is voiced

Before any voicing procedures are begun the piano must be adjusted to its best condition, since many uneven sounds perceived as voicing problems may actually be created by other faults within the action, keyboard, and strung back. The piano must be accurately tuned to concert pitch, with its strings well seated on the bridges, and the action and keyboard well regulated to ensure it produces an even, powerful, and accurate response. This includes the reshaping of the hammer heads and subsequent realignment so that they strike their strings squarely and simultaneously, as their smooth shape and striking action is essential for good tone. Only once these basic functions have been restored can a piano's tone be accurately judged. If it is then thought to be too loud, harsh, or brittle, it can be made mellower by softening the hammer felt. This is achieved by stabbing the felt with sharp needles in a very controlled and precise manner. If overdone or misdirected, the compression manufactured within the hammer head has the potential to collapse beyond repair and the

dangers to the technician's supporting hand are all too obvious. If the tone is judged to be too mellow, then the hammer felt can be hardened by the application of hard-setting chemicals, such as cellulose. Before using these in the top treble, though, a technician must be sure that the weak tone is caused by the hammer felt being too soft and not by the striking position of the hammers. Once the overall tone of the piano is perceived to be right, then the individual hammers are needled so that the tone blends from hammer to hammer over the entire compass.

Only an experienced and trusted technician should be asked to voice a piano, for it is a job of great skill, concentration, and understanding.

voicing a piano

To mellow the sound of a piano, the density of the hammer felt is softened by needling.

1–2. Support the hammer head and shank to protect the glue joint and delicate center-pin from the anticipated heavy pressure.
3. Accurately stab the shoulders of the hammer felt with one or more needles that protrude from various tools at different lengths. The depth and number of times that the felt needs to be stabbed vary from hammer to hammer but the same treatment must be applied to both shoulders to keep the tension in the individual hammer's felt equal.

Piano voicing is an exact art: the tone of the entire compass of hammers must be even at all levels of playing from pianissimo through to fortissimo. The voicer primarily only needles the hammer shoulders; attacking its nose would result in the tension of the hammer felt collapsing.

protecting your piano

The piano has a unique role, in that it is thought of as a piece of furniture as well as a musical instrument. Protecting its external condition is important not only to retain the piano's value but also to add beauty to the home.

finish care

Various finishes have been used on piano cases throughout history. Early instruments used alcohol-soluble spirit varnishes, such as French polish, and oil varnishes were used after the mid-nineteenth century. Today lacquer and polyester are in use. Unfortunately there is no single cleaning technique or solution suitable for all pianos.

Certain precautions can be taken to protect a piano's finish and avoid possible damage. Do not keep the piano in direct sunlight, as this will age the finish prematurely and cause its color to fade. Not only will excessive changes in relative humidity affect the internal workings of a piano, but the expansion and contraction of the casework panels can cause crazing and in extreme conditions separate the finish material from the wood itself. If the piano is subjected to too much moisture, the removable panels can expand

Polishing out a high-gloss surface demands a great deal of skill and endurance.

care of specific types of finish

FRENCH POLISH AND SPIRIT VARNISH: French-polished finishes are best cleaned using a 5 percent solution of acetic acid in water to remove the grease and grime that naturally accumulates. If the surface has been treated with a coat of wax from typical furniture polishes, then this can be removed using a dewaxing agent available from finishing suppliers. Once this has been removed, then the original finish should start to shine. Once back to the original finish, a polish reviver can be used if necessary, which will cut back the polish to give it more shine.

LACQUER AND POLYESTER
• Use a feather duster to remove the excess dust and then finish with a slightly damp soft cotton cloth. Care should be taken to wipe in the direction of the wood's grain or, in the case of satin-colored finishes, the finish flow, and this will avoid a swirling pattern being left. This procedure should also lift fingermarks.

• High-gloss polyester finishes need only to be kept clean to maintain their gloss, whereas gloss lacquer finishes may need polishing after they are cleaned. In this case use a good-quality, nonaerosol furniture polish, and avoid applying pressure to sharp edges since the finish can easily wear.

• Avoid using any type of polish on polyester or lacquer satin finishes, because they will leave the surface looking shiny but scratched.

so much that they jam inside the fixed panels, resulting in strain and perhaps damage when they are removed.

We have already mentioned the acoustical reasons not to place anything on top of a piano but this should also be avoided to protect the finish. Make sure lamps or other objects have a soft felt pad under them to help prevent scratches, and never put vessels containing liquid near a piano, since spilled water can mark finishes and in extreme cases can lift veneer.

It is only natural to want to dust a piano to keep it clean and looking beautiful, but be aware that dust is an abrasive and thus will scratch if wiped with a dry cloth. It is advisable to use a feather duster to remove the excess dust and then finish with a slightly damp soft cotton cloth. If heavier cleaning is required, then you will need to know the type of finish used on the piano. This can be found out by consulting the piano maker's manual in the case of a new piano, or your technician.

Whatever the finish, do not use furniture polishes that contain silicone, as this will work its way into the wood and complicate any future repairs or refinishing. Cheap polishes can also soften finishes and so should be avoided. Aerosols are just as damaging, since their spray can land on parts of the piano other than its case, harming key coverings and corroding strings and tuning pins.

On most finishes a technician trained in finish touch-up can repair a dent, chip, or scratch quite invisibly.

cleaning keys

It is important for a pianist of any level to practice on a clean keyboard that is in good condition. Not only can a dirty keyboard feel uncomfortable under the fingertips, but also marks, rather than the orientation of the keyboard, can come to distinguish a particular note. The natural keys are covered using plastic, celluloid, or ivory

and the three are easily distinguishable from one another. Plastic coverings are colored a solid white and have no grain pattern, celluloid sometimes has an artificial line pattern to give the effect of a grain and is often colored off white, while ivory is a translucent shade with an individual grain. The sharp keys are covered in either ebony (or another hardwood stained black) or plastic, and these too are easily distinguishable. Whatever the material, the keys can be wiped clean by using a slightly damp white cotton cloth and water. Use a different cloth for the naturals than for the sharps, to prevent the black polish from staining the white keys, and never use a colored cloth because the dye might affect the color of the key covering. Do not allow water to run down the side of the keys, and use a dry cloth to dry off any excess moisture immediately. After cleaning leave the fall open to allow air to circulate and dry the keyboard thoroughly. Never use a furniture polish or any other chemical cleaner on the keyboard, because this can soften the covering, as well as leave a slippery residue. A technician can polish jaded ivory naturals and ebony sharps by using a high-speed buffing wheel with a very fine cutting compound to restore their shine. Water should also be used very sparingly to clean plastic coverings marked with felt-tip pen; for ivory, use a small amount of acetone applied with a clean white cloth.

cleaning the keys

1. To remove the build-up of dirt and grime on the surface of the piano's keys, wipe them with a slightly damp white cotton cloth, using only water as the cleaning agent.
2. Being careful not to exert pressure on the lip of the key top, the natural keys can be lifted up to 0.08 inch (2mm) in order to gain suitable access.
3. Once they have been cleaned, the key tops should be wiped with a similar dry cloth to remove any remaining film of water and the fall should be left open to air the keyboard.

glossary

Action A collection of levers, primarily consisting of the hammers, dampers, and all other moving parts and supporting rails found above the keyboard.

Agraffe A brass string guide with a bridge that spaces and levels the string.

Back-touch rail A baize-covered wooden rail on which the tail of the keys rest.

Balance pin A 2 to 3-mm plated pin on which the key pivots.

Balance rail A central hardwood rail of the keyframe that acts as the fulcrum of the keys into which the balance pins are inserted.

Batt pin An oval-shaped plated pin that positions the keys in their rest position and guides them through their travels.

Beats A term referring to the sensation caused by two strings vibrating at slightly different frequencies.

Belly The piano's soundboard, bridge, belly-bars, and liners.

Bridge The surface on which the strings bear; the bridge determines their speaking length. The long bridge—attached to the soundboard—is made of a hardwood such as beech. The top bridge has a metal bearing surface either cast into the iron frame or set within an agraffe.

Bridge pin A small metal pin driven into the wooden bridge to determine the string spacing upon it.

Bushings Felt liners glued to wooden parts that rub against metal pins within the action and keyboard. Used for silent and reduced-friction operation.

Capo d'astro The top bridge on a grand piano that is normally cast into the frame. Some exceptions exist where it is cast into a separate unit and mounted onto the iron-frame so that it can be removed for resurfacing.

Capstan A domed screw inserted into the back of the key. Usually made of brass, it is regulated in height to fill the gap from the back of the key to the heel of action. Its wooden form is called either a pilot or a dolly, depending whether it is lubricated or covered with cloth.

Celeste see *moderator*.

Check A refinement in the piano action that catches the hammer after it has struck the string, to allow a comfortable touch and a speedier repetition.

Cheek The side part of the piano case at each end of the keyboard.

Chipping up This term refers to the initial string-tensioning and first tunings of a newly strung piano.

Clavichord A small, rectangular stringed keyboard instrument; the strings are set in vibration by brass tangents that sit on the rear of the key. The tangents also act as a bridge.

Clavicytherium The upright form of the harpsichord. Triangular in shape the soundboard is raised at 90° to the keyboard.

Clavier The generic German term for keyboard.

Crown Curve of the piano soundboard.

Damper A soft felt-covered action part that stops the vibration of the strings.

Depth of touch The distance that the key can be pressed down, usually set at around 10mm. Also called *key dip*.

Escapement The disengagement of the hammer from the force of the key and action levers. Also called *set-off*.

Fall The casework part that covers the keys when the piano is not in use.

Front-touch rail The foremost rail of the keyframe which governs the depth that the keys can travel.

Hammer butt The part of the upright piano hammer that is pushed by the jack.

Hammer head The primary part that distinguishes the piano from other stringed keyboard instrument. It consists of a wooden moulding covered at one end with dense felt that strikes the strings.

Harpsichord A wing-shaped stringed keyboard instrument that contains quilled-jacks that pluck the strings.

Heel of action The base of the action lever at the point that it contacts the capstan.

Hitch pin A steel rod driven into the iron frame around which the non-tuneable ends of the strings are seated.

Hopper see *jack*.

Iron frame A cast metal component of the piano structure that is responsible for withstanding the strings tension.

Jack A boot-shaped wooden lever that connects the lower parts of the action through to the hammer and forms an essential part of the escapement mechanism. In earlier actions it is called a *hopper*.

Kapsel A metal or wooden fork attached to the rear of the key in which the hammer pivots (in Viennese or Prellmechanik actions).

Keybottom A solid wooden base on which the keyframe either sits or is attached.

Key chasing A cloth lined mortise that works on the balance pin, found protruding on the top of all keys at their center.

Key top Covers the surface of the natural keys. Traditionally made from ivory, it is now usually made from celluloid or plastic.

Keyframe A wooden framework on which the keys operate, consisting of the back-touch rail, the balance rail, and the front-touch rail.

Knee lever A lever attached to the underside of the key-bottom. Operated by the player's knee, it most commonly lifted the dampers.

Lost-motion Any travel in the key that does not pass through the action.

Moderator A stop that places a thin strip of celeste felt between the hammers and the strings to soften the volume. Operated by the middle pedal on most upright pianos, it can also be called the *celeste* or *practice* pedal.

Natural keys A lower set of keys that equate to notes C to B excluding the accidental keys. Traditionally covered with ivory, they are now made from celluloid or plastic.

Over-damper An upright piano action in which the damper operates above the hammer head.

Prellmechanik A twentieth-century term used to describe the South German or Viennese action in which the hammer was mounted directly on the back of the key.

Pressure bar A brass rod that ensures that the strings are securely held down over the top bridge in an upright piano.

Repetition lever A spring-loaded lever that supports the hammer allowing the jack to return quickly without the key necessarily returning to rest.

Set-off see *escapement*.

Scale design A calculated combination of a string's diameter, speaking length, flexibility, and tension to give the best resulting tone, volume, and sustain.

Sharp key Accidental raised keys traditionally made of ebony but today more likely to be made of black molded plastic or a stained hardwood.

Soundboard A wooden board made of spruce that vibrates at the same frequency of the strings and so amplifies their volume.

Stossmechanik The German term for an action where the hammer is mounted on a separate rail and not on the key.

Square piano A rectangular horizontal piano that derived its shape from the clavichord.

Una-corda Meaning "one string," this stop adjusts the position of the keyboard and action sideways, so that the hammer heads miss one of the trichord and bichord strings. More commonly employed on grand pianos, it is operated by the left pedal.

Under-damper A type of upright piano action where the damper operates below the hammer head.

Viennese action see *Prellmechanik*.

Wippen A rocking lever that transmits the motion of the key to the hammer.

Wrest pin A 7mm-diameter steel pin around which the string is wound. By turning the wrest pin, the string's tension can be altered and therefore its tuning. A small hole is drilled through the top of the pin to anchor the string and a fine thread is wound around its base so that it can be extracted from the wrest plank.

Wrest plank A tough laminated, hardwood piece into which the wrest pins are driven. Its strength and accurate fitting beneath the iron frame are essential to the stability of the piano's tuning.

index

bibliography

Bielefeldt, Catherine C.
The Wonders of the Piano
Belwin-Mills, 1984

Cole, Michael
The Pianoforte in the Classical Era
Clarendon Press Oxford, 1998

Colt, C.F.
The Early Piano
Stainer and Bell, 1981

Crombie, David
Piano Evolution, Design and Performance
Balafon 1995

Dolge, Alfred
Pianos and their Makers and *Men who
have made Piano History*
Dover Publications, 1972

Ehrlich, Cyril
The Piano: A History
Oxford University Press, 1990

Fine, Larry
The Piano Book
Brookside Press, 1990

Gill, Dominic
The Book of the Piano
Phaidon Press, 1981

Harding, Rosamund
*The Pianoforte: Its History Traced to the
Great Exhibition of 1851*
Gresham Books, 1978

Hilderbrandt, Dieter
A Social History of the Piano Century
Hutchinson, 1988

Hollis, Helen Rice
*The Piano: A Pictorial Account of its
Ancestry and Development*
David and Charles, 1975

Kentner, Louis
Piano: Yehudi Menuhin Music Guides
Macdonald Futura, 1980

Keys, Ivor
Mozart: The Music in his Life
University Press, 1980

Komlos, Katalin
Fortepianos and their Music
Clarendon Press Oxford, 1995

The New Grove Musical Instrument Series
Early Keyboard Instruments
Macmillan, 1989

Palmieri, Robert
Encyclopedia of the Piano
Garland Publishing, New York and
London, 1996

Pierce, Bob
Pierce Piano Atlas
Larry E. Ashley, 1997

Pollens, Stewart
The Early Pianoforte
Cambridge University Press, 1995

Ratcliffe, Ronald
Steinway
Chronicle Books, 1989

Reblitz, Arthur A.
Piano Servicing Tuning and Rebuilding
Vestal Press, 1988

Rowland, David
*The Cambridge Companion to
the Piano*
Cambridge University Press, 1998

Sumner, William Leslie
The Pianoforte
Macdonald and Jane's, 1978

Unger-Hamilton, Clive
Keyboard Instruments
Phaidon Press, 1981

Van Barthold, K. and Buckton, D. *The
Story of the Piano*
BBC, 1975

Wainwright, David
The Piano Makers
Hutchinson and Co., 1975

White, William B.
Theory and Practice of Piano Construction
Dover Publications, 1975

Wolfenden, Samuel
*A Treatise on the Art of Pianoforte
Construction*
Gresham Books, 1982

Zilberquit, Dr. Mark
*The Book of the Piano:
An Illustrated History*
Paganiniana Publications, 1987

Plus numerous articles printed in
Europiano, FoMRHI Quarterly, and *The
Piano Technicians Journal.*

credits

Quarto would like to thank and acknowledge the following for permission to reproduce the pictures that appear in this book.

Key: b=bottom, t=top, c=center, l=left, r=right

AKG-London, 8 tr, 9 bl, 10 bl,18 tl, 32 bl,33 bl,34, 35 cl, 35 br, 36 tr, 37 br, 38 bl, 39 br, 40 tr; **Astin-Weight Piano Makers**, photos by Mr Ray Astin 59; **Baldwin Piano & Organ Company** 7, 60, 61, 120,124t & c; **Bayerisches National Museum**, Munich 23; **C. Bechstein Pianofortefabrik** 44, 62, 63; **Bernisches Historisches Museum**, Berne 29 bl; **Julius Blüthner Pianofortefabrik**, photos by Jens Drescher 45 r, 61, 64, 65, 123b; **L. Bösendorfer Klavierfabrik** 31b, 66, 67; **Bridgeman Art Library** 17; **The British Piano Manufacturing Co** 86(Knight), 107 (Welmar); **John Broadwood & Sons Ltd** 38t, 68, 69 (manufactured by Ladbrooke Pianos Ltd, 32 Bristol Street, Birmingham B5 7AA); **Chas. H. Challen (1804) Ltd/Vienna Music Sdn Bhd** 4, 5, 60, 70; **Chappell & Company** 71; **Dampp-Chaser Corporation** 141, 142t; **Fazioli** pianoforti srl, www.fazioli.com 72, 73; **Feurich** 74, 75; **August Förster** 76, 77, 121; **Germanisches National Museum**, Nuremberg 40 bl; **Gesellschaft der Musikfreunde**, Vienna 41; **Grotrian-Steinweg Pianofortefabrikanten** 78, 79; Company Archive, **Harrods Limited**, London 125; **Hungarian National Museum/Judit Kardos**, Budapest 36 bl; **Rud. Ibach Sohn** 80, 81; **Irmler Piano GmbH** 117; **Kawai Musical Inst. Mfg. Co** 82, 83, 124b; **Anna M Koopmans** for William E. Garlick Collection, New York 19; **Kunsthistorisches Museum, Vienna** 24 br; **Manchester Art Gallery** 24 cl; **Mason & Hamlin** 88, 89; **Robert Morley & Company Ltd** 114, 119; **Museum of Musical Instruments**, Leipzig University, 8 br, 9 tr, 10 tr, 12 t,14 cl, 14 br, 15 br, 16 br, 30 bl; **Petrof** 90, 91; **Pianos Pleyel**, www.pleyel.fr 92,93; **Powerhouse Museum**, Sydney, Australia. " 2002. Photo: Marinco Kojdanovski 106 r; **Louis Renner GmbH** 50, 51; **Ann Ronan Picture Library** 11, 33 tr, 122, 139, 140; **Rönisch** 1, 87 (produced by Pianofortefabrik Leipzig GmbH); **Russell Collection of Early Keyboard Instruments**, University of Edinburgh by permission of the Curator 21; **Samick Musical Instruments Co** 42, 45 l, 94, 95; **Carl Sauter Pianofortemanufaktur** 31t, 96, 97; **Wilhelm Schimmel Pianofortefabrik GmbH**, Friedrich–Seele-Strasse 20, D-38122 Braunschweig, Germany 43,48, 98, 99; **Ed. Seiler Pianofortefabrik** 100, 101; Courtesy of **Sotheby's** 28 br; **Steingraeber & Söhne**, Bayreuth, Germany 102, 103; **Steinway & Sons** 2-3, 6, 20, 26 bl & br, 104, 105, 113; **Stuart & Sons** 106 (logo); **V & A Picture Library** 28 tr; **Yamaha-Kemble Music Ltd**, www.uk-piano.org/kemble 84, 85, 108, 109, 123 t; **Young Chang** 110, 111.

All other photographs and illustrations are the copyright of Quarto Publishing plc. While every effort has been made to credit contributors, we would like to apologize in advance if there have been any omissions or errors.